BRITISH POLITICAL IDEOLOGIES

CONTEMPORARY POLITICAL STUDIES SERIES

Series Editor: John Benyon, *Director, Centre for the Study of Public Order, University of Leicester*

A series which provides authoritative yet concise introductory accounts of key topics in contemporary political studies.

———

BRITISH POLITICAL IDEOLOGIES

———

Second edition

ROBERT LEACH

 PRENTICE HALL
HARVESTER WHEATSHEAF

LONDON   NEW YORK   TORONTO   SYDNEY   TOKYO   SINGAPORE
MADRID   MEXICO CITY   MUNICH

First published 1996 by
Prentice Hall Europe
Campus 400, Maylands Avenue
Hemel Hempstead
Hertfordshire, HP2 7EZ
A division of
Simon & Schuster International Group

© Prentice Hall Europe 1996

Typeset in 10/12 pt Times
by Photoprint, Torquay, Devon

Printed and bound in Great Britain by
T J Press (Padstow) Ltd, Padstow, Cornwall

Library of Congress Cataloging-in-Publication Data

Leach, Robert.
   British political ideologies / Robert Leach. — 2nd ed.
     p. cm. — (Contemporary political studies series)
   Includes bibliographical references and index.
   ISBN 0-13-518176-3 (alk. paper)
   1. Political science — Great Britain. 2. Right and left (Political
science) I. Title. II. Series: Contemporary political studies
series (Prentice Hall)
JA84.G7L39 1996
320.5' 0941—dc20
                                                   95-48445
                                                     CIP

British Library Cataloguing in Publication Data

A catalogue record for this book is available from
the British Library

ISBN 0–13–518176–3

1 2 3 4 5   00 99 98 97 96

CONTENTS

PREFACE TO FIRST EDITION

This book provides a simple introduction to the extremely complex and controversial subject of British political ideologies. It is intended primarily for both undergraduates and A level students, although hopefully it will also interest any intelligent layperson who desires to know more about liberalism, socialism, conservatism and other political creeds.

The scope and breadth of the book inevitably requires a somewhat brief and perhaps over-simplified treatment of great themes and complex ideas. Moreover, although I have tried to be as dispassionate and detached as possible in discussing a wide range of sharply opposed viewpoints, it is only too likely that my interpretation of some ideologies will be seen as partial or narrow. I can only repeat that this book is intended as an introductory text. Those who seek further illumination are advised to delve more deeply into the extensive literature on political ideas, some of which is indicated in the bibliography.

I would like to thank John Benyon, the series editor, and Clare Grist of Philip Allan for their help and advice. Several colleagues at Leeds Polytechnic have read part of the manuscript, and I would like to thank in particular Brendan Sheehan and Janie Percy-Smith for their detailed and constructive advice. I also owe a debt to my students, particularly on the BA Economics and Public Policy degree, for sharpening my ideas.

I would also like to acknowledge a few longer-term debts – to my late mother, and my father, for the support they gave to my education, and my shifting, eccentric academic pursuits, and to my old history teacher, Michael Cherniavsky, who first stimulated my interest in political ideas and much else besides. My greatest debt is, however, to my wife, Judith, without whose constant encouragement and support this book would certainly never have been written.

PREFACE TO SECOND EDITION

A commission for a second edition is gratifying to an author's pride, but carries little additional academic kudos. Had I realised how much work would be involved I might not have agreed to it so readily. Those familiar with the original book will notice several changes. There are three completely new separate chapters on nationalism, feminism and the Greens, various other additional sections and diagrams, as well as some necessary updating to take account of developments in the last few years. I have also taken the opportunity to undertake some restructuring of material, for example on the chapter on labourism and socialism. As a result it is now a considerably bigger book; whether it is a better book I leave my readers to decide. The debts I acknowledged in the preface to the first edition still apply, although sadly Michael Cherniavsky has since died. For this revised version I owe particular thanks to my colleague Janie Percy-Smith, who gave valuable advice for the material on feminism (although convention requires that I acquit her of any blame for the final result), the anonymous reviewer of an early draft of my chapters on the Greens, and all at Prentice Hall, including Clare Grist (who inveigled me into undertaking the revision), Ruth Pratten, and Ian MacQuarrie. My greatest debt is, however, once more to my wife, Judith.

1

IDEOLOGICAL DIFFERENCE AND CONSENSUS IN BRITAIN SINCE 1945

Introduction

Why is the study of political ideology important? This opening chapter seeks to answer this question by reference to British politics in the post-war period. One view suggests that British politics has been more characterised by consensus (or agreement) than ideological differences. This view is critically examined in terms of three periods. The first is the period popularly associated with consensus politics, from the end of the war until the late 1960s. The second covers the period of apparent ideological polarisation in the 1970s and early 1980s. The third relates to the presumed establishment of a new ideological consensus from the late 1980s and more particularly the 1990s. The implications of the (real or alleged) consensus are explored, particularly the notion that it involves the end of ideology. The argument advanced here suggests, by contrast, that political behaviour and public policy can only be understood in terms of the underlying ideological assumptions of participants in the political process, and this is as true in periods of apparent consensus as it is in terms of overt ideological conflict.

Consensus and the end of ideology?

In 1960 Daniel Bell confidently proclaimed 'The End of Ideology'. This scarcely involved a revolution in thinking about politics, rather the confirmation of a trend which was already well under way. Political ideologies seemed at best irrelevant, at worst positively dangerous in the post-war western world. Between the wars Europe had been an ideological battleground as the rival creeds of communism and fascism contended for supremacy. The defeat and discrediting of fascism, and the excesses of Stalinism provoked a reaction against what were now lumped together as 'totalitarian' ideologies (Talmon, 1960; Arendt, 1967). Moreover, the very term 'ideology', which had always had rather ambivalent connotations, was also substantially discredited. All systems of political thought, all 'isms' were widely regarded as suspect. 'Ideological thinking' was held to involve a blinkered, dogmatic approach. Political opponents were stigmatised as 'ideological'. Both individual politicians and political parties were at pains to deny that they were themselves ideological. Pragmatism was elevated into principle.

This was accompanied by a new optimism that some of the most important problems in society could be solved, or at least substantially alleviated, by the application of the appropriate techniques. It was widely reckoned that the economist Keynes had found the answer to mass unemployment. The new tools of demand management seemed to promise that never again should millions be made unwillingly idle. The deliberate pursuit of economic growth also suggested that society could look forward to a steady increase in living standards, which would effectively eliminate poverty and materially reduce inequality. New breeds of professional technocrats confidently advocated and applied solutions to a variety of social problems.

The 'End of Ideology' was perceived as a world, or at least a western world, phenomenon, but it seemed particularly applicable to Britain. In Britain the new policy solutions were embraced by all major political parties, and all mainstream politicians. Partisan rhetoric was of course still employed, but in practice there did not seem to be much difference between socialist and Conservative approaches to education, health, housing, town planning, industrial relations, and most of all the management of the economy.

This was widely recognised at the time. Crossman (1981, p. 30) quotes Boothby on the new Conservative ministerial appointments in 1951: 'Rab Butler Chancellor! Why, that's Gaitskell all over again, but from Cambridge.' This proved a prophetic observation. The term 'Butskellism' was soon employed to describe the essential similarity of the economic policies pursued by the two chancellors, and later to characterise a whole era of 'consensus politics'.

Socialism and conservatism, once seen as starkly opposed alternatives, increasingly appeared to blend into each other. At one level it might be suggested that socialism had been absorbed into the political culture and system. Macmillan had once provocatively declared that conservatism had always been a paternal form of socialism, and there were indeed right-wing critics who suggested that the post-war Conservative governments were heavily infected with the socialist virus. As for the Labour Party, revisionists argued that socialism must adapt to changed circumstances. Nationalisation was now irrelevant. Socialists should pursue greater equality by distributing the benefits of economic growth through a progressive tax system and social welfare. Their critics could see little difference between this revised socialism and 'one-nation' conservatism. There appeared to be one orthodox view of the world which had assimilated some socialist and some progressive conservative values.

The conventional psephological wisdom suggested a successful electoral strategy required capture of the middle ground. Political parties were perceived as vote-getting machines. Parties competed for votes in much the same way as firms competed for business. In this context political ideologies were perceived as awkward electoral baggage, better jettisoned. Parties, like firms, should study the market to find out what the punters wanted, and endeavour to supply it. Economic analysis suggested that, in a two-party system, vote maximisation would necessitate both parties adopting similar centrist positions on the political spectrum (Downs, 1957). This analysis seemed to be confirmed by the experience of two-party politics in both the United States and the United Kingdom. Robert McKenzie's (1963) massive study of political parties in Britain suggested that major apparent differences in organisations and principles masked a substantial convergence of practice.

Such an analysis attributes a rather passive role to the electorate. However, many observers saw the political consensus extending beyond Parliament and parties to the nation as a whole. British political culture was considered to exhibit the characteristics of homogeneity, deference and consensus (Punnett, 1987, ch. 1). Class differences were perceived as declining, while other differences were generally regarded as insignificant (Jennings, 1966). Partly this was attributed to growing prosperity. The inter-war recession and its associated miseries had created a fertile political climate for the growth of extremist political ideologies, although even then in Britain communism and fascism had not advanced beyond the political fringe (see Chapter 7). In the post-war era of full employment, welfare provision and rising living standards, radical proposals posed more of a threat than a promise. The language of class politics seemed singularly inappropriate in a 'property-owning democracy' in which an increasing proportion of the old working class were buying their own homes, running their own cars, and enjoying foreign holidays. The phenomenon of 'embourgeoisement' was seen as particularly threatening to the electoral prospects of Labour (Abrams *et al.*, 1960) and the party was urged to shed its old 'cloth cap' image and acquire a more modern, classless approach. In fact this was already happening at constituency level, where middle-class intellectuals were increasingly displacing manual workers as the leading local party activists (Hindess, 1971).

For some observers this apparent growing social consensus mirrored fundamental changes in the economy and society. Britain was no longer a capitalist society in the old sense of the term, thus the social divisions associated with nineteenth-century industrial capitalism were outmoded. Ownership of capital was more widely diffused, and besides the important decision-takers were now technocratic managers rather than owners. Control had thus been effectively divorced from ownership, and in any case was increasingly subject to influence from a democratically elected government committed to national economic objectives. There was a sizeable and growing public sector, including nationalised industries which provided substantial leverage over the economy as a whole. The economy was now more properly 'mixed' than 'capitalist' and ideological thinking based on old social and economic cleavages was thus increasingly irrelevant (Crosland, 1956).

The political consensus on this analysis represented more than mere pragmatic electoral considerations. It reflected an altered economic and social reality where fundamental conflicts of interest had been eradicated. Political ideologies which substantially reflected interests based on these now outmoded divisions, such as old-fashioned socialism, or for that matter *laissez-faire* liberalism seemed doomed to extinction.

The neglect of political ideas

So, for all kinds of reasons, political ideologies seemed to have a sharply diminished significance in post-war Britain. They were perceived as highly suspect, involving a dogmatic adherence to outmoded convictions, and the antithesis of a modern, pragmatic approach to politics. They were certainly not regarded as a respectable field for academic study. The study of modern politics was increasingly devoted to means rather than ends, political behaviour rather than political ideas.

This was indeed taken to be the very essence of a scientific approach. All social science had been heavily influenced by the logical positivists. Metaphysical speculation was out. Dispassionate examination of social phenomena was in. For the study of politics this involved a greater emphasis on what was quantifiable, such as elections and voting. Of course, more careful regard for evidence and improved statistical analysis provided a valuable corrective to some of the intuitive assumptions and unsubstantiated generalisations which had been current in earlier political studies. But the emphasis on the more easily quantifiable sometimes involved a relative neglect of some aspects of the study of politics.

Ideas were in one sense not neglected. On the contrary, systematic opinion polling produced a wealth of data, not previously available, on the ideas of ordinary people on a whole range of issues. This kind of data was heavily drawn upon in work on voting and on more ambitious efforts to describe and compare political cultures (Almond and Verba, 1963). In the study of political parties there has been detailed analysis of, for example, motions submitted by constituency parties to the Annual Party Conference, which provides important insights into the nature and character of grassroots party activism. However, although such expressions of opinion were carefully categorised, measured and analysed, the actual substance of the opinions was not generally considered a proper subject for political science.

Traditional political theory remained until recently a substantial but rather specialised area of study, essentially antiquarian in its approach, devoted to the detailed exegesis of the great texts of Hobbes, Locke, Bentham and Mill. The implication was that the study of political ideas was scarcely relevant to the modern world. The study of political theory at institutions of higher education, where it was still carried out, generally stopped short in the nineteenth century with Mill and possibly Marx. Twentieth-century political thinkers and twentieth-century political ideas were not considered subjects worthy of academic study.

The rebirth of ideology

It was soon clear that the announcement of the end of political ideology was at least premature. From the late 1960s or early 1970s the post-war political consensus was fractured, and replaced by ideological polarisation as far as the two major British political parties were concerned (Plant, in Drucker *et al.*, 1983). Variants of Marxism and classical liberalism, ideologies widely regarded as outmoded and irrelevant in the era of consensus politics, showed renewed vitality. This was accompanied by a proliferation of new (or at least newly recognised) perspectives outside the former two-party consensus. A revived nationalist fervour in Scotland and Wales, an essentially new breed of feminism, the increased relevance of ethnic divisions in politics, and the green movement all helped to produce a far more diverse political scene where a wide variety of ideas contended for attention.

None of this could have happened had not the old political consensus been broken. It was never of course as monolithic as some conventional analysis suggested (including that above in the first section of this chapter). There were always some important differences even between the front benches in Parliament, and certainly there were significant dissenting elements who opposed the prevailing orthodoxy in both major parties. And right through the 1950s and 1960s there were individual thinkers who continued to peddle what were then deeply unfashionable views – thinkers who in some cases have since been hailed as major prophets.

Yet it may still be argued that the consensus was no myth, largely perhaps because the prevailing orthodoxy actually seemed to work. In one sense the consensus broke down because the orthodox prescriptions stopped working. The optimism that the major social and economic problems were solved or at least were soluble was displaced by hard evidence to the contrary. The rediscovery of poverty, increased public awareness of homelessness, the apparent failure of much previous housing and planning policy, the growth of family breakdown with accompanying social problems, evidence of growing social unrest culminating in riots in major cities, these all helped to dissolve comfortable assumptions of a society which was good and bound to get better.

Recognition of these problems, although clearly significant and chastening, did not immediately involve the destruction of the political consensus, however. It was possible to argue that they were all in principle soluble, given adequate public funds and appropriate new policies. A plethora of reports produced analysis and recommendations which commanded widespread assent across the political spectrum.

Much more significant was the apparent breakdown of the assumptions on which the whole post-war economic order rested. The simultaneous growth of inflation and unemployment in the 1970s should have been impossible, according to conventional Keynesian analysis. Keynesian remedies were accordingly also discredited. A Labour Prime Minister sadly asserted that spending your way out of a recession was no longer an option. Crosland, the arch Labour revisionist of the 1950s, who had then declared that the country stood on the edge of mass abundance, now bluntly announced that the party was over.

All this had of course considerable implications for the new (or at least newly discovered) social problems identified above. Previously there had been a general assumption that economic growth fuelled by Keynesian demand management would provide the additional resources necessary for social reform. Keynes had helped to make public expenditure respectable, in certain circumstances at least. But the apparent failure of Keynesianism involved a throwback to an earlier era when public expenditure had always been regarded as inherently suspect. Higher public spending was seen as incompatible with a healthy, growing economy. Policy prescriptions for social problems which required higher public spending were increasingly seen as unrealistic in some quarters, and prompted a search for radically different solutions which did not involve 'throwing [government or taxpayers'] money' at them. Thus the previous consensus which had substantially existed on a whole range of issues – child poverty, care of the disabled, homelessness, inner city policy – was dissolved. Analysis and prescription increasingly reflected fundamentally divergent assumptions.

For if Keynesian economic science was found to be deeply flawed, the search was on for new paradigms. Not surprisingly this involved a re-emergence of the ideologies which Keynesianism had apparently displaced, socialism and old-style liberalism. In both major parties there were those who sought a return to fundamentals. For many socialists, if Keynesian-style economic planning could not deliver full employment, social reform, and significant progress towards greater equality, then the case was made for a return to common ownership and socialist planning. Equally for many Conservatives if Keynesian analysis and prescriptions coupled with a moderate consensus approach on industrial relations and social issues generally could not deliver economic growth, a degree of social harmony, and electoral success, the gut reaction was to turn back to free market values.

On the left there were of course always Marxists and others who argued that what was represented in the 1950s and 1960s as the end of ideology involved instead the general acceptance of one dominant ideology. The new post-war Keynesian orthodoxy, it was pointed out, rested on certain assumptions about society and human nature. Keynes was supporting an essentially capitalist economy and society, where the ownership of productive wealth remained heavily concentrated. Substantial inequalities were implicitly endorsed. Moreover, the so-called 'mixed economy' of the post-war years remained in most important respects a capitalist economy. Keynesian planning involved a degree of government manipulation of economic aggregates at the macro-economic level, leaving market forces to operate at the level of individual enterprises and whole industries. Economic science thus served to legitimate a distribution of income and wealth which remained profoundly unequal.

The left also questioned pluralist assumptions about the nature and distribution of political power, and suggested that much which passed for value-free political science was actually highly ideological. Power and influence was not widely dispersed, as liberal pluralists suggested, but concentrated. The whole economic and social system served to reinforce the values of capitalism, free markets and private enterprise. While conventional economic and political theory suggested that individuals were the best judge of their own interests, radicals suggested that this was not necessarily so. Real choices were not presented, but even if they were, the effective conditioning of the people through education, the mass media and the whole socialisation process would ensure the rejection of radical alternatives to the status quo.

Neo-liberals started from quite different assumptions. For them it was axiomatic that the expressed interests of individuals were their real interests. Individuals naturally pursued their own self-interest, and were the best judge of that interest. Socialist suggestions to the contrary implied paternalism, condescension and bureaucratic interference summed up in the saying 'The man in Whitehall knows best'. Neo-liberals sought to return power to individuals, with the implicit assumption that individuals did have real economic power (through the market) and, perhaps to a lesser extent, political power (through the ballot box). Collective provision was always suspect as it involved imposing preferences, interfering with individual freedom, and distorting market choice.

To neo-liberals the era of consensus politics had not shored up private enterprise and the capitalist system, as Marxist critics alleged, but had fundamentally undermined it. Keynesian economics had legitimised a massive growth in public spending which had stimulated inflation and harmed the economy. The vested interests of public service employees and recipients of benefits provided powerful pressures for an ever-expanding public sector. Electoral competition forced the parties to respond to the demands of these and other interests in a public auction of promises. Both parties also sought to 'buy off' labour unrest and wider social unrest by making expensive concessions in terms of pay, benefits, and participation in policy-making. Such policies had undermined incentives and destroyed the natural discipline of the labour market. High welfare spending could not solve social problems. On the contrary it sapped individual initiative, and created additional social problems. Keynesianism was thus far from being a neutral technocratic tool of economic management. It involved, rather, creeping socialism.

Thus Marxists and neo-liberals provided strongly contrasting critical analyses of the assumptions behind the formerly prevailing ideological consensus. Yet it would be simplistic to suggest that consensus was replaced by an ideological polarisation between Marxist socialism on the one hand and classical liberalism on the other. On the right there were (and remain) significant neo-conservative as well as neo-liberal elements in the general critique of consensus politics, and there were (and remain) considerable differences of emphasis among free market advocates. On the left there were, as always, sharply conflicting tendencies.

Nor of course was the rejection of Keynesian economics and consensus politics anything like universal. Some Keynesians suggested that there was nothing essentially wrong with the traditional Keynesian remedies. Others suggested that Keynes had been vulgarised and misinterpreted, and that his real message was as valid as ever. Still others suggested that an inadequate political and administrative system had failed to apply a Keynesian approach properly (Hutton, 1986), an analysis which chimed in with a growing critique of British political institutions. Another line of argument assumed a continuing national consensus around moderate centrist views; ideological polarisation at Westminster was the artificial product of an outdated electoral system and adversarial procedures in Parliament (Finer, 1975). Many who shared these views coalesced around a revived political centre.

Cutting across these contending schools of thought were other political perspectives which reflected differences based on nation, ethnicity and gender, and an essentially new green ideology. Thus a political scene which in 1960 had plausibly appeared to involve the end of ideology, or, rather, the general acceptance of a dominant ideology, was apparently replaced twenty years later by one which involved a maelstrom of competing ideas and perspectives. Ideology was back in fashion.

From ideological polarisation to a new consensus

Yet as the 1980s wore on and gave place to the 1990s the competition between these different perspectives increasingly appeared unequal. The free market ideas of the neo-liberals was rapidly established as the new orthodoxy, both in Britain, and in the wider world.

In Britain four successive Conservative election victories consolidated a virtual counter-revolution which effectively reversed many of the policies and underlying assumptions of the post-war ideological consensus. The nationalised industries were progressively privatised and other public assets sold off. Trade unions were subjected to new controls, effectively weakened and marginalised. Competition was injected into the administration of public services. The control of inflation rather than the reduction of unemployment was established as the dominant goal of economic policy. The replacement of Mrs Thatcher by John Major in 1990 led to some change in style, but little in substance.

The revived fundamentalist socialism in the Labour Party of the early 1980s gradually gave place to a cautious revisionism under the Labour leaders Kinnock, Smith and Blair. Commitments to leave the European Community, to give up nuclear weapons and to reverse Conservative privatisation and trade union legislation were progressively abandoned, and replaced by a cautious pragmatism. The symbolic commitment of the party to public ownership, expressed in Clause 4 of its constitution, was formally ditched, and the links with the trade union movement weakened. Increasingly it appeared that 'New Labour' now accepted the ideas of the free market and competition previously associated with the New Right.

If old socialism presented little of a threat to the dominant neoliberal ideology in Britain, neither apparently did any of the other new or revived competing political perspectives. In the middle of the 1980s it briefly appeared that the alliance of the old Liberal Party and new SDP might restore the fortunes of the political centre, and the moderate ideas associated with the old Keynesian consensus. However, this ambitious attempt to break the mould of British politics foundered, leaving a slightly remodelled Liberal Party with some electoral prospects but little in the way of a really distinctive political philosophy. Meanwhile, the peace movement was marginalised by the end of the Cold War, the nationalists only gradually recovered from their collapse in 1979, the Greens failed to capitalise on an apparent electoral breakthrough in 1989, while the women's movement appeared more fragmented as it faced something of an anti-feminist backlash.

Thus in Britain the ideological polarisation of the 1970s and early 1980s apparently gave place to a new consensus around the dominant free market values associated with Thatcherism and the New Right. This essentially mirrored changes outside Britain. Privatisation and competition were pursued by governments across the western world, even governments which were ostensibly socialist. Yet the most dramatic changes came in what had been the communist world.

Ever since the Russian revolution of 1917, but particularly since 1945, Soviet-style communism apparently posed a sharp alternative to liberal capitalism, an alternative which had been in some cases imposed, but often willingly embraced by a large and growing proportion of the world's countries. The 'really existing socialism' of the Soviet Union, eastern Europe, China and much of the third world for decades provided a radically different ideology from the political and economic system of the liberal capitalist west (Hobsbawm, 1994b).

The astonishingly rapid collapse of Soviet communism, coupled with economic liberalisation (albeit combined with continued political repression) in China, has effectively removed the threat to western capitalism. The Cold War was over and the west had won. The implications for political ideologies were apparently profound. Not only was Soviet communism discredited: it was soon declared 'that socialism is dead and that none of its variants can be revived' (Dahrendorf, 1990, p. 38). Meanwhile Francis Fukuyama (1992), echoing Daniel Bell thirty years earlier, proclaimed the 'end of history'. If, as Mrs Thatcher was fond of stating, there was 'no alternative' to her policies in Britain, it now seemed that on a world scale there was now 'no alternative' to the values of liberal capitalism.

If Fukuyama is right and ideological conflict is effectively at an end, there would be little point in studying political ideologies, except perhaps to explore and expose the misconceptions of the past. Yet it already appears that Fukuyama's verdict is as premature as Daniel Bell's.

In the first place, if there is a new ideological consensus it involves not the end of ideology (still less of history), but, as with the previous Keynesian consensus, the dominance of a particular ideology. This ideology may remain dominant, but the experience of earlier periods of consensus suggests at least the possibility of challenge and supersession. Indeed, there are already signs that the consensus, if it ever existed, is cracking. In Russia and eastern Europe the transition to the free market has been sufficiently problematic to stall economic reforms. In some countries former Communists have been restored to favour while in others it seems that communism has been replaced not by capitalist democracy but by right-wing nationalism, religious fundamentalism, or even fascism. In the west some of the problems of an unregulated free market are being rediscovered. The triumphalism of the New Right has been replaced by doubts.

Moreover, the whole end of history thesis depends on the assumption that the only really important issues dividing humanity are issues of economic management, and the relative advantages and disadvantages of the free market and state planning. Yet the continuing bitter divisions over national identities, religious faith, race and ethnicity suggest that this assumption is grossly wide of the mark in much of the world. In Britain, the political issues which people care about sufficiently to bring them onto the streets include race, gender, sexual orientation, abortion, civil liberties, environmental protection and animal rights. The passions people bring to such causes reflect ideological perspectives which are not primarily economic.

Conclusion

It has been argued here that neither in Britain nor the wider world have we been witnessing the end of ideology. On the contrary, it could be argued that political differences have increased in range and depth. In addition to old familiar cleavages based on social class there are new or revived cross-cutting allegiances based on race, ethnicity, nationality, religion and gender. The apparent dominance of one perspective following the collapse of communism is far from total and is unlikely to prove permanent.

While some political differences are over the best means to achieve agreed ends, others reflect sharply opposed perspectives on the world. Indeed, one reason why it is often so difficult to resolve political differences is because they involve irreconcilable underlying assumptions. Governments and politicians often suggest that their prescriptions follow strictly from a common-sense evaluation of the facts or the situation, and a concern for the general public interest. Yet inevitably much policy analysis and prescription does not involve the application of neutral techniques but essentially ideological assumptions and interests, which can be challenged from a different ideological perspective. Ideologies not only may explain why particular policies emerge, but also how they are subsequently rationalised and justified.

Such considerations require some further exploration of what has has hitherto been taken for granted – the nature of political ideologies. This first chapter has established the importance of the study of political ideologies for an understanding of the mainsprings of political behaviour and public policy. It is now necessary to examine the nature and content of ideologies, the purposes they serve, the ways in which they are transmitted, and the links between ideology and policy. These will be among the subjects of the second chapter.

Guide to further reading

There is a wealth of literature on post-war British politics. The most useful single-volume history is by K. O. Morgan (1992), *The People's Peace: British history 1945–1990*. On consensus politics see D. Kavanagh (1990) *Thatcherism and British Politics* and D. Kavanagh and P. Morris (1994) *Consensus Politics*. The debate over the existence and extent of consensus is usefully summarised by A. Seldon in B. Jones *et al*. (1994) *Politics UK*, which provides a good up to date account of British government and politics. S. H. Beer (1982) *Modern British Politics* and R. McKenzie (1963) *British Political Parties* are still useful for an appreciation of the politics of the 1950s and 1960s. McKenzie emphasises the similarities in organisation and policy of the two major parties, while Beer presents a persuasive but now dated view of a one-nation conservatism as committed to collectivism as its socialist opponents. Very different assumptions underpin S. Finer's (1975) *Adversary Politics and Electoral Reform*.

On the wider debate over the end of ideology/history, see D. Bell (1960) and F. Fukuyama (1989, 1992). The implications of the collapse of communism for political ideologies worldwide is discussed provocatively by, among others, R. Dahrendorf (1990) *Reflections on the Revolution in Europe*, E. J. Hobsbawm (1994b) *Age of Extremes*, and R. Miliband (1994) *Socialism for a Sceptical Age*.

2

IDEOLOGY

Introduction

The last chapter established the importance of ideologies, but deliberately avoided or postponed some of the fundamental issues surrounding the study of ideologies. This chapter seeks to remedy that
omission, and addresses a number of questions. What is ideology and
what purposes do ideologies serve? How do ideologies relate to
power and interests on the one hand and science and truth on the
other? How can we classify and compare ideologies? How are
ideologies transmitted? How far do ideological considerations influence public policy? It will become apparent that there are no
generally agreed answers to these questions, rather that the concept of
ideology is itself contested, subject to rival interpretations.

What is ideology?

In the previous chapter it was suggested that ideology often has a
pejorative connotation, associated with blinkered dogmatism, extremism and illusion (McLellan, 1986, p. 1). It is also a highly contested
concept. Many key words used in political, philosophical and social
science discourse are unfortunately used in widely different senses,
and the term 'ideology' has been defined and employed in extremely
varied and even contradictory ways. One recent account identified

some twenty-seven distinctive 'definitional elements' drawn from the mass of literature on the subject (Hamilton, 1987).

Here the concept of ideology will be taken to mean any more or less coherent system of beliefs or views on politics and society. This is the more inclusive, neutral definition of the term derived from writers as diverse as Gramsci and Mannheim which is now fairly generally used at least in academic writing on ideology (Seliger, 1976, p. 14; Greenleaf, 1983, vol. 2, p. 7; Evans, 1984, p. 131; Hamilton, 1987, p. 38). Yet it has to be admitted that the more pejorative and restricted use of the term has a long history, both among Marxists and non-Marxists (McLellan, 1986).

It is impossible to ignore Marx and his successors on the subject of ideology, not only because the concept is central to Marxist thought, but because so many of the issues they have raised are still live. Crucially, there is the question of the relationship of political ideas to material interests and questions of power and domination on the one hand and science and truth on the other. Are political ideologies ultimately just rationalisations of self-interest? Do they simply reflect the interests of dominant groups? Is it impossible to adjudge between the rival claims of ideologies, or are some 'true' and others 'false', some scientifically based and others unscientific?

Marx was concerned with the source of ideas. One of his targets was idealism, the philosophical approach derived ultimately from Plato but featuring especially Kant and Hegel which suggested that ideas are the ultimate reality, and the motive force in human history. Against this, Marx presented his own materialist conception of history in which ideas derive from the material circumstances of humanity: 'Life is not determined by consciousness, but consciousness by life' (Marx, ed. McLellan, 1977, p. 164).

Thus ideas reflect social and economic circumstances. Marx moreover saw society as deeply divided, so that the moral and political ideas expressed at any time reflect ultimately conflicting class interests. But the prevailing ideas, Marx suggested, will reflect the existing power structure, the current pattern of domination and subordination, partly because those with economic and political power will be well placed to control the dissemination and legitimation of ideas, through, for example, education and the mass media. Thus 'the ideas of the ruling class are in every epoch the ruling ideas' (Marx, ed. McLellan, 1977, p. 176).

It follows that subordinate classes will not necessarily recognise the real basis of society, nor their own exploitation, but will hold a distorted, mistaken view of reality. Marx commonly used the term 'ideology' to describe this distorted view that a social class, such as the industrial proletariat, might have of its own position in society as a whole. Much of the prevailing wisdom of his day, such as the ideas of the classical economists, Smith, Malthus and Ricardo, Marx regarded as ideological rather than scientific. Their theories served the interests of capitalism. By contrast, Marx thought his own method provided a powerful tool for penetrating below the surface and understanding the real economic and social forces which shape change. Thus Marxism was science rather than ideology.

This identification of ideology with illusion and distortion and what Engels later called 'false consciousness' (McLellan, 1986, p. 18) is of course highly pejorative. However, Marx sometimes used the term in a more neutral sense, and this is the sense in which later Marxists, such as Lenin, Gramsci and Lukács have developed the discussion of ideology. Thus the need to counter the dominant ruling-class ideology with a proletarian or socialist ideology was assumed. The latter naturally could not be identified with illusion or false consciousness. The use of the term 'ideology', then, implied nothing as to the truth or falsehood of its content.

Yet this later non-pejorative use of the term ideology by Marxists is still tied to class interests. Relating political ideas to material interests is certainly a fruitful approach. It does make sense to ask who is putting forward particular doctrines and why, and whose interests they serve. Frequently the answers will be suggestive, although of course the establishment of an interest does not neces-sarily disprove a theory. Moreover, it is not that difficult to relate major political ideologies with class interests. Thus conservatism historically was associated with the landed interest, liberalism with financial and industrial capital, and socialism with the industrial working class.

Non-Marxists would generally reject the close association of ideologies with class interest. Thus conservatives or liberals would argue that their ideas have a universal relevance, and are to the general benefit of all. But one does not have to accept these claims uncritically to ask whether political ideologies always and essentially have to articulate class interests, for where does that leave per-spectives which reflect other divisions in society, such as those based on religion, ethnicity or gender?

In practice, Marxists have tended to regard such divisions as either artificially fostered to weaken working-class unity (e.g. nationalism and religion) or derived ultimately from more fundamental class divisions (e.g. race and gender). But of course there are those for whom issues of race, gender, religion or nationhood are quite fundamental rather than secondary, so that these issues inform their whole perspective on politics, power, decision-making and public policy. Thus feminism or nationalism may be regarded just as much as political ideologies as those which more plausibly relate to class divisions such as socialism or liberalism.

Yet feminism, nationalism or racism can still be associated with material interests, if not the economic class interests of classical Marxist theory. The Greens arguably present a greater difficulty for Marxists, as their ideology is not ostensibly related to the interest of any specific group within existing human society, but to generations yet unborn, to other species, and to the universe as a whole. While it is possible to relate green ideas to social interests, this may not be the most useful approach to understanding the ideology.

Modern, particularly American, social scientists have also, like Marx, employed the term ideology in a highly pejorative and re-stricted manner, but in a quite opposite sense to his. Thus non-Marxist economists, sociologists and political scientists emphasised the need for detached, value-free, rigorous empirical research – which they saw as the essence of the social science method. Marxist analysis was regarded, by contrast, as dogmatic, unscientific and 'ideological'. Ideology was thus identified with a blinkered adherence to a system of thought without regard to evidence. Communism and fascism were ideologies, while the liberal pluralist ideas on which post-war western society rested were scientific and non-ideological.

Both Marxists and non-Marxists then have tended to define ideology in a restricted sense, but they have reached diametrically opposed conclusions over which political perspectives should be regarded as ideological. Marx saw ideology as a rationalisation of the status quo, as a self-interested justification of the existing distribution of wealth and power. Many non-Marxists have regarded the status quo in the west as unideological, and the post-war consensus was taken as marking the 'end of ideology'. Revolutionary creeds that threatened consensus like communism were ideologies. Marx most of the time (but by no means all Marxists) and Marx's most virulent modern critics have also both used the term in a highly pejorative way. Thus an ideology is someone else's perspective. To describe a position as 'ideological' is to condemn it.

Such an interpretation of ideology is ultimately rather sterile. Partly for that reason, there is an increasing academic consensus that the term is more usefully employed in an inclusive and neutral, non-pejorative way. Here ideology will be taken to mean 'any system of ideas and norms directing political and social action' (Flew, 1979, p. 150). The use of the term 'ideology' does not therefore by itself imply any kind of judgement on the validity or otherwise of the ideas discussed. Ideology is not to be contrasted with science. Moreover, ideologies are not to be identified exclusively with either the preservation or the overthrow of the status quo. Ideologies may thus be conservative, reformist or revolutionary. They may be 'moderate' or 'extremist'. Further, although ideologies are often associated with conflict, a system of beliefs which commands general or even universal assent within society may still be characterised as an ideology. Thus the era of consensus politics did not involve the end of ideology, simply the widespread dominance of a single ideology, a situation which for some writers, such as Gramsci, might constitute the norm rather than the exception.

An ideology implies a connected set of beliefs, a whole perspective on the world, rather than a single political principle. Yet it may involve inconsistencies and even contradictions. Moreover, ideologies can be held at a variety of levels. They may be systematically articulated, through for example the writings of major thinkers, or expressed more selectively and persuasively through political pamphlets of speeches, or they may be essentially latent, and unsophisticated, expressed if at all in shorthand slogans and symbols. Hayek's *Road to Serfdom*, the advertising slogans of Saatchi and Saatchi, the speeches of Margaret Thatcher, the Union Jack, and the headlines in the *Sun* newspaper are all aspects of modern Conservative ideology.

Finally, no definite position is taken here on the vexed question of the relationship between ideology and interest. This may seem craven, or worse, depriving the study of a coherent theoretical framework for analysis (some may feel), but a degree of agnosticism does have the merit of not closing down in advance what might prove fruitful areas of study. An idealist position might preclude any investigation of the social background, interests and motivations of those holding particular views. A thoroughgoing materialism would not allow any discussion of the elements of mainstream ideologies in terms which their adherents would allow or understand. Furthermore, it might on a priori grounds dismiss all major British ideologies as rationalisations for capitalism with various shades of emphasis. This may be a quite tenable position, but it does rather undermine the case for any extensive examination of ideologies.

In the developing literature there is work on political ideologies within both the materialist and idealist traditions. A good example of a sophisticated Marxist approach is Stuart Hall's 'Variants of liberalism' (in Donald and Hall, 1986) which suggests a subtle interaction between changing class forces and the evolution of liberal ideas which is never crudely reductionist. By contrast, Robert Pearson and Geraint Williams (1984) treat ideologies in an essentially idealist way. Their procedure is to expound first the ideas and principles of particular political ideologies, such as liberalism, conservatism and socialism, and then explore how these ideas were applied in the form of public policy. Their work fits within a political thought tradition which tends to assume that ideas are worth studying in themselves, and is less concerned with where they have come from.

Classifying ideologies

One of the oldest ways of classifying ideologies involves locating them on the familiar left–right political spectrum. The terms derive from the seating positions in the National Assembly in France in 1790, when the most revolutionary groups sat on the left and the more conservative or reactionary sat on the right. Since then the terms 'left' and 'right' over time have acquired a universal currency. In many legislatures, particularly where the chambers are semi-circular, seating arrangements still mirror those of the revolutionary National Assembly, but even in countries like the United Kingdom where they do not, politicians, parties, and political programmes are freely classified according to the terminology of left and right.

A 'scale' suggests that the terms are essentially relative, and that is how they are employed. Indeed, further sub-categories are often used, such as 'far (or hard) left', 'extreme right' or 'centre left', to describe the position occupied on the spectrum more precisely. Frequently it is suggested that a certain politician, party or trade union is more left or more right than another, and the terms are also commonly used to describe intra-party factions. This can be confusing. Thus a particular politician or group in the British Labour Party might be described as 'right wing', strictly within the context of his party, while more generally he would be regarded as 'on the left'. Similarly, factions within the Conservative Party are often loosely termed left, right or centre to explain their ideological position relative to others within their party, while they all essentially belong to the right. This emphasises the importance of context in interpretation.

Yet if the classification is virtually universal, it is not unproblematic. What is the scale really about? A common interpretation is that the scale measures attitudes to change, with those seeking revolutionary change on the left, and those opposed to all change on the right, with cautious reformers somewhere in the middle. Thus socialists and communists are on the left, conservatives on the right and progressive liberals in the centre.

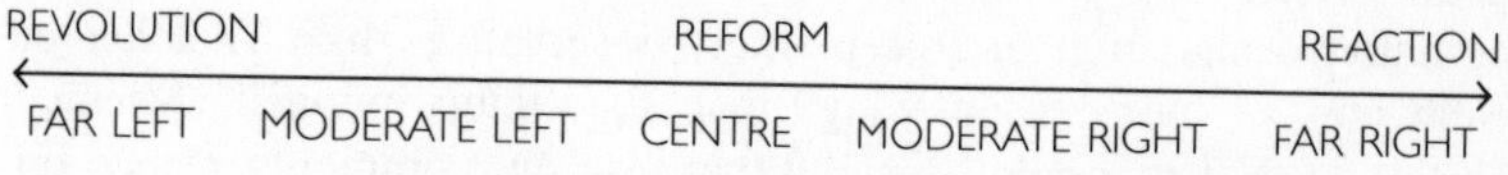

REVOLUTION   REFORM   REACTION

←——→

FAR LEFT   MODERATE LEFT   CENTRE   MODERATE RIGHT   FAR RIGHT

Figure 2.1   Left and Right: revolution and reaction

However, this causes some difficulties where the revolutionaries succeed, and establish a new status quo, as for example was the case with the communist regimes in Russia and eastern Europe. Logically it might be supposed that these Communists should then have been called 'right', while their opponents who desired massive change to displace them should have been described as 'left'. But in practice the Communists continued to be regarded as 'left' whether they constituted the revolutionary opposition or the new status quo. Similarly, there is a problem with what is sometimes described as the 'radical right', which might be considered almost a contradiction in terms if 'right' means opposition to change. Thus the Conservative Prime Minister Margaret Thatcher instituted radical change, although she and her allies were generally considered further to the right than the

rather more cautious one-nation Conservatives whom they had effectively displaced.

Another way of interpreting the left–right scale is in terms of
attitudes to authority – with those championing individual liberty on
the left, and those emphasising discipline and order on the right. This
also does not always accord with general usage. Thus anarchists and
communists, both generally considered on the left or far left, tend to
display radically different attitudes to authority, and there are similar
differences between the libertarian and authoritarian right. It might be
noted in passing that the notion of 'totalitarianism' developed by
some western theorists in the post-war period, implied that both
communism and fascism, conventionally placed at opposite ends of
the left–right scale, were essentially similar in subordinating individual liberty to state authority.

Perhaps rather more promising is a definition in terms of attitudes
to state intervention in the economy, with 'left' associated with
collectivism and 'right' with the free market. This definition would
appear to be more consistent with the description of communists and
socialists as 'left' regardless of whether they constituted the establishment or the opposition. Moreover, it is also consistent with the
common designation of free market conservatives like Thatcher or
Redwood as more 'right wing' than the 'interventionist' Michael
Heseltine. Yet it should be noted that fascism, commonly placed on
the far right, favoured some state direction and autarchy rather than
the free market.

COLLECTIVISM			LAISSEZ-FAIRE
STATE DIRECTION	STATE INTERVENTION	STATE WELFARE	FREE MARKET

←──→

COMMUNISM   SOCIALISM   MODERN LIBERALISM   ONE-NATION CONSERVATISM   NEW RIGHT

Figure 2.2   Left and Right: collectivism and *laissez-faire*

These ambiguities and inconsistencies should be noted, but ultimately the terms 'left' and 'right' are too familiar and indeed useful
to be discarded. Thus they will be employed freely in this book,
particularly in the earlier chapters, and the classification adopted is
conventional, despite the problems discussed above. However, as the

FAR LEFT	MODERATE LEFT	CENTRE	MODERATE RIGHT	FAR RIGHT
COMMUNISM	SOCIALISM	LIBERALISM	CONSERVATISM	FASCISM

Figure 2.3 Left and Right: conventional ideological spectrum

discussion above perhaps implies, this left–right political spectrum is more readily applicable to some ideologies than others. In particular there is a problem in locating nationalism, feminism, and the Green ideology on a left–right continuum. They each cut across or render irrelevant the familiar distinctions based on economic intervention or social class interests. Nationalism in different times and places has been associated with ideas across the political spectrum from the far left to the far right. Feminism is generally linked with the left, but there is some question over whether it should be. Although most Green activists are also more commonly associated with the left, the familiar Green slogan 'neither left nor right but forward' suggests they see themselves on another dimension altogether. Thus some would argue that 'left' and 'right' describe the old obsolete politics, while the women's movement and the Green movement in common with other currents of thought such as post-modernism or communitarianism represent a new politics.

Constituents of ideologies

The broad and somewhat loose definition of ideology adopted here rather precludes any categorical assumptions over what an ideology should or should not contain. It may confidently be asserted that all political ideologies contain, implicitly or explicitly, descriptive and prescriptive elements. The prescriptive elements may normally predominate, but any prescription for social action must ultimately rest on some assumptions, however crude, about the nature of existing society and human behaviour. There is thus a picture of the world as it is, which may be more or less accurate or highly distorted, and there is a picture of the world as it should be, which may approximate to what is perceived as the existing picture, or be far removed from it. There is usually some conception also, rudimentary or highly developed, of how the ends which are desired are to be achieved.

Thus three elements may be broadly identified: an interpretation of existing social arrangements, a vision of the future and a strategy for realising that future. Of course for those who are broadly happy with existing social arrangements, the vision of the future may closely resemble the present, and the strategy will be one of seeking to maintain the status quo. Those profoundly dissatisfied with the present will contemplate strategies for achieving some kind of revolution.

A view of existing social arrangements will commonly include some assumptions about human nature and individual motivation, and indeed such assumptions can be seen to lie behind both the ideas of most of the great political thinkers of the past, and, perhaps more implicitly, behind modern political ideologies. Indeed, it is not difficult to divide political theorists into optimists and pessimists on the subject of human nature. Plato, Machiavelli and Hobbes, for example, were all fairly pessimistic about the capacity of human beings to live together sociably and co-operatively, without a considerably element of coercion or brainwashing, while Aristotle, Rousseau and, in the last analysis, Marx, had a more optimistic view of human potential for fruitful co-operation.

Among modern political ideologies, fascism makes some fairly cynical assumptions about the pliability of man, while anarchism involves what some might consider hugely optimistic assumptions about human nature. Of mainstream ideologies socialism is essentially optimistic, and traditional conservatism rather pessimistic about human nature. Between these two, old-style liberalism, drawing heavily on classical economics, sees individuals motivated by self-interest, but suggests that the net consequence of all pursuing their self-interest will be the greatest common good.

A linked consideration is the potential for changing human nature, from which a further question naturally arises. Is human nature the same everywhere, or is it substantially the product of the environment? Does vicious behaviour reflect the immutable nature of humanity, or is it the product of a particular environment, which might be changed? Anarchists, for example, believe that power corrupts. A society without hierarchies of authority, and without government in the sense of coercive power would lead to more co-operative and civilised human behaviour. Socialists tend to think that highly self-interested competitive behaviour is the product of the capitalist economic system rather than a universal human characteristic. They also suggest that substantial inequalities in human capacities and attainments are not innate, but can be reduced through enlarging opportunities. Conservatives are usually rather more sceptical about the scope for improvements in human nature, although they may consider religious belief, or stable family background as possible ameliorative factors. Some feminists would draw a major distinction between male and female human nature, suggesting that men are naturally aggressive and competitive, while women are naturally caring and co-operative, although other feminists would suggest that this behaviour is largely culturally determined, and that men could learn to be caring. The capacity for changing human behaviour is clearly important to some ideologies, to the extent that prescriptions for the future may require people to behave in different ways.

This highlights the question of the relationship of the individual to society. Most of the ancient Greeks, including both Plato and Aristotle, saw man as a naturally social and political animal. Aristotle considered that the man outside political society was either a beast or a god, sub-human or superhuman. A proper human existence was not conceivable outside society. At the opposite extreme liberalism has often tended to see society as an artificial construct, requiring a conscious and deliberate effort to bring it into being, and having no meaning apart from its constituent individual elements. Mrs Thatcher lies comfortably within this liberal political tradition in her assertion that there is no such thing as society, only individuals and their families. By contrast, both traditional conservatism (or Toryism) and socialism have tended to view the individual as inseparable from society, with individuals, groups and whole classes bound inextricably to each other through ties of mutual dependence, although of course conservatives would tend to see these unequal relationships in essentially benign terms, while socialists would interpret them in terms of exploitation, at least within existing capitalist society. Finally, in this connection it may be observed that what have been described as totalitarian ideologies involve, in theory at least, the total subjugation of the individual to the national whole.

Ideologies will commonly involve all kinds of other assumptions about the way society currently operates: the extent of equality within society, the organisation of work and industrial relations, community relations, authority and power structures, and a host of further issues. Some of these assumptions may be substantially accurate, while others may be wildly inaccurate, but perceptions of how the world is inevitably colour perceptions of how it should be, so that description and prescription are closely interlinked. In the 1970s, for example, it was widely believed that trade unions ran the country, and that Mr Jack Jones, then General Secretary of the Transport and General Workers Union, was more powerful than the Prime Minister – purportedly a description of the then existing state of affairs. Not surprisingly perhaps in view of this widespread conviction, many people also thought that trade unions were too powerful (an evaluation) and that their power should be reduced (a prescription).

Prescriptions for the future are thus bound to depend on perceptions of present arrangements and attitudes towards them. Some people may be more fearful than desirous of change – for all sorts of reasons. They may be substantial beneficiaries of existing social arrangements. They may pessimistically fear that change is likely to be for the worse. They may be persuaded, perhaps against what others would regard as their objective interests, that change is impossible, dangerous, or undesirable. The essence of conservatism, as the term implies, is to avoid major change, and a radically different future is neither sought nor desired, although a degree of gradual reform may be countenanced. Some reactionaries, in the proper sense of the term, may seek a future which resembles a past, real or imaginary, which they regret; others may strive for a future which is nothing like the present or immediate past. The construction of utopias has been a favourite pastime of political thinkers since classical times.

The problem with utopias is how to achieve them. The proposed utopia may be far more appealing than existing society, but how does one progress from (a) to (b)? Ideologies thus generally involve some assumptions about social change, although this element can in practice be fairly weak. Marx was critical of some of his socialist predecessors for lacking any coherent theory of social change. They had a socialist vision of the future, but no realistic strategy for achieving that socialist vision. A major debate among socialists since Marx's day has been over the prospects of the parliamentary road to socialism – whether socialism can be achieved solely or mainly through the ballot box and the election of governments with parliamentary majorities. Some socialists deny that this is possible. Parliamentary socialists tend to respond that the alternatives are even more problematic.

For conservatives the problem is rather how to maintain social stability, and avoid social unrest and revolution. The choice may often seem to lie between granting reforms to appease dissatisfied elements, or refusing any concessions for fear that these will only fuel demands for further change and create more instability in the long run. In general, conservatives are much more sceptical of the scope for deliberate social engineering than liberals or socialists, and more wary of the possible dangers of change.

Levels of ideology

Political ideologies may be expressed at a number of different levels, from the relatively sophisticated to the crude or even latent.

Some 'great thinkers' studied within the political theory tradition have clearly made a significant contribution to particular political ideologies: Marx to socialism, and, perhaps, Burke to conservatism or Mill to liberalism. But there are writers who have attracted particular attention from other political thinkers or from modern academics who have had relatively little obvious impact on subsequent political movements: Hobbes, for example, generally rated as the most important political thinker that Britain has produced. It may of course be true that many of Hobbes' ideas have generally permeated the British political tradition, but it is difficult to identify him positively with a particular ideology.

Often writers who would not be categorised as major political thinkers have had a wider influence, and perhaps contributed more towards the development and acceptance of particular ideologies. Harriet Martineau, who wrote little fables embodying the principles of classical economics, Edward Baines, the polemical editor of the *Leeds Mercury*, and Samuel Smiles, the purveyor of Victorian homilies on self-help and other virtues were all more widely read and understood than Ricardo or Nassau Senior, and in some ways can be considered more typical of *laissez-faire* liberalism.

At another level, the pronouncements and achievements of active politicians, which would not command space or attention in histories of political theory, may play a critical role in the development of ideologies and be important for their subsequent interpretation. There are very few 'great texts' which provide much of a guide to an understanding of conservatism. Many interpretations place particular emphasis on the contribution of past politicians, especially Prime Ministers, such as Peel, Disraeli, Salisbury, Baldwin, and most recently Mrs Thatcher, to the development of conservatism. Some of these politicians did articulate their ideas with varying degrees of sophistication in articles, novels, or carefully constructed speeches and manifestos, but the ideas of others must be substantially derived from their behaviour and output in office. For while political ideologies, almost by definition, influence political behaviour, they can also sometimes appear as *post hoc* rationalisations of political behaviour, although few politicians would put it quite as bluntly as Herbert Morrison, who declared that socialism was what the Labour government did.

Ideologies are not just the possession of the political classes, however. They are held by the masses, and although there may be a difference in sophistication between the elite and mass versions of particular ideologies, normally they recognisably belong to the same kind of outlook on life, and interrelate. Mrs Thatcher acknowledges the influence of the everyday maxims acquired during her upbringing in that celebrated grocer's shop in Grantham (Young, 1989, p. 5) but also acknowledges a debt to Adam Smith and Hayek (Thatcher, 1977), and it is difficult to assess which has made the more significant contribution to what has come to be termed 'Thatcherism'.

It can be confidently asserted that it is the everyday maxims which have a greater resonance with the wider public. Newspaper headlines, slogans and graffiti, and non-verbal symbols, such as the British bulldog, or Britannia, or photographic images may reinforce or express particular ideological approaches. Some political ideologies are indeed almost entirely lacking in sophisticated intellectual expression. The Nuremberg rallies and the slogans painted in Mussolini's Italy, 'Believe, Obey, Fight', 'Live dangerously', 'Better one day as a lion than a thousand years as a sheep', perhaps tell us more about the nature of fascism, and certainly had more influence on political behaviour than the generally rather thin fascist theoretical literature.

Ideologies then can be interpreted and analysed at a number of different levels – from sophisticated intellectual constructs down to inferences from political behaviour. The clenched fist may seem a long way removed from Marx's *Das Kapital* but they are both aspects of one ideology. The different levels are also intricately interrelated. It should be re-emphasised, however, that the non-rational or irrational ways in which ideologies are sometimes made manifest does not necessarily invalidate their interpretation of the world or their message. To take an obvious analogy, it would not generally be regarded as fair to judge the truth of some of the world's major religions from the sometimes crude utterances and bizarre practices of their less educated adherents. On the other hand, such behaviour may tell us as much about a particular religion as the sacred texts associated with it. Both require investigation for a full picture.

Power, influence and indoctrination

Consideration of the ideological perspectives of the masses raises some awkward questions on the transmission of ideas – over, for example, the potential for deliberate indoctrination. There are some celebrated fictional accounts of thought control, and plenty of real life illustrations of more or less successful attempts to mould opinion, by no means all of which are to be found in so-called totalitarian states. For example, the allied authorities in Germany after the war embarked on a deliberate counter-indoctrination programme which employed many of the means of their Nazi predecessors: censorship of newspapers, burning of books, screening teachers for ideological soundness, and the like.

Most attempts to influence people's minds on political issues are less extensive and systematic than this, but there is still a certain amount of quite conscious manipulation, even in a supposed liberal democracy like Britain. For example, both prior to and during the privatisation of the former public utilities television commercials were extensively and expensively employed to promote the activities of 'your local electricity business' and 'your local water business'. Quite apart from other questions raised by these commercials, the use of the term *business* was clearly deliberate and significant. Although the term can be employed by academics in a broader sense, its popular association is with the private sector, involving decidedly different associations from the word *authority* or *board* previously used. It both prepared the public for the privatisation of these industries, and promoted the values and ideas associated with the private sector and commercial enterprise.

If deliberate manipulation of people's minds by the government or the dominant element in society was regularly employed and always successful, there would be no ideological conflict, just the universal acceptance of one ideology. Plato wanted to eliminate conflict in this way in his ideal state, and there have been celebrated recent fictional examples, such as Orwell's *1984* and Huxley's *Brave New World*. Real live governments have found it rather more difficult to stifle all dissent. However, at the very least it can be said that they have the means at their disposal to influence opinion.

The role of the media in shaping opinion is another controversial area. The liberal pluralist assumption was that people were exposed to a wide range of sources and views, enabling them to make up their own mind on political questions. Academic research in the 1960s suggested that people used the media to reinforce their own ideas, and tended to filter out information which did not match their pre-conceived attitudes. This implied that the media influence on attitudes was relatively slight. Moreover, at that time there was a rough balance in the partisan leanings of the national press, and any newspaper bias was assumed to be modified by a strictly non-partisan television.

These comforting conclusions have been somewhat undermined of late. The narrow concentration of ownership and control of the media has reawakened fears of the power of the press (Newton, in Drucker *et al.*, 1986). Recent elections have involved a clear party bias in the national press, and mass circulation tabloids exhibit extensive and quite deliberate political propaganda, although this is not realised by all their readers (Seymour-Ure, 1974). The assumption of television neutrality has also increasingly been challenged by the radical left and some of the right (Glasgow University Media Group, 1976, 1982). Additionally and critically, more recent research is less con-fident of the capacity of people to resist or filter out the extensive political propaganda to which they are exposed. The views of the masses – the popular expression of political ideologies – may reflect media influence. Dearlove and Saunders (1984, p. 352) conclude 'It is too crude to suggest that the papers tell us what to think; but they do to a large extent tell us how to think it.'

Too much emphasis should perhaps not be placed on deliberate indoctrination by governments or media propaganda. Far more sig-nificant, it might be argued, is the largely unconscious process by which beliefs are transmitted and sustained from the elite to the masses, and across generations. Existing institutions, work practices, patterns of social organisation, habits and beliefs may generally be taken for granted. In some cases it may require a considerable effort to even imagine alternatives. The weight of tradition is always likely to be a major constraint on political thinking, which will tend to rationalise the status quo, and serve the interests of those who benefit principally from the status quo. Thus the ideas of established dominant groups will tend to be fairly generally accepted throughout society, without any deliberate action to ensure this. And while the dominant ideology may not be all-pervasive, some of its core assumptions at least may gain wide acceptance among subordinate groups.

Parkin (1972, ch. 3) usefully distinguishes between dominant, subordinate and radical meaning systems. The dominant value system 'will tend to set the standards for what is considered objectively "right"' throughout society. Parkin points out that these generally accepted standards will affect artistic values and linguistic usages, as well as the more critical rules for the allocation and distribution of resources. The subordinate value system is grounded in the direct experiences of the local working-class community, but is 'essentially accommodative' involving adaptation towards, rather than endorse-ment of, or outright opposition to, dominant values. Parkin instances trade unionism as an example of a subordinate value system. While trade unionism springs directly from working-class experience, and involves attempts by the organised working class to secure better wages and conditions through collective bargaining, it does not normally amount to a fundamental challenge to the existing economic system, but rather can be seen as an accommodation with capitalism. A radical value system involves a clear alternative to the existing social and political order, such as might be presented by a socialist party. Parkin's own analysis suggests how difficult it is to secure mass support for such a radical alternative value system. It seems unlikely to emerge spontaneously from working-class experience, and although Parkin suggests that an organised working-class party may be able to articulate and sustain a mass following for a radical alternative, he also acknowledges how far in practice socialist parties have abandoned radical aims, and sought accommodation with the existing capitalist order.

It is not necessary to follow Parkin's argument in every particular to recognise that there is a clear connection between the distribution of economic and political power on the one hand, and ideological competition on the other. The battle of ideas is inevitably fought with loaded dice. The failure of some political perspectives, such as radical feminism, or anarchism, or dark green environmentalism, to gain a wider following may reflect inherent weaknesses in the ideology. Alternatively, it may be an indication of the overwhelming difficult-ies any radical perspective faces in combating the mass of routinely accepted assumptions bound up with the existing economic and social order. Yet it may not just be radical left-wing views which fail to secure a fair hearing. Both neo-liberals and neo-conservatives have claimed that the post-war progressive Keynesian consensus effectively excluded their ideas from political debate until recently.

Theory and reality – ideology and public policy

It is the constant two-way interplay between ideas and action which is perhaps the essence of political ideologies. Ideologies evolve and develop through experience of reality. Marx's writings may be reinterpreted by every age, but the texts remain the same. Socialism as a political ideology has had to evolve to take into account developments as varied as a universal adult franchise, two world wars, the Russian Revolution, the General Strike, the Great Depression, the welfare state, Keynesianism and economic growth, decolonisation and the emergence of the third world. Such developments inevitably provoked some reassessment of cherished nostrums – some might argue not enough, and indeed would suggest that conservatism has been more adaptable. A common consequence has been internal tension and division: between socialism and social democracy, for example, which are now sometimes presented as essentially separate ideologies. There was a similar tension within liberalism around the turn of the century between old-style free market liberalism, and the New Liberalism. In such circumstances the reformers feel that they are extending and updating principles to take account of a changed world, while traditional adherents feel that fundamental principles are being ignored or betrayed. There has been a similar debate among conservatives since the Second World War over the extent to which conservatism should make concessions to the altered circumstances and altered expectations of the post-war world.

But if ideologies are constantly evolving and adapting to changed circumstances, they are also constantly influencing political and social action. Ideological perceptions influence, for example, whether people vote, and how they vote. They will influence how individuals, groups and communities will react to proposed and actual developments which adversely affect them – from passive acquiescence, through various forms of lobbying to civil disobedience and ultimately violence. They will influence the kind of demands which are made of government and how these are pursued. They will also quite fundamentally affect legislation and other outputs of government.

Public policy not only reflects ideological assumptions, but in turn can influence people's ideological perceptions. The sale of council houses is an obvious illustrative example. The policy may be said to reflect Conservative convictions on the merits of private ownership, and free market values. But the opportunity which many council house tenants took to purchase their own houses, arguably had an impact on their political perceptions, and subsequently their political behaviour, including perhaps their voting behaviour.

The relationship between ideology and public policy has become a fruitful area of study. Laying bare the ideological assumptions behind particular measures provides a useful approach to policy analysis, which avoids the bland consensus interpretations of much social and political history. There is often the implication that particular outcomes were the only possible course of action following the cumulative endeavours of enlightened reformers of all convictions and none, working in the general public interest. Uncovering the ideological assumptions behind particular policies does not of course necessarily invalidate them, but does provide a basis for criticism and the analysis of alternatives. Why, for example, did Beveridge consider the insurance principle so important in his social security scheme? He might have recommended that benefits should be financed out of general taxation (as in effect they substantially have been). Beveridge's own liberalism, and the broadly small 'l' liberal assumptions of much of the then political establishment provides some explanation.

Objectivity and bias in the study of ideologies

The discussion of ideology in this and the previous chapter should warn the reader that this is not a subject where one can expect objectivity. Clearly, accounts of specific ideologies are written from a particular point of view which may be more or less sympathetic to the ideology concerned. Much of the literature on feminism or the Greens is written by committed supporters, and some is frankly propagandist. By contrast, a substantial proportion of the academic writing on nationalism is in varying degrees hostile to the nationalist ideology, and some is clearly aimed at discrediting its assumptions. Such obvious bias by both proponents and antagonists is scarcely surprising. Ideologies are generally action-oriented – paraphrasing Marx, they seek to change the world, not just to interpret it. Those who are ideologically committed seek converts to their cause. Even academics who affect greater detachment inevitably have their own views which consciously or unconsciously influence the way they treat their subject.

Moreover, as we have seen, the study of ideology itself inevitably reflects ideological preconceptions. There are very different views on the definition and nature of ideology, and the relationship of ideology to power and interests on the one hand and science and truth on the other. There are widely different perspectives on human nature and motivation, and on the capacity of human beings for rational thought and the pursuit of rational self-interest. The relationship of the individual to society is very variously interpreted, with conflicting assumptions over the impact of environmental and social pressures on behaviour, and radically different implications on the capacity for individual judgement and responsibility.

All this suggests some problems for students, both in terms of reading and interpreting what others have written on specific ideologies and ideology in general, and in terms of formulating and presenting their own views. The contested nature of the subject matter may suggest that in the study of ideologies anything goes, allowing a free rein to the ventilation of personal prejudices. Such an attitude is misguided. As in any subject for academic study there is an obligation to standards of accuracy over detail and rigour in analysis. Views attributed to particular thinkers, politicians, parties or ideological perspectives require supporting evidence. The reasoning behind inferences and causal connections should be explained. Above all, awkward facts which do not fit a favoured interpretation should not be ignored. A particular standpoint or theory may ultimately be rejected, but in academic discourse there is a presumed obligation to present it fairly and accurately first.

Political ideologies are the very stuff of controversy, which is why many find them a subject of fascinating interest. But this means that no one who comes to the study of political ideologies can be free of preconceptions, while many will have strongly held views. In some cases, further study may lead to some modification of previous convictions, or possibly even a major change in political allegiance. It is perhaps rather more likely that initial political opinions will not be significantly altered. The aim of academic study is the promotion of greater understanding, not conversion. Even so, it is difficult to divorce academic enquiry entirely from political allegiance, and the two are not necessarily inconsistent. Commitment to a particular political position should not preclude some reasonably dispassionate examination of its development, supporting interests, core principles and problematic areas. Equally, opposition to a particular ideology is not compromised by an attempt to understand its appeal to others. There are advantages to be derived from 'knowing your enemy'.

Even an ideology such as fascism which may inspire general repugnance requires some reasonably detached analysis to explain its apparent attractions to millions between the wars, and its possible continuing appeal today. Was it the product of a particular time and place, or was it related to more common and enduring aspects of human behaviour? Did it draw its support from one particular section of society or social class, or was its appeal fairly general? Can that appeal be best understood in terms of psychological factors, such as a presumed need for order and authority, or in terms of economic circumstances, such as unemployment and inflation? Did it secure converts by pandering to the basest human instincts, or were some attracted by an element of idealism and self-sacrifice? These are not wholly academic questions – indeed they might have considerable implications for the future of humanity – but they are best addressed using dispassionate and rigorous academic enquiry rather than glib answers based on prior assumptions.

A one-sided or inadequate view of an ideology may not reflect prior prejudice on the part of the reader, but simply weaknesses or bias in the source material. The best safeguard against falling for a partial, narrow or eccentric interpretation of an ideology is to read widely but always critically. Contrasting interpretations, and both hostile and sympathetic treatments should be deliberately sought out. Such an approach will help to identify both points of agreement and controversy. In all reading a questioning, sceptical approach should be adopted. Nothing should be taken on trust (including what is written here!). It is often useful to attempt to discern the author's perspective. To know that a particular writer is a Marxist or belongs to the New Right may assist in interpretion, and also suggest critical questions.

Guide to further reading

Useful extended definitions of ideology and related concepts are provided in various specialist dictionaries such as those by R. Williams (1976), A. Bullock and O. Stallybrass (1977), R. Scruton (1983) and T. Bottomore (1991). These are handy reference works from which to begin an exploration of the numerous highly contested concepts discussed throughout this book, but the reader should be warned that the treatment of ideas even in such reference books reflects the different perspectives of authors. A good introduction to the issues surrounding the nature of ideology is given in D. McLellan (1986) *Ideology*. There are thoughtful chapters in A. Vincent (1995) and by I. McKenzie in Eccleshall *et al.* (1994). Still the most authoritative modern source is M. Seliger (1976). The best introduction to the relationship between power and value systems is still Parkin (1972) *Class, Inequality and Political Order*.

A number of useful studies have explored the relationship between ideology and public policy: for example, Fraser (1984) *The Evolution of the British Welfare State*, George and Wilding (1985) *Ideology and Social Welfare*, Pearson and Williams (1984) *Political Thought and Public Policy in the Nineteenth Century* and, above all, W. H. Greenleaf's (1983) massive *The British Political Tradition*.

3

THE BRITISH POLITICAL TRADITION

Introduction

This chapter will seek to explain and justify the emphasis of this book on British political ideologies. It argues that political ideologies in Britain, although clearly linked with wider currents of thought, developed in distinctive ways. It seeks to establish a connection between a British political tradition and key formative developments in British history.

Although any account of the British political tradition must be selective and inevitably oversimplified, it is worth attempting, as it is impossible to explain the distinctive development of British political ideologies without reference to the historical context within which they have been shaped. The choice here has been to centre on the long-term impact of particular historical developments. More specifically, this account focuses on the impact on British political thinking of six major historical influences: first, the Reformation and religious upheavals of the sixteenth century, second, the political upheavals of the seventeenth century, third, the establishment of the British Constitution and political stability from the eighteenth century onwards, fourth, the impact of industrialisation over the last two hundred or so years, fifth, the effect of war and finally, the legacy of empire.

While reference is made to the ideas of major political thinkers in the context of these historical developments, their thought is not systematically explored. It is argued that British history itself has shaped British political ideas. This is more obviously the case where the focus, as here, is on the evolution of broad political ideologies which can be examined at a number of levels from the highly articulate and conscious elaborations of key thinkers and political leaders, to the largely unconscious and implicit assumptions of the masses.

Why British political ideologies?

Most, if not all, of the ideologies referred to in the opening two chapters are essentially international. Moreover, the specifically British contribution to these ideologies has not been particularly impressive in intellectual terms. Britain appears almost a backwater in the evolution of socialism, with few thinkers or politicians warranting extended consideration in any general history (e.g. Lichtheim, 1970). Ideologies of the right are less internationalist and more culture-specific, yet it might still be suggested that with the partial exception of Burke, Britain has provided no sustained intellectually coherent defence of conservative or reactionary politics to compare with continental or American writing. British conservatism is thus largely empty of explicit theoretical content, and its essence has to be inferred from practice. The British contribution to liberalism is rather more impressive, although the general insularity of British thinking about politics is again evident from the general ignorance in this country of the European liberal tradition. While continental accounts of liberalism pay due tribute to British liberal thinkers, the compliment is rarely returned. Even Arblaster's (1984) stimulating book on western liberalism is somewhat Anglocentric. Nor is the British element in more recently developed ideologies any more significant. Green and feminist thinking have been more impressively explored in other countries.

So why *British* political ideologies? It might be objected that any account of ideologies centring on Britain is bound to leave out a great deal of what is important. Not only does it necessarily involve a somewhat intellectually impoverished account of socialism and conservatism, it also virtually omits altogether some ideologies which are important on an international scale such as anarchism. But in general a concentration on British ideologies might be held to reflect and confirm an insularity in the British intellectual tradition which is less than admirable.

However, that very insularity provides a kind of justification. British political ideologies are clearly related to wider ideologies which transcend national boundaries, and as such obviously susceptible to foreign influences – an account of British socialism which made no reference at all to Marx might reasonably be regarded as deficient. Yet they are also to a degree *sui generis*, of their own kind. British liberalism, conservatism and socialism have all developed in a distinctive way. All mainstream British ideologies have been influenced by a British political, economic and social history which has exhibited some markedly different features from experiences elsewhere. There is thus a British political tradition which has left its mark on all our major political ideologies, even those which, like socialism, are ostensibly internationalist in assumptions. And it goes without saying that it is these British variants of political ideologies which influence British political behaviour, and British public policy.

To attempt to demonstrate how British history has influenced the development of British political ideologies might seem a far more perilous enterprise than a conventional account of British political thought. The past is not 'given'. Contemporaries disagreed about the meaning and significance of the momentous events such as the Reformation or the English Civil War which they lived through, and historians have continued to disagree about them ever since. Key episodes in British history have been repeatedly reinterpreted.

Moreover, while these episodes have clearly had an effect on subsequent thinking about politics, it is equally true that later political ideas have contributed to the reinterpretation of the past. Sometimes a powerful myth has been created with the benefit of hindsight, and from the standpoint of victorious groups and interests, and this in turn has reinforced the dominant ideology. Something of the sort perhaps occurred with the so-called Glorious Revolution of 1688. The interpretation of history is often a critical ingredient in political ideologies, and the winners who have emerged from the struggles of the past have not surprisingly sought to rewrite that past to suit their own interests.

Inevitably, then, our understanding of the past is influenced by our understanding of the present, and equally our modern political ideologies involve an interpretation of the past. This is more obvious in some other countries than in Britain. In France the interpretation and reinterpretation of the last 200 years of French history have been an inseparable element of ideological conflict.

The impact of the Reformation and the religious upheavals of the sixteenth century

The English Reformation begun by Henry VIII may seem a somewhat remote starting-point for an exploration of the British political tradition, the more particularly as Britain was then a geographical expression rather than a political reality. Yet it was an event of quite fundamental importance in this country's history, with not only major immediate consequences, but long-term political implications, some of which have persisted to the present day.

It is a truism that, following the Reformation, England was no longer part of the Roman Catholic family of nations. That alone, however, had major implications for the content and style of its politics. The politics of Catholic countries today have a different flavour from those where Catholics are in a minority. Church–state relations have èvolved differently. In some cases the Church has been built into the state, in other cases the state and the Church have been at odds (Italy before Mussolini's Concordat, or France under the Third Republic). Either way, religion has generally continued to play a more significant part in politics. It is sometimes explicitly recognised in the Constitution. It has spawned Catholic political parties, and Catholic trade unions. It has influenced voting, and church leaders have not on occasion shrunk from giving explicit instructions to their flock over how to exercise their vote. The close involvement of the Church in politics, and sometimes its association with a wealthy establishment, has also often provoked an anti-clerical reaction among liberals and socialists. There is thus an anticlerical tradition among French, Spanish and Italian liberals, republicans, radicals and socialists which is largely absent in Britain.

A more problematic, contestable legacy of the English Reformation was the early development of capitalism. It was Weber who suggested that Protestantism, or more specifically Calvinism, was particularly congenial to the development of values which favoured capitalist accumulation. Tawney (1938) and others have applied Weber's thesis to England, associating Puritanism with the spirit of mercantile and subsequently industrial capitalism. The evidence is suggestive, but inconclusive, yet if there is anything in the theory, then the initially rather arbitrary and accidental removal of England from the Catholic sphere had momentous long-term implications for the country's economic development, and ways of thinking about economics and politics. Samuel Smiles' little Victorian homilies on self-help might be seen as an expression of an essentially 'Protestant ethic' which can be traced back to the Reformation.

While the connection between the Reformation and the rise of capitalism is speculative and contentious, the continuing divisive effect it had, not only on religious conviction and observance but also on society and politics, is almost too obvious to require restatement. Within England the Reformation established religious divisions which have persisted to the present day. Henry VIII of course had no intention of establishing freedom of conscience in religious matters. He had merely substituted himself for the Pope as Head of the English Church. He sought to impose a new, only slightly altered orthodoxy to replace the one he had overthrown. Yet his successors failed to impose a uniform religious system. Catholicism could not be restored, as Mary and later James II discovered, but it also could not be totally suppressed. Nor, it transpired, could the sovereign impose uniformity of religious observance on Protestants.

Scarcely anyone in the sixteenth or early seventeenth centuries championed religious toleration, however. True believers of all per-suasions hoped for the triumph of their righteous cause, and the more passionate adherents were prepared to die for it. The divisions in English society which the Reformation caused to an extent cut across class and other divisions. They remained bitter for centuries. Cath-olics became a persecuted and feared minority – a potential Trojan horse within the nation. Guy Fawkes day was not in the seventeenth and eighteenth centuries a harmless diversion but a rather grisly reminder of potential Catholic treachery. Effectively Catholics re-mained second-class citizens until Catholic Emancipation in 1829. Puritans also suffered from persecution from the reign of Elizabeth onwards, and the subsequent division between Anglicans and Non-conformists had enduring consequences. Thus in the late seventeenth century the Tories emerged as the party of the established Church of England, while the Whigs championed the right to dissent and religious toleration. These divisions remained important for the Conservative and Liberal Parties in the nineteenth and early twentieth centuries.

Religion then inspired far more political controversy, and had a larger impact on party allegiances and voting behaviour than economic issues. While today of diminished significance, it still affects the ethos and character of modern political parties. For example, the Labour Party inherited something of the Whig/Liberal Nonconformist tradition, and this is one of the factors which explains the distinctive flavour of British socialism.

But the English reformation did not just sow the seeds of religious divisions with enduring political implications. It virtually established England as a sovereign nation-state. Whatever his motives, Henry VIII had effectively asserted England's sovereign independence against the universalist claims of the papacy. This was a symbolic act which both reflected and assisted trends already in progress. The final loss of the Hundred Years War had forced the Tudors to concentrate their attention on the government of England, and allowed the development of an English nation-state and an English national culture.

Before the sixteenth century it might be questioned whether there was much of a distinctive English, let alone British, tradition of thought. England was part of a western Christian culture. Latin was the lingua franca of the educated classes, and virtually all serious writing on theology, philosophy and history was in Latin. Moreover, from the Norman Conquest for a couple of centuries or more the language of the upper classes had been French. Significantly the Parliament Rolls were still recorded in French for many years after the nobility had learned to cope with English. It was only in the later Middle Ages that a vernacular literature began to re-emerge.

The Reformation thus helped the development of an English culture and intellectual tradition. This was most obvious in poetry and drama in the sixteenth century, although it led on to the remarkable scientific and philosophical speculation which was a feature of Britain in the seventeenth century. Of course, some of this might have happened anyway, but the Reformation certainly removed some impediment to speculation, and ensured that much of the intellectual discourse was within a native English/British context. Not that Britain was cut off from intellectual currents in Europe. There was still a European community of scholars, well aware of each other's work. But within that community there was emerging a distinctive British tradition of thought.

This developing national culture was paralleled by the growth of nationalist sentiment, clearly evident in Shakespeare's plays. This was relatively early compared with its development elsewhere. In later centuries English nationalism hardly needed to be crudely asserted, because English nationhood was an incontrovertible fact, unlike German, Italian, Polish or Czech nationhood. Yet nationalism has been and remains an important constituent of modern British political ideologies – most obviously of conservatism, which has successfully hijacked nationalist symbols for party purposes, but also for British liberalism and labourism. Within liberalism for a long time there was a tension between internationalist ideals and national interests – notably in the division between the Liberal Imperialists and pro-Boers at the turn of the century, while British socialism or labourism has been markedly insular and infected by nationalist assumptions.

It was perhaps also the early emergence of English national sentiment which has made British nationalism a somewhat partial and questionable enterprise. Possibly because the notion of 'Britain' is so difficult to disentangle from the notion of 'England', it has never commanded the universal allegiance of Scots and Welsh, whose own nationalism is in part a reaction against an English nationalism which is no less real for being expressed through cultural and economic hegemony rather than articulated in overtly political form.

These were among the long-term political consequences of the English Reformation. The more immediate political implications of the Reformation were both profound and contradictory. On the one hand, it confirmed and extended what has come to be called the 'Tudor despotism'; on the other, it unleashed subversive forces which were ultimately to destroy that despotism.

In making the breach with Rome Henry VIII had made a dramatic assertion of royal power as well as national sovereign independence. The English Reformation was initially imposed from the top for what might euphemistically be called reasons of state. Yet the relative triviality of the King's original motivation only serves to underline the apparently total nature of the authority which he wielded. He had firmly subordinated the power of the Church to the secular power of the monarchy. He was to be the Head of the Church, the disposer of its wealth, and the arbiter of its doctrines. All this paved the way for what Dickens (1959) termed a 'lay-dominated society', and what Elton (1953) described as the 'Tudor Revolution in Government'. Henry had apparently laid the foundations for an absolutism which was unknown to his medieval predecessors, but which was to become only too familiar over much of Europe in the next two centuries.

Yet the Reformation also unleashed intellectual currents which the royal power found difficult to control. Henry VIII was not mainly actuated by religious conviction, but he had aligned himself with Protestant currents of thought on the continent which had already proved potentially politically subversive. Many Protestants wanted more than the substitution of royal power for papal power on questions of religious belief and observance. Their convictions were to plague Henry VIII's Tudor and Stuart successors. Moreover, if the spiritual authority of popes and priests could be questioned and overturned, similar questions could be asked of secular power. A direct relationship between the believer and God, without the necessary intermediary of an ecclesiastical hierarchy, was a notion which was corrosive of authority and hierarchy in general. This was a point which the Elizabethan divine, Richard Hooker (1554–1600), fully realised. If individual conscience was to be the only guide and restraint on matters of faith and conduct, then the result, he argued, would be anarchy. James I made a similar point more succinctly in expressing his opposition to Presbyterianism: 'No bishop, no king'. Freedom of conscience in matters of religious faith would breed scepticism towards secular authority (Hill, 1980, ch. 5).

It was not surprising then that Puritans figured prominently in the parliamentary opposition to Elizabeth and the early Stuarts, nor that some Puritans later embraced republicanism, and a few egalitarian principles. Individual liberty of conscience in religion thus implied a similar individualism or liberalism on political questions. For those on the other side, like Hooker, the claims of authority in religious matters were bound up inseparably with political authority and social hierarchy. The connection was to be powerfully demonstrated in the seventeenth century.

The English Civil War and the Glorious Revolution

The legacy of the seventeenth century for British politcs hardly requires emphasising. After all, the period saw the emergence of the Whig and Tory parties, key features of the modern British constitution, and a ferment of political ideas, many of which have an enduring significance. Yet it will also be argued that there was a negative as well as a positive legacy. The rejection of revolution and 'extremism' and the preference for gradualism and the politics of pragmatism and compromise which many would see as a marked feature of British political culture is perhaps the most important consequence of the conflicts of the seventeenth century. Similarly, the virtual absence of republicanism in modern British politics is in marked contrast with its fashionability for a time in the seventeenth century, and these features are hardly unconnected.

Indeed, the legacy of the seventeenth century is contentious. There is, unsurprisingly, substantial disagreement among historians over the causes of the Civil War and its essential nature. For a long time a 'Whig interpretation' of seventeenth- and eighteenth-century history predominated. Only more recently have the ideological assumptions behind the Whig interpretation of history been recognised and challenged. But it does not follow that more recent interpretations have successfully stripped away the distortions imposed by ideological assumptions and restored some kind of unvarnished truth. The writing of history inevitably involves selection and emphasis which reflects presuppositions and ideological assumptions in the author.

Essentially, Whig historians saw the seventeenth century in terms of an ultimately successful struggle by Parliament on behalf of the people against royal absolutism. This struggle established the sovereignty of Parliament, the principle of government by consent, religious toleration, and the balanced British Constitution. All this provided the very foundation of British freedom and prosperity.

This was history viewed with the benefit of hindsight of later constitutional developments, and history moreover written by the victors from their own distinctive ideological perspective. It was subsequently challenged by 'revisionists' who declined to see seventeenth-century political upheavals in terms of clear conflicts between opposed principles. The early seventeenth century, they suggested, was rather a period of ideological consensus, with leading parliamentarians sharing the constitutional convictions of the Stuarts. It has even been argued that in some respects it was the opponents of Charles I who were the real reactionaries, while the policies of the King and his advisers, Laud and Strafford, were enlightened and progressive. This 'revisionist' version of seventeenth-century history has been challenged in its turn from a variety of perspectives (Cust and Hughes, 1989).

Here we are concerned essentially with the impact of the seventeenth-century political upheavals on the British political tradition. In that context the myth is more important than reality. While the Whig interpretation has become partially discredited among historians, it has seeped into later British thinking about politics. Moreover, if the motives of the protagonists are ignored, and the actual outcome of these political upheavals is considered, there remains an element of truth in the 'Whig interpretation'. In retrospect the seventeenth century saw the end of any prospect of establishing a royal absolutism – and this marked off the British political tradition from developments over most of Europe. Elsewhere the authority of kings and princes was maintained and enhanced – to establish an 'age of absolutism'. Significantly many of the reform-minded thinkers of the eighteenth-century Enlightenment on the continent sought change from above rather than below, and met with some superficial response from the 'benevolent despots' who flattered them with their attention.

In Britain the monarchy survived, but royal power progressively declined. The idea of absolutism has virtually disappeared from British political discourse since the seventeenth century. But during most of that century the whole issue of royal authority was very much alive and endlessly debated. Royalists had to demonstrate and justify what had previously been taken for granted. Filmer (1588–1653), for example, attempted to buttress the royalist cause by supplementing the familiar argument for the divine right of kings with a patriarchal analogy derived from Aristotle. Hobbes (1588–1679), by contrast, ignored these traditional arguments. His justification for yielding unconditional obedience to the sovereign power was ultimately utilitarian – because of the peace and security which the sovereign could supply.

Yet although Hobbes was convinced that he had found a surer basis for authority, his ideas were unpopular with the royalists who burnt his books and tried to secure his prosecution for atheism. It is not difficult to see why. His arguments justified obedience to any sovereign who was able to deliver peace and security: to an Oliver Cromwell, or in theory at least, to a sovereign Parliament. But both Hobbes and his royalist critics were on the losing side. It was other ideas which won the day and became embedded in British political thinking.

Hobbes had preached virtually unconditional obedience to the sovereign power, while the contrary ideas of limited government and government by consent gained ground and became implicit and to a degree explicit in the post-1688 revolutionary settlement. Hobbes had also taught that sovereignty, or supreme power, cannot be divided, while Locke (1632–1704) and others suggested that it not only could be divided, but should be. The idea of the balanced constitution and the separation of powers, anathema to Hobbes, was soon widely associated with the British political system, both by domestic and foreign commentators. Of course, such ideas were imperfectly realised in practice. The constitutional principle of parliamentary sovereignty, and the actual political dominance of the Cabinet point to a concentration of power. However, the idea of the balanced constitution and government by consent became part of the British political tradition. Although in origin Whig, these ideas permeated virtually all subsequent political thought, including conservatism.

Significantly, British right-wing ideas have not been reactionary in the sense that the French right was reactionary. The Tories (and, later, Conservatives) remained essentially the party of monarchy, but of constitutional monarchy. They accepted limitations on the authority of government, and most of them even changes in the dynasty, albeit reluctantly. They have not been 'ultras' defending fundamental principles. Compromise, gradualism and an acceptance of change have been more generally the hallmarks of British conservatism in action.

If the seventeenth century destroyed royal absolutism, it also established ultimately religious pluralism and a degree of cultural diversity. It took a century and a half after the English Reformation to confirm finally that the old orthodoxy would not be re-established, nor effectively replaced by a new uniformity, even though it required another century and a half before dissenters and Catholics were freed from their civil disabilities. Religious toleration was finally if reluctantly conceded on virtually all sides as a matter of practical necessity, and subsequently became a key point of political principle, generally if not universally accepted.

Effectively the seventeenth century confirmed and extended the individualism which was always perhaps implicit in the Protestant reformation. In this Hobbes and Locke, who were at odds on so much else, were at one. Social behaviour could only be understood in terms of individual psychology and motivation. Society was essentially just an aggregate of individuals – so much so indeed that it had to be

Thomas Hobbes
1588–1679
(*Leviathan*)

John Locke
1632–1704
(*Second Treatise on Civil
Government, Essay on Toleration*)

(Associated with Civil War)   (Associated with 1688 revolution)

Individualism

|

State of nature

|

Natural liberty and equality

|

Contract
(to establish society and government)

Absolutism	Limited goverment
Sovereignty not divisible	Division of powers
No citizen rights	Rights to life, liberty, and property
No toleration	Religious toleration
No right to rebellion	Government by consent
	Limited right of resistance

Figure 3.1 Hobbes and Locke – opposed conclusions from similar
assumptions

artificially created. Both Hobbes and Locke used the notion of a
contract to establish a society and government, although neither of
course invented the idea which had been current for some time. The
notion of rational self-seeking individuals underpinned their assumptions over the origins and development of civil society and government, and was the explicit premiss behind their entire political
theory.

Such individualist assumptions fitted easily with an empirical,
sceptical mode of thinking, which became the hallmark of the British
philosophical and political tradition. Scepticism over ultimate
truths and values and a rejection of authority entailed a relativism
and an absence of fanaticism (or principle, depending on one's

point of view) which has permeated all mainstream British political ideologies.

Religious diversity was paralleled by a degree of political diversity in the sense that the existence of rival political parties or factions with different personnel, ideas and interests was, albeit reluctantly, accepted. The Whig and Tory parties originated in the seventeenth century. Recent historians have effectively destroyed the old portrayal of pre-nineteenth-century political history in terms of a two-party conflict, yet the futher implication that the terms 'Whig' and 'Tory' were virtually devoid of meaning is surely going too far. While they involved nothing like modern political parties, they clearly implied distinct political outlooks to contemporaries, even if there were inevitably subtle shifts in Whiggism and Toryism over the years. British politics in the eighteenth century did involve, to a degree, a choice of men and measures. Opposition, from being regarded as at best factious and at worst treasonable, became legitimate. 'Outs' could hope to become 'Ins', at least within reason.

For of course the establishment toleration of political differences had fairly clear limits. Certain views and perspectives were beyond the pale. The restoration in 1660 had effectively narrowed the scope of political debate. Views which had been vigorously canvassed and indeed widely held only a few years before, such as the radical democratic and embryo socialist ideas of the Levellers and Diggers, were henceforth proscribed and effectively excluded from serious political dialogue. They never completely disappeared, but went underground – to resurface occasionally in subsequent abortive rebellions, risings, disturbances and plots in the late seventeenth, eighteenth and early nineteenth centuries – but they were outside the mainstream British political tradition.

A clear example is republicanism, which was a vigorous creed among the political classes of the mid-seventeenth century. It is an obvious point, but one which requires emphasis, that a King was beheaded in England, and a Republic established, a full 140 years before the beginning of the French revolution. Moreover, this republicanism was justified and celebrated in political pamphlets and treatises. But whereas in France republican principles eventually triumphed, in Britain not only the republic, but also republicanism, proved short-lived. In the nineteenth century there were periods when republican sentiments were expressed, and feared by the political establishment, but proved little real threat to the survival of the

monarchy. By the twentieth century the open espousal of republicanism was not practical politics. Elsewhere republicanism and democracy are regarded as almost synonymous. In Britain even a party
which regards itself as socialist has never dared to challenge the
future of the monarchy.

More generally, a revolutionary tradition was born and died in the
seventeenth century. What happened in the middle of the century can
reasonably be described as a revolution. Yet this experience of
revolution seems to have effectively killed off revolutionary aspirations in subsequent British politics and bred a distrust of 'extremism'
which is still a feature of our modern political culture. A legacy of the
political turmoil of the mid-seventeenth century might be the subsequent characteristic British preference for pragmatic compromise
and gradualism. The so-called Glorious Revolution of 1688 was not
an exception to this generalisation. It was really not a revolution
at all, more a successful *coup d'état* which effectively confirmed
and extended the main outlines of the post-restoration political
settlement.

The British Constitution and the British political tradition

The Growth of Political Stability in England was the apt title of a
major work by the modern historian of the eighteenth century J. H.
Plumb (1966). In the seventeenth century England had been a byword
in Europe for division and political upheaval, and an awful warning
to rulers elsewhere. Yet by the end of the eighteenth century Britain
seemed the very model of political and social stability. By and large,
that reputation for stability has been preserved until the present day.
A succession of revolutions and violent political currents on the
continent left Britain virtually unscathed. After 1688 there were no
marked breaks in British political history. While the British system of
government has changed considerably since then, it has changed
through a process of gradual evolution.

Some of the main institutions of the modern British system of
government were already in place by the end of the seventeenth
century: King, Lords and Commons, of course, coupled with the
Cabinet and embryo political parties. But if the institutions were
established, their role, interrelationships and degree of power within

the overall system of government were yet to be determined. The post-1688 revolutionary settlement actually settled very little. What came to be known and celebrated as 'the British Constitution' emerged over time.

That constitution has enjoyed a good reputation over the years. It has been admired by foreigners, certainly from the eighteenth century onwards, and there have been perennial attempts to export its real or perceived elements abroad. It has also attracted a remarkable degree of acceptance, and even veneration right across the domestic British political spectrum, at least until very recently. Conflict between the parties on constitutional issues has been rare, and when it has occurred, as in 1832, or 1909–11, it has been resolved relatively quickly, and a new constitutional consensus established. There have been a few heretics such as Paine (ed. Foot and Kramnick, 1987) or Bentham (see Dinwiddy, 1989) who have taken a distinctly jaundiced attitude towards the British Constitution, but theirs has been a minority voice. Acceptance of the main elements of the British Constitution is common to all mainstream British political ideologies. The institutions and processes of British government, and the ideas and myths associated with them are thus important elements of the British political tradition.

But if the British Constitution has been almost universally praised, it has been very variously described, for it has long been somewhat opaque and mysterious. All constitutions are open to interpretation, but the lack of an authoritative written document renders the British constitution particularly liable to very diverse and even contradictory interpretations. The writers who have praised it from the eighteenth century onwards have identified its essence very variously – a mixed (or balanced) constitution, the sovereignty of Parliament, constitutional monarchy, the rule of law, Cabinet government, representative government – the list is endless. Of course some of these contradictions are more apparent than real, and others may be considered to reflect altered realities over time. Even so, imprecision is of its essence, and helps to explain the breadth of its appeal across the political spectrum. It is because the British Constitution seems to be compatible with widely divergent political ideologies with very different underlying assumptions that it has enjoyed such widespread approval.

Thus although the British Constitution perhaps owes most to the Whig/Liberal tradition, it has also been embraced by the Tory/

Conservative right and the Labour/Socialist left. Those on the right find reassurance in the survival of traditional institutions. Reforms have generally been reluctantly accepted, and even promoted, however, to preserve the substance of the system. Thus most Tories accepted the 1688 revolution and the revolutionary settlement, and generally, and with more reluctance, accepted the Hanoverian succession. Peel's Conservatives accepted parliamentary reform, and Disraeli persuaded his party to initiate further reform. Ultimately, if ungraciously, the Conservative Party acquiesced in the reduction in the power of the House of Lords. The principle of representative democracy, once anathema, was also gradually accepted as it became clear that it was compatible with the maintenance of property and the prospects of future Conservative government. The British right, unlike the right in relatively recent times in France, Germany, Italy, Spain, and other western countries, has thus championed rather than sought to overthrow the liberal democratic system of government and its associated symbols and values.

Employing a different terminology from their reactionary opposite numbers, but with similar subversive aims in view, radicals and socialists in other countries have often sought to 'smash the state'. In Britain such hostility to the state has rarely been expressed, partly perhaps because there has never been any clear conception of what constitutes the state. Instead, works on British government present a picture of a rather confusing collection of institutions, some old and some comparatively recent, which have an imprecise shifting relationship with each other. Radicals and most socialists in this country have not sought to oppose the state but have been generally prepared to use existing institutions, suitably reformed if necessary, to achieve their objectives. Thus the Chartists, although associated with some revolutionary disturbances in the mid-nineteenth century, sought to amend rather than overthrow the Constitution. The craft unions established from the mid-nineteenth century onwards were generally content to work within the existing parliamentary framework. Almost inevitably, the socialism which the British Labour Party eventually embraced was a socialism which saw the state as an ally rather than the enemy, the solution rather than the problem (Barker, 1978, p. 48).

The plasticity of British institutions gives some justification for the benign view of the state held by radicals and socialists, and its capacity for adaptation to socialist purposes. The monarchy has been transformed from an executive to a non-executive role. The House of Commons which represented less than 5 per cent of the adult population in the eighteenth century is now elected by universal suffrage. The House of Lords has been insensibly but rapidly transformed from an hereditary to a nominated chamber. The Prime Minister, once the increasingly constrained choice of the sovereign, is now the formally elected leader of a political party. Of course, it is possible to take a more jaundiced, less optimistic, view of such developments, suggesting that they are quite consistent with a continuing concentration of power and wealth in British society (Dearlove and Saunders, 1984), but this has not been the mainstream consensus verdict on the British system of government. British socialists have generally agreed that an extensive democratisation of society and the state has indeed taken place, and in so far as this democratisation is still defective, further reforms may complete the process. The past adaptive capacity of the system reassures radicals that other changes might equally be possible – the election of the Cabinet by the majority parliamentary party for example. Thus the existing state apparatus has not generally been seen as an obstacle to the achievement of socialism, rather the reverse.

In these circumstances the bulk of the British left has been as enthusiastic about the British Constitution as the Conservative right. Leading Labour politicians and socialist thinkers have written books substantially endorsing the main outlines of the British system of government. While a renegade right-wing Conservative like Enoch Powell may appear poles apart from a socialist like Michael Foot on economic issues, their thinking on constitutional questions has often seemed remarkably similar.

The impact of industrialisation – interests and power

Industrialisation substantially transformed British politics. A far larger, more concentrated, urbanised population employed in a much wider range of occupations and with new patterns of work and organisation radically changed the balance of interests in society and the nature of the demands made upon the political system. The emergence of mass political movements, the extension of the franchise, the rapid growth in the functions of government, the size of public expenditure and the state bureaucracy, were all products of industrialisation (Hobsbawm, 1969, especially chs 4 and 6).

Yet the changes wrought by industrialisation, which are closely paralleled by the experiences of other industrialising countries, over-layed rather than obliterated the political ideas and practices of a pre-industrial age. What is remarkable about Britain compared with countries like France, Germany and Italy is how little industrialisation changed the style and substance of politics. An economic and social revolution did not produce a political revolution. Old institutions survived. Traditional parliamentary parties acquired national organisations. Old political cleavages based on religion remained. The new political classes adopted much of the traditional ways of thinking about politics. Overall, the relationship between social class and political allegiance continued to be complex.

Land, the overwhelming source of wealth and influence until at least the seventeenth century, was challenged increasingly by commerce from then on, and by manufacturing industry from the nineteenth century. In the nineteenth century the declining but still powerful landed interest was substantially associated with the Tory Party, although some of the greatest aristocratic landowning families were traditionally Whig. Nineteenth-century liberalism, essentially a blending of traditional Whiggery with radicalism and Peelite conservatism, was increasingly tied to the manufacturing interest and a fast-developing professional middle class.

The changing economic structure of the country involved massive changes also in the geographical distribution of population, wealth and political power. The new urban centres of the North and Midlands prospered at the expense of the counties. A predominance of Tory landowning squires in the House of Commons was gradually replaced by Nonconformist merchants and industrialists from places like Manchester, Birmingham, Leeds and Bradford. But behind these was a developing urban working class whose numbers and concentration made them a greater potential threat to the social and political establishment than the old labouring classes had ever been.

Superficially, then, it is possible to associate the three mainstream British political ideologies of conservatism, liberalism and socialism with the distinctive class interests of, respectively, the declining landed interest, manufacturing and financial capital, and the urban industrial working class. It is not too difficult to interpret some of the political history of the nineteenth century in such class terms. The

1832 Reform Act, and the 1835 Municipal Corporations Act were victories for the urban manufacturing interests over the landed interest, and the Repeal of the Corn Laws in 1846 can be seen as a highly symbolic turning point in the relative fortunes of landowners and industrial capitalists.

Yet such an analysis involves a considerable element of over-simplification. Class interests were never that clear-cut, partly because of the substantial interpenetration of the landed and manu-facturing interests. Successful businessmen bought land and acquired titles and sought to merge with the landed gentry. Old declining families looked to marriage alliances with the new wealth to recoup their failing fortunes. Moreover, many of the political classes did not align automatically where their class interests apparently lay. Some great landowners supported repeal of the Corn Laws, while some industrial capitalists opposed it. Religious beliefs, personal con-nections, political ambitions and a shifting intellectual climate were among the factors influencing the day-to-day judgement of politicians.

Had conservatism remained tied to a declining landed interest it would have been doomed. Thus as a result of industrialisation it would have faded into impotence like most of the parties of the traditional right on the continent of Europe. Instead the party increas-ingly picked up support from the manufacturing interest, and turned itself into a party looking after the interests of property in general. More surprisingly it also picked up some support from the working class, whose political importance was growing with the progressive extension of the franchise.

The British working class was slower to seek a distinctive political vehicle for its own advancement than its counterparts in Germany and France. Working-class radicals and trade unionists were generally content to work as a pressure group within the Liberals until the late nineteenth century and even beyond, while in some parts of the country, such as Lancashire, an aversion to the politics of their Liberal bosses coupled with the growing patriotic and imperial appeal of the Tories established a significant Conservative working-class electorate. Once a Labour Party was belatedly established, although overwhelmingly working-class in terms of support and even for a time in terms of the social composition of the parliamentary party, its intellectual leadership was provided by the professional middle classes, who later provided also its parliamentary leadership.

In these circumstances political creeds could not simply reflect class interests. Conservatism has always claimed to stand above class and for the nation. Although the source of the Conservative Party's income, its social composition, at the higher levels especially, and some of its policies in government might throw some doubt on that claim, Conservative politicians and voters have sufficiently convinced themselves of its truth to affect their behaviour. Liberals, from increasing desperation born out of electoral decline, preached partnership and an end of the confrontation between the two sides of industry. Labour was the only party which might once have profited from whole-hearted class politics, but generally eschewed the language of class warfare in favour of the ideals of co-operation and economic efficiency. Perhaps the British working class was never sufficiently class-conscious, either actually or potentially, for such a class appeal to succeed. There are all sorts of possible reasons for this, from Methodism to rising living standards, although of course the British working class was substantially imbued with the dominant political tradition and its values of patriotism, compromise and gradualism. It had also come to accept many of the ideas associated with industrial capitalism, particularly with regard to what was considered feasible or desirable in the economic sphere.

The impact of industrialisation – *laissez-faire* and collectivism

Quite apart from the complex effects it had on social structure and political allegiances, industrialisation had a more direct impact on economic and political ideas. It clearly sharpened even if it did not create the debate over the benefits of free markets and state intervention. But the legacy of industrialisation here was more complicated and contradictory than is often supposed. Certainly, industrialisation was aided by the relaxation of old barriers to trade and industry, and it is no accident that it was also accompanied by the celebration of the market in classical economic theory. *Laissez-faire* ideas were popularised by writers like Harriet Martineau who reached a wider audience than Smith, Ricardo and Malthus.

Yet social and economic historians who have questioned whether there ever really was an age of *laissez-faire* in Britain have a point. Industrialisation was also associated with, and arguably produced, a massive growth in state intervention. It created some new needs and problems, and raised others in more acute form, while the economic growth promoted by industrialisation also made available more resources to deal with them. Although *laissez-faire* ideas seem to have permeated the political culture of the early and middle years of the nineteenth century, the same period saw the beginnings of state intervention in a range of new fields.

The contradictions can be plainly seen in the thought of the utilitarians. They had strong intellectual and personal links with the classical economists, and fully accepted free market values and precepts. Yet their own reform programme also involved a growth in the state. Bentham's own elaborate schemes for a new rational system of administration involved the establishment of a professional bureaucracy. Bentham's secretary Chadwick was closely involved with the making and administration of the New Poor Law, which, although founded on rigorous free market principles, required the establishment of an extensive bureaucratic machine to implement it. Chadwick's subsequent involvement in the Public Health movement of the 1840s was to push him much further in the direction of state intervention, and away from the *laissez-faire* principles he had once espoused – as he himself came to admit. John Stuart Mill was both the last of the great classical economists, and, as son of Bentham's collaborator, James Mill, the heir of the utilitarian tradition, but some of his writing shows sympathy with socialist ideas, and his thought was a significant influence on Fabianism.

W. H. Greenleaf (1983) has seen the tension between libertarianism and collectivism as the major theme of the British political tradition. It is a tension within as well as between political ideologies. Greenleaf himself has described conservatism in terms of a continuing struggle between rival collectivist and libertarian traditions. From the late nineteenth century if not earlier, liberalism might be interpreted similarly. The New Liberalism justified and advocated state intervention in ways which seem markedly at odds with the old liberalism, but the tensions within liberalism had long been evident, and in some respects the New Liberalism can be seen as a kind of *post hoc* rationalisation of the interventionist practice of the Liberal Party in action at both the municipal and the national level for some time. The tension between libertarianism and collectivism can even be seen in British socialism. The Fabians eagerly embraced state intervention but the trade unions who provided the bulk of the membership, money and muscle in the Labour Party were more interested in free collective bargaining than in state welfare, and were distinctly suspicious of compulsory insurance schemes which eroded workers' take-home pay.

This somewhat schizophrenic attitude towards the role of the state is perhaps unsurprising. The growth of government was both massive and unprecedented. Overall, it was not willed, and came about despite an initial general presumption against government intervention. It developed piecemeal and haphazardly, not according to any ideological blueprint. Often, as with education, direct state involvement was only reluctantly accepted after voluntary efforts had proved insufficient. There were widespread fears of centralisation, collectivism and compulsion, but at the same time a growing realisation that the trend was largely inevitable and irreversible. The theoretical justifications for state intervention in terms of the New Liberalism or Fabian Socialism came after half a century of expansion in government expenditure and services, although of course these ideas were employed to support further growth.

Interpretations of Britain's economic history over the last 200 years still inform present-day ideological thinking. Consciousness of a comparatively poor economic performance this century, particularly in relation to Britain's industrial and commercial predominance in the mid-nineteenth century, has provoked various diagnoses of the nature of the British disease, and various suggested remedies. A common inference is that the British economy flourished under the relatively unfettered enterprise of the nineteenth century, and has stagnated under the burden of state interference and taxation in the twentieth century.

Such an interpretation owes more to myth than reality. The agricultural revolution which preceded and facilitated the industrial revolution involved, through the enclosure bill procedure, compulsion on a massive scale. The growth of railways from the start involved extensive legislation and state regulation. Even the overseas markets and overseas investment on which Victorian prosperity substantially depended owed much to Britain's political pre-eminence and Victorian foreign policy. Free trade followed the flag.

In some respects, though, the British experience of industrialisation was distinctive, and helps explain its association with *laissez-faire* ideas. As Britain was the first country to industrialise, the process was necessarily unprecedented and unplanned. Industrialisation elsewhere had a model to imitate, and it could be, and in many countries was, deliberately assisted and promoted by government action. Without such state help, other countries could not have competed effectively. In Britain such intervention was less obvious, and where it occurred, less goal-directed.

Free trade has been an enduring principle in British politics (although needless to say it has not always been practised). The attachment to free trade is unsurprising because it apparently produced prosperity for Britain in the nineteenth century. It was then less popular elsewhere. Napoleon III got into considerable trouble with some of his erstwhile supporters in France when he signed the Cobden Treaty with Britain in 1860, and cheap British goods were then no more popular with American or German manufacturers. It was only when Britain was later faced with the successful competition of other countries in the early twentieth century that the issue of tariffs and protection was raised by Joseph Chamberlain and his supporters. But although economic circumstances had changed, and, arguably, Britain's economic interests had also altered, the attachment to free trade persisted. Protection briefly captured the Conservative Party, but proved an electoral millstone. The more recent conversion of the Conservatives to the virtues and values of the free market, has enabled the party to draw on a deep well of libertarian ideas in the national consciousness, which in turn is partly a result of this country's distinctive experience of industrialisation.

The impact of war

A survey of the impact of Britain's distinctive economic, social and political history on its political thought can scarcely overlook the effects of the experience of war on ways of thinking about politics and government. War, like industrialisation, can scarcely be described as a peculiarly British experience. Even so, as with industrialisation, the British experience has been in some respects distinctive.

It is a commonplace observation that war tends to reinforce a national consciousness at the expense of internal conflicts and divisions which transcend national boundaries. The patriotic sentiments aroused in wartime have frequently had a strong peacetime legacy. Memories of the common national purpose in wartime – the 'Dunkirk spirit' – are invoked years afterwards to encourage a rejection of divisive attitudes in industrial relations and other spheres. Yet wars can divide as well as unite, and almost all the wars in which Britain has been engaged from the Dutch Wars of the seventeenth century to the Falklands War in 1982 have involved a dissentient minority opposed to the whole enterprise.

Yet these divisions have rarely had much enduring political significance. From the sixteenth century onwards, Britain rarely suffered defeat, and never suffered conquest and occupation. Thus the British never had to choose between collaboration and resistence, a choice which left a bitter legacy of division in post-war domestic politics over half of Europe.

Britain has also not had to cope with other legacies of war – frequently shifting political boundaries with parcels of land, and their helpless inhabitants, shunted backwards and forwards with changing military fortunes, and millions of refugees left homeless by the altered political map. Most European countries were less fortunate, and the political demands of the dispossessed have been a significant feature of their domestic politics.

Foreign armies also can bring new ideas and political change in their wake. French revolutionary ideas were thus carried to Germany, Italy and Poland in the early nineteenth century, while Soviet communist institutions and principles were introduced into eastern Europe after the Second World War with the Russian army. Britain remained immune from such foreign influences. Moreover, because of Britain's apparent success, war did not arouse the same doubts about independence, sovereignty and nationalism which impelled other European countries to pursue international co-operation and European integration with rather more drive and conviction. The insularity of Britain's political thinking was confirmed rather than undermined by the experience of war.

British commentators have emphasised instead the impetus war gave towards collectivism (Greenleaf, 1983, vol. 1, pp. 47ff.). This is well documented in terms of new specific forms of state intervention, and in terms of the growth of public expenditure and taxation. Clearly, war directly provoked increased state expenditure and in-creased state intervention in the interests of military victory. Also it seems plausible that the public grew sufficiently accustomed to higher levels of government intervention, expenditure and taxation, to accept their continuance into peacetime. In addition, shortcomings revealed in wartime have provided a powerful stimulus for economic and

social reform. The Crimean War, the Boer War, and two world wars have thus played a part in stimulating domestic reform. Mainstream historians of the evolution of state welfare (e.g. Fraser, 1984) have emphasised the role of war as a catalyst in that process, while for some critics of the trend to greater state intervention, war has been a potent element in the collectivist ratchet.

Two points might be made about the connection between war and the growth of collectivism. First, in so far as it is valid, it is scarcely a uniquely British experience, and can therefore not be invoked to explain what is sometimes (surely incorrectly) held to be a peculiarly British attachment to state welfare and collectivism. Secondly, it is in any case exaggerated. War perhaps accelerated trends which were already well in process, but the growth of state intervention and state welfare took place over a century and a half in which peace rather than war was the norm.

The legacy of empire

It is difficult to impress on younger generations the significance once attached to the British empire. Even at the end of the Second World War it still appeared that Britain headed the most extensive empire the world had ever seen. The coronation of Queen Elizabeth II in 1953 was accompanied by the issue of commemorative stamps with the Queen's head from literally hundreds of Dominions, Colonies and Dependencies. The reality was already otherwise, of course. The older dominions had been independent sovereign states for many years. India and Pakistan had secured independence from the post-war Labour government. The bulk of the rest of the empire was effectively wound down with astonishing rapidity. In retrospect, the débâcle of Suez in 1956 marked the end of British pretensions to imperial and great power status. Within a few years, in a decisive shift in policy, the Conservative government of Harold Macmillan applied to join the European Economic Community.

The empire was a factor of enormous importance for British economy, society and politics. Arguably, it had been a major source of economic strength and prosperity. Lenin had plausibly suggested that it was imperialism which had allowed the older European countries to avoid social upheaval and revolution. The working classes had not experienced the squeeze on living standards anticipated by Marx, partly, Lenin and others claimed, because they benefited from the exploitation of the colonies. Whatever the truth of the matter, certainly the empire was popular with a large section, perhaps the bulk, of the British working class, may be as a consequence of effective propaganda (Mackenzie, 1986). Schwarz (1986, in Donald and Hall) suggests that 'in the last decades of the nineteenth century, the social and political institutions attempting to instil the imperial ethic into the culture of the working class multiplied beyond belief'. Pride in the empire reinforced nationalist and royalist sentiment.

Paradoxically, the empire may also have contributed to economic and political decline. Arguably it was a diversion of energies, a factor in delaying political and economic modernisation. Talents which might have been employed in manufacturing were drawn into colonial administration, and contributed to the perpetuation of an anti-industrial culture among the British establishment. The empire might also have provided a soft cushion when declining competitiveness in non-imperial markets might otherwise have forced a painful but necessary transformation of the economy (Hobsbawm, 1969, p. 191). Parts of the empire had never been particularly profitable, and increasingly in the twentieth century the burden of maintaining it imposed strains on the British economy. A defence capacity on a world scale had to be maintained. The status of sterling as an international reserve currency constrained domestic economic policy.

The loss of empire, although not entirely painless, did not involve quite the same trauma and humiliation experienced by the French in Indo-China and later Algeria. Yet there were painful problems of adjustment as British politicians strove to maintain great power status despite the end of the imperial role. The legacy of Britain's imperial past was a major factor in preventing a wholehearted conversion to Europe. There were also major implications for domestic society and politics.

Not the least of these has been substantial immigration from former colonies in the post-war era, and the effective conversion of Britain into a multiracial and multicultural society. This direct legacy of empire has introduced new issues and new tensions into British politics, and established new sub-cultures and ideological perspectives. It is, moreover, at least arguable that deeply ingrained imperialist assumptions of British superiority over 'lesser breeds

Period	Main features or events	Political consequences	Key figures

Reformation 16th century	Breach with Rome
	Dissolution of monasteries
	Elizabethan Church
	    Settlement
	Persecution of Catholics and
	    Puritans
		Tudor despotism
		Lay society
		Religious differences
		English national culture
		Protestant ethic, rise of
		    capitalism?/individualism
		Challenge to authority?
			Henry VIII
			More
			Cranmer
			Hooker

Political upheavals of 17th century	Civil War, 1642 Execution of Charles I Commonwealth Restoration, 1660 'Glorious Revolution' of 1688	Constitutional monarchy Parliamentarism Distrust of extremism Whigs and Tories Religious toleration?	Charles I Cromwell Hobbes Filmer Locke Halifax
Political stability 18th century	Act of Union Whig oligarchy George III Growth of empire American War of Independence French Revolution	British identity? Growth of British constitution Parliamentary sovereignty Cabinet and Prime Minister Separation of powers?	Walpole Bolingbroke Chatham Fox Pitt Burke Paine

Industrial revolution – 19th century especially	Capitalism
	Factory system, urbanisation
	Extension of franchise
	Professionalism
	Communications revolution –
	    railways, roads, mass
	    newspapers, etc.
		Power to cities and industrial
		    and professional middle
		    classes
		Free trade
		Laissez-faire?
		Growth of government
		    intervention, public
		    services, bureaucracy
		Trade unionism
			Smith
			Malthus
			Ricardo
			Bentham
			Peel
			Bright
			J. S. Mill
			Gladstone
			Disraeli
			Spencer

Impact of war, 19th and 20th centuries	Napoleonic War Crimean War Boer War First and Second World Wars	National unity New ideas? Social reform, increased public spending	Lloyd George Keynes Beveridge Attlee

End of empire – post Second World War	Independence for India,
	    Caribbean and African
	    colonies, etc.
	Suez crisis, 1956
	Immigration Acts
	UK joins EC 1973
	Irish troubles
	Devolution debate
		Loss of world role
		'Coloured' immigration
		Racial tension and racism,
		    multicultural Britain
		Divisions over Europe
		Scottish and Welsh
		    nationalism
			Churchill
			Macmillan
			Powell

Figure 3.2   Historical influences on the British political tradition

without the law', and over 'peoples half-devil and half child' (Kipling) have contributed to modern white racism.

Loss of empire has also posed a question mark over the future of the United Kingdom. The Scots and Welsh had, like the English, substantially profited from the empire. Its loss meant they were no longer partners in a great imperial enterprise. Rather, they might appear as England's first and last colonies. Other factors of course contributed substantially to the growth of Scottish and Welsh nationalism, but the virtual disappearance of the empire transformed horizons, and helped stimulate some reassessment of the real and supposed benefits of Union.

Conclusion

Inevitably, this brief account of the impact of British history on British political thinking will provoke some sharp disagreements over particular details and overall trends. Clearly there is room for very considerable argument over precisely how the experience of a distinctive history has shaped ways of thinking about politics. Moreover, while plausible connections can be asserted, it is impossible to prove causation, so that any conclusions must, necessarily, be highly tentative. However, even though it is so difficult to operationalise the relationship between a nation's historical experience and its political thinking, this is insufficient justification for not even making the attempt. The assumption here is that an understanding of distinctive British political ideologies such as Fabian socialism or 'one-nation' conservatism, and their relationship with each other must relate to a distinctive history. Any focus on what is specifically 'British' in British political ideologies requires some speculation on the nature of the British political tradition and culture.

Guide to further reading

The range of this chapter is so wide that it is only possible to indicate possible avenues for further study which readers may wish to pursue. Those wanting to explore the historical background may look at Elton and Neale on the sixteenth century, Hill on the seventeenth, Plumb and Pares on the eighteenth, Gash and Ensor on the nineteenth and

Taylor on the twentieth century. Thompson's writings provide a useful corrective to mainstream perspectives, and Hobsbawm is illuminating on economic history. There is a useful introduction to political thinkers in Thomson, and those seeking more depth might try Plamenatz, Skinner or Hampsher-Monk. Macpherson is provocative on Hobbes and Locke, but the literature on these writers is vast, and some may prefer to sample them direct. For a survey of the interplay between history and ideas from the nineteenth century onwards, Greenleaf is almost indispensable.

4

LIBERALISM

Introduction

To begin an account of modern British political ideologies with liberalism may appear perverse. At one level liberalism seems a substantially outmoded and irrelevant ideology. After all, the modern Liberal Party has been reduced to a peripheral force in British politics now for well over half a century, despite a more recent partial revival under the new name of Liberal Democrats. While the fortunes of liberalism as a creed should not necessarily be associated with those of a political party, some critics have been equally dismissive of liberal ideology (Arblaster, 1984). For some, the eclipse of liberalism was an almost inevitable historical tendency, as liberalism was associated with a particular phase in the development of industrial capitalism.

However, a form of liberalism was already making a comeback in the west even before the collapse of Soviet-style communism apparently heralded the triumph of liberal capitalism. Moreover, some interpretations had always seen liberalism as the hegemonic ideology of the modern age. All modern mainstream political ideologies, including Marxism, may be regarded as variants of liberalism. Such an analysis can be readily applied to post-war British politics. From the war to the 1970s the dominant political and economic orthodoxy was essentially derived from the New Liberalism which had flourished early in the century. Indeed, Keynes and Beveridge, the twin gurus of that post-war consensus, marked the culmination of New

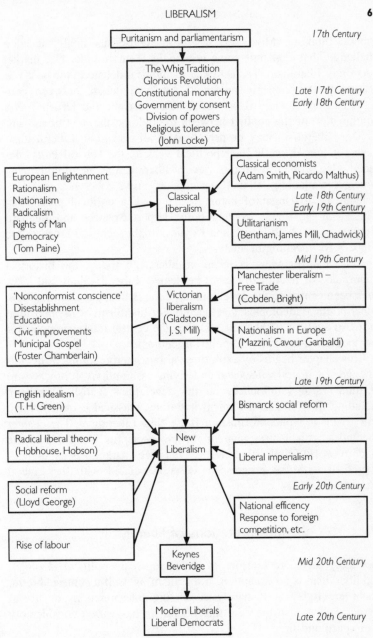

Figure 4.1 The Liberal tradition

Liberal thinking. Moreover, when this consensus finally faced a challenge, that challenge came principally from an older free market version of liberalism. The essential ideological debate in the post-war era might be plausibly presented not as a debate between conservatism and socialism, nor even between right and left, but as a continuation of the conflict between the old and the new liberalism.

Thus liberalism may be perceived as all-pervasive. Liberal ideas have conquered, while their political vehicle, the Liberal Party, has faded. One problem with this view of liberalism as an all-embracing hegemonic ideology is that any clear identity, coherence and consistency is in danger of being lost. Indeed, a political philosophy which can apparently contain both Herbert Spencer and Leonard Hobhouse, and both Hayek and Keynes, might seem too broad or too slippery for meaningful analysis.

But whatever view is taken of liberalism today, the historical importance of liberalism cannot be denied. Liberal values and ideas have been central to the development of the British political tradition. Other political ideologies developed out of liberalism or in opposition to it. An analysis of liberalism is thus the central reference point for any examination of British political ideologies.

This chapter begins by exploring various interpretations of liberalism and key liberal values and underlying assumptions. It proceeds to examine various influences on the developing British liberalism, including the Whig and Radical traditions, classical economics and utilitarianism, Nonconformism and the New Liberalism. The chapter concludes with a discussion of the prospects for liberalism in the modern world, contrasting the revived free market values of neo-liberalism with the progressive ideas associated with the Liberal Democrats.

Interpretations of liberalism

Inevitably there are tensions in any mainstream political ideology, and liberalism is no exception. 'Liberalism' is itself a contested term. There are today still sharply conflicting interpretations of liberal ideology. It is also the case that liberalism has varied considerably over space and time.

Most accounts of the evolution of liberal thought occupy at least three centuries. Strictly speaking, the term should not be used before the early nineteenth century, when it became current (Manning, 1976, p. 9; Gray, 1986, p. ix). Yet the roots of liberalism have generally been traced back much earlier, at least to the seventeenth century (Arblaster, 1984, p. 11), and it would be pedantic to deny the description 'liberal' to writers and politicians who are generally regarded as within that liberal tradition. This has allowed some latitude to later commentators in claiming for liberalism thinkers who have also been claimed for other and opposed ideological traditions. Thus Burke and Hume have both sometimes been claimed for liberalism as well as conservatism (Gray, 1986, ch. 3). The point is not just academic, for the inclusion or exclusion of particular thinkers subtly serves to redefine the essence of liberalism.

In the first half of the nineteenth century liberalism appeared a revolutionary creed on the European continent, where absolutist or reactionary regimes generally prevailed. The cause of individual liberty was there inextricably bound up with national self-determination. Movements for national freedom or national unity were closely associated with demands for civil and political rights and for constitutional limits on government.

By contrast, Britain's national integrity and independence seemed then to be unproblematic, while absolutism had been defeated and parliamentary sovereignty apparently established in the seventeenth century. British liberalism certainly involved support for constitutional government and national self-determination in Europe, but with these goals already substantially achieved at home, the domestic liberal programme necessarily concentrated on other objectives.

A distinction is sometimes made today between economic and political liberalism. Some recent neo-liberal accounts suggest that the ideology essentially involves a belief in free markets. This was never true of nineteenth-century continental liberalism, which was primarily a political creed. Even in the case of Britain, the centrality of free markets to liberalism has been exaggerated. Victorian liberalism stood for political reform at home and support for national and constitutional movements abroad. Its inspiration was derived more from religion, and specifically radical nonconformism, than from classical economics.

From the late nineteenth century onwards, British liberalism explicitly repudiated *laissez-faire* and accepted the need for state intervention, particularly in the area of social welfare. This New Liberalism has been variously regarded as a natural and inevitable development out of the old liberalism (Hobhouse, 1911), as an aberration (Arblaster, 1984, ch. 16) or even as a betrayal (Gray, 1986, pp. 32–3).

Today the term 'liberal' has distinctly different connotations in different parts of the world. It is not even easy to place it on the standard 'left–right' political spectrum. The modern British Liberal Party is still within the New Liberal tradition and has long been regarded as centre, or even left of centre. In continental Europe, liberalism is generally associated with the right. However, in the United States the term 'liberal' has become almost a term of abuse for radical-progressive and crypto-socialist ideas. At the same time the 'liberal' label has been adopted by advocates of the free market like Hayek and Friedman and their New Right disciples.

It is thus not possible to present a view of liberalism which would command universal acceptance. However, there is fairly general agreement over some of the underlying assumptions behind liberalism, and some of the key liberal ideas and values, even if there is not always equal agreement over their subsequent development and interpretation.

Liberalism: underlying assumptions

Individualism is perhaps the most fundamental assumption underpinning liberal ideas. For the liberal, individual human beings, rather than nations, races or classes are the starting-point for any theorising about society, politics or economics. Society is seen as an aggregate of individuals, and social behaviour is explained in terms of some fairly basic assumptions about individual human psychology (Macpherson, 1962; Arblaster, 1984, chs 2, 3). Indeed, some thinkers within the liberal tradition saw society as an essentially artificial creation. They postulated a prior state of nature in which neither society nor government existed. The state of nature was generally perceived as a hypothetical model rather than historical fact, but the implication in either case was that society and government were thus deliberately created by rational individuals in their own self-interest. Liberals today still tend to see society as an aggregate of individuals. There can be no social interests beyond the interests of the individuals which constitute society. The individual is logically and morally prior to society.

Rationalism is another core liberal assumption. Liberals not only consider that individuals pursue their own self-interest but are also the best judge of that self-interest. No one else, not rulers, nor priests nor civil servants, can interpret for the individual what is in his or her own best interest. That can only be determined by the exercise of individual reason. Moreover, liberals have been generally optimistic that the application of rational principles will produce not only greater individual satisfaction but also more social progress.

But it is of course freedom which is the quintessential liberal value. Liberals require that individuals should be free to pursue their own self-interest (Mill, 1859). This was originally interpreted in a predominantly negative sense. The individual should be as far as possible free from external constraints. In the early history of liberalism this freedom from constraint entailed firm limits to the power of government to interfere with individual liberty. An important application of this was the principle of toleration. This particularly applied initially to religious belief and observance and was vigorously championed by Locke (1689, ed. Gough, 1966). It was to receive its most eloquent expression from John Stuart Mill (1859, ed. Warnock, 1962) who used the negative conception of liberty to demand full freedom of thought and expression.

Subsequently, some liberals emphasised the freedom to enjoy certain benefits, a more positive conception of liberty, which might entail extensive state intervention to enlarge freedom (Green, 1881; Hobhouse, 1911; Berlin, 1967). The conflict between these two sharply contrasting views of freedom and their widely divergent practical implications has been a major theme in the development of liberalism over the last hundred or so years.

Bound up with the debate over the interpretation of liberty is a similar argument over the emphasis to be placed on equality. For if liberalism has always involved a commitment to liberty, however defined, it has also involved some egalitarian assumptions. Individual human beings are seen as in some important respects naturally equal. Moreover, it is an implicit liberal premiss that one person's preferences are not to be valued more highly than another's – assuming equality in the consideration of interests. Thus liberals have stressed equality before the law, and equal civil and political rights, although there has not always been agreement over what these should entail in practice. Egalitarian considerations have also led many liberals to justify social provision of education and other collective provision in order to establish greater equality of opportunity.

But a commitment to an equality of worth and opportunity has generally been quite consistent with a liberal acceptance of considerable inequality of income and wealth. Indeed, liberalism has also been closely associated with a defence of private property rights as a crucial element of individual liberty. Critics of liberalism have thus tended to see the liberal commitment to equality as at best highly theoretical and at worst nakedly hypocritical (Arblaster, 1984, pp. 84–91), while even sympathetic commentators have suggested that liberals have been generally prepared to sacrifice equality to liberty.

Liberals themselves have argued that freedom entails the freedom to be unequal, but they have also tended to assume that individual liberty is not inconsistent with social justice. Liberals argued that the pursuit of rational enlightened self-interest would produce the greatest public welfare. Although liberalism is based on the assumption of self-seeking individualism, it has never involved the cynical equation of might and right. Rather, liberals have embraced the language of justice, and attempted to make it consistent with the pursuit of rational self-interest (Rawls, 1971). There is implicit in such arguments some fairly optimistic assumptions about human nature and the scope for reconciling individual and collective goals.

It is here that liberalism parts company with traditional conservatism on the one hand, and socialism on the other. Conservatives have been more pessimistic about human nature and sceptical over enlightenment and the potential for individual rational conduct (see Chapter 5, below). Socialists, while sharing with liberals a more optimistic view of human nature, have not accepted that individual self-interest and social justice can be so easily reconciled (see Chapter 6, below).

There are some underlying problems here which will require some later elaboration and discussion. For the present it is sufficient to note that the tension between considerations of individual liberty and the sanctity of private property on the one hand, and assumptions about equality and social justice on the other, have been a major theme in the evolution of liberal thought.

But while there are clearly major differences and tensions within the liberal tradition, it is not that difficult to describe liberals or liberalism in terms which would command a wide element of agreement. Stuart Hall (Donald and Hall, 1986, p. 34) suggests that liberals are 'open-minded, tolerant, rational, freedom-loving people, sceptical of the claims of tradition and established authority, but strongly committed to the values of liberty, competition and individual freedom'. This is a description by a non-liberal which most liberals would probably be happy to endorse. Hall goes on to argue that nineteenth-century British liberalism 'stood for individualism in politics, civil and political rights, parliamentary government, moderate reform, limited state intervention, and a private enterprise economy'.

The Whig tradition

Liberalism in Britain grew out of the Whig tradition. It is easier perhaps to distinguish liberalism from Whiggism than it is to distinguish conservatism from Toryism, but even so, the Whig tradition slides naturally and imperceptibly into the liberal tradition, to the extent that it is not possible to mark precisely where the one ends and the other begins. Whigs originated in the seventeenth century as the party which opposed royal absolutism, and championed religious dissent. The Whigs in turn were the political heirs of the religious and parliamentary opposition to the early Stuarts. Whigs supported the rights of Parliament, and sought to place limits on royal power. Writers like Locke (1632–1704) sought to ground this political programme in abstract principles. There were natural rights to life, liberty and property. Government should rest on the consent of the governed, who were ultimately justified in rebellion if their rights were infringed. There should be constitutional limits on government, and a division between the executive and legislative powers (Locke, 1689, ed. Gough, 1966; Macpherson, 1962; Dunn, 1969). These ideas came to be enshrined, albeit somewhat imperfectly, in the British Constitution following the Glorious Revolution of 1688. They later helped to inspire or justify the American and French Revolutions, and a radical tradition in British politics.

Yet there were always contradictory tendencies in Whiggism. Behind fine sentiments there were material interests to advance and defend. The great Whig aristocrats and their allies among the merchants and bankers sought to preserve their own power, property and privileges from a perceived threat from the crown. The massive inequalities in income and wealth in eighteenth-century England were for them unproblematic (Arblaster, 1984, ch. 8). Locke spoke for their interests in defending rights to life, liberty and property. In fact, liberty was not in the seventeenth and early eighteenth centuries the rather abstract principle it was to become, but a word closely associated with property. This was particularly the case with its commonly used plural 'liberties' which had a connotation close to the word 'privileges' with which it was often combined (Hill, 1980, pp. 36–8).

Moreover, the Whigs in general had no wish to spread power beyond the ranks of the propertied. Arblaster (1984, p. 169) suggests that their triumph in 1689 'resulted in political reaction' with further restrictions on the very limited right to vote and the extension of the life of Parliament from three to seven years. Thus the constitution which they developed and defended was essentially oligarchic and conservative. Worse still, it could only apparently be successfully operated on the basis of graft, corruption and jobbery. Through the period of the Whig ascendancy in the eighteenth century, patronage greased the wheels of government. Parliamentary seats, offices under the crown and commissions in the army were bought and sold.

Power was furthermore shamelessly exercised for the benefit of the wealthy. Prodigious fortunes were made out of war, the slave trade and India. Wealthy landowners used enclosure procedures to enrich themselves at the expense of the rural poor, and all in the name of agricultural progress. The game laws were ruthlessly enforced, as naked an example of class legislation as can be found. It is not difficult in the face of such evidence to conclude that there was no more behind the political principles of the Whigs than class interest.

Yet Whig principles were capable of a radical as well as a conservative interpretation. 'No taxation without representation', the slogan of the parliamentary opposition to the Stuarts, became the cry of the American rebels against George III, and many Whigs found it difficult to deny the justice of their case. The Declaration of Independence (1776) was based on classic Whig principles. The French Revolution was more divisive, but was initially welcomed by most leading Whigs. Despite the reaction which the subsequent course of the revolution provoked, the Whig leader Charles James Fox continued to defend its principles if not always its practice, and consistently championed civil liberties in England until his death in 1806.

Perhaps it was their effective exclusion from power for the greater part of the period from 1783 to 1830, which permitted some reaffirmation and development of Whig principles. Free from the messy compromises of government, Fox's followers could proclaim their continued attachment to 'Peace, retrenchment and reform'. Parliamentary reform became a Whig cause, with unsuccessful bills introduced into Parliament in 1797 and 1810, providing some precedent for the Great Reform Bill of 1832 (Watson, 1960, pp. 361–2, 450–1). The Foxite Whigs could also claim some credit for British abolition of the slave trade, the one positive achievement of their participation in the brief 'Ministry of All the Talents', in 1807 (Watson, 1960, pp. 440–1). Moreover, the traditional Whig demand for religious toleration was reaffirmed in the cause of Catholic emancipation as well as Protestant dissent.

The defection of the 'Old Whigs' and the accommodation within the Foxite remnant of the party of a new generation of radicals, such as Whitbread, Brougham and Romilly, with a strong commitment to reform, helped preserve or re-establish a politically progressive Whig tradition which ultimately merged into liberalism (Watson, 1960, pp. 436–7). The 1832 Reform Act was a key element in the transition. It can be seen in one sense as the culmination of the Whig tradition. Grey, the Prime Minister responsible for its successful passage, had, as Fox's loyal lieutenant, personally introduced the unsuccessful reform bill of 1797. In another sense, the Act serves to underline the cautious, essentially conservative nature of the Whigs (Wright, 1970, pp. 31–6). It was a strictly limited measure, allowing for some redistribution of parliamentary seats, and a very modest extension of the franchise, to incorporate elements of the respectable propertied middle classes.

Yet even so it provided the foundation for Victorian liberalism by gradually but decisively changing the political geography of Britain. The new urban centres gained at the expense of the shires, manufacture and commerce at the expense of land. Whig aristocrats as well as Tory squires ultimately lost influence to the urban-based business and professional middle classes, and it was the latter who were to provide the effective muscle behind Victorian liberalism. Whiggism had developed in a pre-industrial age, in a predominantly rural society in which land remained the overwhelming source of wealth. It was an

approach to politics which was increasingly anachronistic in
an industrial capitalist society, although the Whigs remained an
important but diminishing element within the liberal coalition until
the late nineteenth century.

Those who would see liberalism in terms of the economic liberalism of the classical economists tend to see the political aspects of
liberalism as almost accidental by-products of free market values.
Such a view involves a wilful neglect of the Whig foundations for
British liberalism, for the Whig/Liberal tradition of thought is essentially a political tradition, concerned with constitutional and governmental issues and questions of civil liberties. Whiggism may have
served economic interests but it was never essentially an economic
doctrine. It was about parliamentary sovereignty, government by
consent, freedom of conscience and religious observance, no taxation
without representation, and a host of other slogans and proclaimed
principles, no doubt very imperfectly applied for the most part. It was
not about free trade or free markets. Whig foreign trade policy in the
seventeenth and eighteenth centuries was opportunist but essentially
mercantilist. The aim was to secure, through colonisation, Navigation
Acts and war as large a British share of world trade as possible.

Radicals

Alongside the Whig tradition, at times interwoven with it, at times in
opposition to it, there is a radical tradition which has had a marked
effect on both British liberalism and, subsequently, socialism. Yet the
term 'radical tradition' if it is to be used at all, must be employed
more loosely. The Whigs were bound together to a degree by
considerations of party, interest and a common intellectual heritage.
Radicals tended to lack even this very loose form of association. The
description 'radical' has been employed to cover a wide range of
politicians, thinkers and ideas, and has rather different connotations
for different periods of time.

Yet although the label is so diffuse and imprecise, it is impossible
to ignore the influence of radicalism on the nineteenth-century British
Liberal Party, and British liberalism more generally. At the parliamentary level the boundary line between Whigs and Radicals was
shifting and imprecise. A succession of radical 'enfants terribles'
were subsequently incorporated into the Whig (and later Liberal)

political establishment. At the popular level radical ideas often enjoyed sufficient support to force concessions from that establishment. Moreover, ideas which were rejected as heretical or even treasonable by one generation, often became another's established orthodoxy.

It was indeed radicals both inside and outside the loose Whig parliamentary grouping which provided the dynamic element in the Whig/Liberal tradition of thought. Although the mainstream Whig politicians of the eighteenth and early nineteenth centuries tended to interpret their proclaimed principles in ways which preserved their own power, property and privileges, it was always possible to give these same principles a far more radical interpretation, as Thomas Paine (1737–1809) did.

In one sense all Paine did was to take the ideas behind the 1688 revolution which had been proclaimed by Locke to their logical conclusion. Once ultimate sovereignty had been transferred from the monarchy to the people, once political equality had been accepted in theory, there was no logical case for restricting participation in the choice of a legislature. Paine himself had earlier accepted some property qualification for voting, but later championed full manhood suffrage (Paine, 1791–2, ed. Collins, 1969). His contemporary, Mary Wollstonecraft (1759–97), went further in demanding full political rights for women, as well as men (Wollstonecraft, 1792, Penguin edn, 1975). Although by turns reviled or neglected in Britain, their ideas were the logical outcome of Whig slogans. Indeed it can be argued that the only coherent way to counter such a revolutionary democratic ideology was by assailing its egalitarian and rationalistic assumptions, as Burke realised.

Whether Paine belongs best within the British liberal or socialist tradition is a somewhat academic point. Recent editors of his work have suggested 'his political theory was vintage liberalism', citing his uncompromising individualism, his sympathies for manufacturers, and his hostility to government (Foot and Kramnick, 1987, pp. 22–9). Ayer (1988, ch. 7), by contrast, talks of 'Paine's blueprint . . . for his Welfare State', and stresses his support for a highly redistributive graduated income tax.

Paine's writing enjoyed what for the time was a massive circulation, despite, or perhaps because of, the government's efforts to suppress them. The Chartists later acknowledged that his philosophy was their inspiration in their 1837 manifesto (Foot and Kramnick,

1987, p. 33). Demands articulated by the working classes and ultimately conceded owed much to the wide if underground dissemination of his ideas.

Yet Paine had less direct influence on the mainstream British liberalism. As a cosmopolitan individual whose ideas had more immediate impact in America and France than Britain, he transcended the parochial British Whig/Liberal tradition of thought, and perhaps belongs more properly to the history of liberalism generally than British liberalism. Moreover, his uncompromising republicanism, his total opposition to the hereditary principle, and his opposition to Christianity, coupled with the vigorous rhetoric in which his ideas were expressed, gave him a wild and dangerous reputation.

In the early nineteenth century there were some radicals with a substantial popular following who were distrusted or persecuted by the political establishment, like Cartwright or Hunt, while others such as Whitbread and Brougham were essentially the progressive wing of the parliamentary Whig party. Also in touch with progressive Whig circles were the 'philosophical radicals' or utilitarians – Bentham and his followers. More difficult to classify is William Cobbett, initially an arch-critic, and later a champion of Paine. Yet Cobbett's radical populism was always essentially harking back to a pre-industrial age, arguably true also of the so-called 'Tory radicals' such as Oastler and Shaftesbury.

Very different was the radicalism of the Quaker manufacturer Bright, who belonged to the new generation of politicians who came to the fore after the 1832 Reform Act, and who in some ways personified the new age. However, Bright in turn lived long enough to be displaced by a new breed of radicals who took over the Liberal Party in the latter part of the century, by which time the term 'radicalism' was beginning to be associated with socialism.

It was radical pressure which committed the Whigs to parliamentary reform in 1832, and later kept up the pressure for further reform in the 1860s and 1880s. The association of radicalism with religious dissent in the second half of the nineteenth century imbued it with a strong moral character, and fuelled demands for non-denominational state education and disestablishment of the Church of England. Radicalism was also strongly associated with the municipal gospel and the growth of local government. At the parliamentary level it was the fusion of Whigs and radicals which created the British Liberal Party.

After the establishment of the Liberal Party in 1859, Whigs continued to predominate in Liberal Cabinets between 1859 and 1886, but at the increasingly important grassroots level, radicals predominated, and this was subsequently reflected in the composition of the parliamentary Liberal party. The formation of the National Liberal Federation in particular signalled the gradual takeover of the party by its radical grassroots supporters, and the increasing alienation of the remaining Whigs. A form of radicalism, always a potent element in British liberalism, thus effectively took it over. Yet it might be noted that it was a relatively restrained, religiously inspired and peculiarly British strand of radicalism which eventually prevailed rather than the fiercely rationalist, republican and universalist radicalism of Thomas Paine.

Classical economics and utilitarianism

If the moral inspiration of Victorian liberalism was derived from radical Nonconformism, it drew intellectual sustenance from the ideas of the classical economists and the utilitarians. It was Adam Smith (1732–90), Malthus (1766–1834) and Ricardo (1772–1823) who virtually founded the modern study of economics, and established the importance of the operations of the market in the allocation and distribution of resources. It was Jeremy Bentham's (1748–1832) 'principle of utility' which was applied to a wide range of institutions and practices. Tradition and long usage were no justification in the face of Bentham's fiercely rationalist analysis. 'What use is it?' was his brutal question, cutting through the mystique in which constitutional and legal issues were generally surrounded. The 'only right and proper end of government' he declared, was 'the greatest happiness of the greatest number.'

To an extent, the classical economists and the utilitarians are difficult to separate. Both shared the individualist assumptions underpinning liberalism. Both stemmed from a similar intellectual climate – the eighteenth-century enlightenment. There were also clear connections between them. Bentham and his associates broadly accepted the *laissez-faire* implications of the economic theories of Smith, Ricardo and Malthus, while Smith's friend and colleague, the philosopher and historian David Hume (1711–76), had earlier laid the foundations for utilitarianism. Some thinkers, like Nassau Senior (1790–1864), had a foot in both camps.

Yet modern neo-liberal writers have identified a fundamental distinction between Benthamism, and the ideas of Adam Smith, and have gone on to suggest that it is Smith and Hume, the great thinkers of the eighteenth-century Scottish enlightenment, who represent the true spirit of liberalism (Gray, 1986, p. 24). Bentham and his followers, by contrast, are blamed for ideas which 'provided a warrant for much later illiberal interventionist policy'. Norman Barry (1986, pp. 19–21) similarly suggests that although 'Bentham is often credited with the liberal label' he is no true liberal.

It is not difficult to understand why neo-liberals opposed to state intervention should be critical of the utilitarians. Their 'greatest happiness principle' involved a potential breach with *laissez-faire* economics. It so happened that Bentham and his associates broadly agreed with Smith that the greatest happiness would be most effectively promoted by free markets, but of course the principle could equally well be employed to justify government intervention, and subsequently was, most notably by Bentham's formidable secretary and disciple, Edwin Chadwick (1800–90). Chadwick had been a key figure in the development and the administration of the harsh New Poor Law, but his later experiences in the public health movement converted him from an orthodox exponent of free market principles to a convinced advocate of state intervention and control in a wide range of issues surrounding water supply, sewage and control of pollution (Finer, 1952).

Bentham himself had been converted by his friend and associate James Mill to representative democracy. If the end of government should be the greatest happiness of the greatest number, it followed that only a government which was freely and regularly elected by the governed, acting in accordance with rational self-interest, could be relied upon to promote the interests of the governed, rather than the interests of the rulers (Dinwiddy, 1989).

Democracy itself can provide a powerful spur for state intervention. There may be electoral pressures for public spending and governmental growth. Yet Bentham has other claims to be regarded as the father of modern bureaucracy. He sought to redesign the whole system of British government from top to bottom on rationalist lines, involving the appointment of professionally qualified, salaried, public officials.

The contradictory implications of Benthamite thinking can be seen clearly in that most notorious of utilitarian-influenced measures, the Poor Law Amendment Act of 1834. Its underlying assumptions were those of free market economics: incentives must be maintained. Thus the able-bodied poor who sought relief must be prepared to enter a workhouse, where their condition would be 'less eligible' than that of the lowest independent labourer. Yet the New Poor Law also involved a comprehensive network of new administrative areas, a new hierarchy of administrative officials, and a novel form of central control and inspection, that had rather different implications for the future.

All this explains why modern neo-liberals have reservations about the utilitarians. Thus Hayek (1975) is critical of what he calls Bentham's 'constructivist rationalism'. Gray (1986) similarly castigates him for believing that 'social institutions can be the object of successful rational redesign', thus his utilitarianism 'had an inherent tendency to spawn policies of interventionist social engineering'. Norman Barry (1986) comments 'its central tenets stress artifice and design in the pursuit of collective ends'.

All this is fair comment, but what is unwarranted is their further suggestion that Bentham and the utilitarians do not really belong to the liberal tradition, while Smith and Hume are the fount of pure liberalism. This involves a *post hoc*, highly artificial, ideal-type conception of liberalism which bears little relation to the British Whig/Liberal tradition, or indeed to the historical experience of liberalism anywhere. The truth is that Bentham and his associates became directly and centrally involved in that Whig/Liberal tradition, in terms of personal connections, ideas and practical influence on policy, while the connection of Hume and Smith with that same tradition is at best tangential. At the personal level Hume wrote a history of England in which contemporaries perceived a strong Tory bias, while Adam Smith's own politics were more Tory than Whig. Ricardo, whose liberal credentials are, by contrast, unimpeachable (Weatherall, 1976), is curiously neglected by the neo-liberals (or perhaps not so curiously in view of the use to which Marx and others later put his labour theory of value).

Certainly the writings of all the major classical economists – Smith, Malthus, Ricardo, Nassau Senior, and, later, John Stuart Mill – contributed significantly to Victorian liberalism. Yet their ideas were extensively vulgarised and oversimplified. While Adam Smith's

'invisible hand' provided a graphic and enduring vision of the
beneficial operation of free market forces, even Smith allowed for
significant exceptions. It was popularisers such as Harriet Martineau,
Edward Baines and Samuel Smiles who reduced the principles of
classical economics to the simple injunctions of '*laissez-faire*' for
governments and 'self-help' for individuals.

Even so, *laissez-faire* was only one strand among many in Victorian liberalism, and public policy was never consistently informed
by the principle. A series of Factory Acts, local and general Public
Health Acts, and Acts to regulate the railways and banks were passed
in the early Victorian period when *laissez-faire* ideas were most
influential. Indeed, economic historians question whether there ever
was an age of *laissez-faire*.

Victorian liberalism

A political ideology is not to be identified with the history of a
political party, yet there is inevitably a strong connection between
particular systems of ideas and their practical political expressions.
An account of British liberalism has perforce to pay some attention to
the composition, support and record of the British Liberal Party,
especially during its heyday in the second half of the nineteenth
century.

Although the term 'liberal' was applied in British politics from the
early nineteenth century, the British Liberal Party was not really
established until 1859 when Palmerston formed an administration
incorporating Whigs, Radicals and former Peelite Conservatives.
Even then the government in the domestic sphere at least remained
more 'Whig' than 'Liberal' until at least the death of Palmerston in
1865, or the emergence of Gladstone (1809–98) as leader and then
Prime Minister in 1868 (Bentley, 1984).

Gladstone himself came to seem the embodiment of Victorian
liberalism. He so dominated the party that he was substantially able to
shape it in his own image. Yet in some ways he was a strange figure
for liberal canonisation. He had started his political career as a
Conservative follower of Peel. Even after he followed his leader into
opposition when the Repeal of the Corn Laws split the Conservative
Party, his final destination was unclear, and some rapprochement with
Derby and Disraeli's Conservatives seemed possible (Bentley, 1984,

pp. 168–9). His pivotal role in Liberal politics after 1859 was thus far from inevitable. He was, moreover, an Anglican landowner with no past reputation as a radical in a party which was becoming increasingly associated with manufacturing, dissent and radical reform. Yet Gladstone was a politician who became more radical and populist with age. Furthermore and crucially, he was inspired by a Christian moral fervour, which struck a receptive chord among his Nonconformist followers. Gladstonian liberalism thus became something of a moral crusade (Vincent, 1966; Adelman, 1970, pp. 6–7).

This Gladstonian liberalism drew on several strands. Parliamentary reform was a theme derived from the Whig tradition. The advocacy of Bright and later Gladstone himself turned it into a populist cause. Proposals for a fairly modest extension of the franchise soon developed into radical Liberal demands for full manhood suffrage (Adelman, 1970; Wright, 1970).

Nonconformism also loomed large. According to the religious census of 1851 almost half of the church-going population of the country was Nonconformist, so that although the 1860s parliamentary party was 'still overwhelmingly Anglican' the Liberals were becoming 'the party of the Nonconformist conscience' (Vincent, 1966, pp. 61–2). It was these pressures which spawned the Liberation Society, which aimed at the disestablishment of the Church of England, and later the National Education League committed to a national, free and secular system of education. The League in turn provided the model for the National Liberal Federation in 1877, which not only established a national organisation for the Liberal Party but also tipped it decisively in the direction of nonconformism and radicalism. By the 1880s the parliamentary party as well as the party in the country was predominantly nonconformist (Adelman, 1970).

A similar attitude to foreign policy and Ireland helped unite Gladstone with the Nonconformists. The importance of foreign affairs to British liberalism is often underestimated. It was support for liberal and nationalist movements on the continent, especially Italian unification, which was one factor which brought Palmerston's 1859 government together, and subsequently kept it together. It was Gladstone's campaign against the Bulgarian atrocities which brought him out of premature retirement and into close collaboration with the Nonconformists. It was the religious fervour behind his mission to pacify

Ireland which both split his party, but also strengthened the moral element in liberalism.

What has been called Manchester liberalism was a significant but retrospectively exaggerated element of the Liberal Party after 1859. Free trade had certainly been clearly established as a liberal principle. Cobden and Bright, the leaders of that classic pressure group campaign, the Anti-Corn Law League, had seen their cause victorious in 1846. Repeal of the Corn Laws symbolically reflected the transfer of power from the landed to the manufacturing interest which both Cobden and Bright represented. Gladstone as Chancellor of the Exchequer in Palmerston's government built on their work by abolishing a whole range of duties, while Cobden himself, although he had declined office, was allowed to negotiate personally the Anglo-French trade treaty of 1860.

Yet free trade did not entail *laissez-faire* in domestic policy. Cobden's opposition to Factory Acts in particular and government intervention in general seemed increasingly out of tune with the times. As for Bright, Vincent (1966, p. 168) claims that his 'theory of history and of politics did not derive from any abstract attachment of *laissez-faire* or political economy, or from any construction of his business interests'. Rather it was a moral and religious fervour which informed his views on economics and foreign affairs, and a detestation of 'privilege' which led him to champion parliamentary reform.

Liberal practice entailed increased state intervention. Major reforms in education, the army, the law and civil service were accomplished by Gladstone's 1868–74 administration. If the record of the 1880–5 administration was disappointing to Gladstone's radical supporters, the passing of the Third Reform Act in 1884 promised the triumph of radical demands for reform over Whig caution. Chamberlain's 'Unauthorised Programme' of 1885, and the 'Newcastle Programme' of 1891 marked a decisive shift towards radicalism in the British Liberal Party.

Behind the evolution of Liberal political practice there was a considerable development in political thinking. Subsequent interpretations of Victorian liberal ideology have concentrated particularly on the massive contributions of John Stuart Mill (1806–73), representing the progressive or revisionist tendencies in liberalism and Herbert Spencer (1820–1903), representing the more old-fashioned libertarian strand.

In most respects Mill was a thorough individualist: 'The sole end for which mankind are warranted, individually or collectively, in interfering with the liberty of action of any of their number is self-protection ... Over himself, over his own body and mind, the individual is sovereign' (Mill, 1859). This sounds like a plea for minimal state intervention, and in some respects it was. Mill was eloquent in denouncing censorship and arguing for full liberty of thought and expression. He was remarkably libertarian on matters of personal conduct also, and it was this concern for individuality which led him, despite his general advocacy of representative democracy, into fears over the 'tyranny of the majority'. He worried about the intolerance of public opinion and the 'despotism of custom' which he saw as a greater threat to individuality than deliberate actions by governments (Mill, 1859, 1861).

In other respects Mill allowed for considerable government intervention, despite his general espousal of the market in *Principles of Political Economy* (1848). Gray (1986, p. 30) quotes Dicey to the effect that Mill is 'a watershed thinker in the development of liberalism' from individualism to collectivism. Greenleaf (1983, p. 103) suggests he was to be a major instrument of the betrayal of traditional Liberal doctrine. But Mill did not transform Victorian liberalism; he largely mirrored it. On education his views (for state aid, and even for limited state provision, but opposed to a general state education) were mainstream. His support for the activities of trade unions and even the sympathies he expressed for socialist ideas were increasingly familiar in radical liberal circles. Only in his support for women's rights was he in advance of his time.

Spencer, by contrast, was increasingly out of tune with the times he lived in. His thought combined *laissez-faire* economics with pre-Darwinian evolutionary theories which emphasised the survival of the fittest. There was, he maintained, 'a universal law of nature ... that a creature not energetic enough to maintain itself must die'. Not surprisingly he was opposed to any welfare measures of the sort which the Liberal Party of his day was increasingly advocating and introducing at both local and national level. But he generally opposed almost all forms of state intervention, and even argued for the privatisation of the Royal Mint.

Just as in some circles there has been a tendency to elevate Smith and Hume at the expense of Bentham in the liberal pantheon, so there has been a similar tendency for much the same reasons to elevate

Spencer at the expense of Mill (Greenleaf, 1983). There is scope for argument over the relative cogency and importance of their writing, but there can be no debate over which was the more representative or influential Victorian liberal thinker.

Liberalism, capitalism and democracy

Liberalism as a political ideology has been closely associated with the rise of industrial capitalism. It pre-eminently was the creed of the bourgeoisie, the owners of industrial and financial capital. Its political objectives involved the enfranchisement of the new middle classes and the effective transfer of political power to the major manufacturing urban centres of industrialised Britain. Its economic theory could be seen as the rationalisation of the interests of capital. Moreover, it was hardly purely coincidental that the British Liberal Party finally emerged in the 1850s, when Britain's industrial and commercial dominance was unchallenged, the British bourgeoisie supremely self-confident, and the working classes as yet largely non-unionised and unenfranchised. The relative decline of British manufacturing, and the rise of labour were part of the background to the subsequent decline of liberalism.

Furthermore, even if one goes back further to the roots of liberalism, it has been argued that Protestant dissent, and more particularly Puritanism, embodied ideas favourable to the spirit of capitalist accumulation, while the political thought of Hobbes, and more especially Locke, involved a 'possessive individualism' which was highly compatible with the mercantile capitalism of the seventeenth century (Macpherson, 1962)

Even so, British liberalism cannot be simply derived from capitalism. The leading Whig parliamentarians, who retained a substantial presence in nineteenth-century Liberal governments despite their diminishing numbers, were large landowners. Many of the rank-and-file Liberal activists were not manufacturers but relatively small shopkeepers and tradesmen (Vincent, 1966). And even before their progressive enfranchisement, a substantial section of the working class had attached itself to the Liberal cause. Liberalism in practice involved a coalition of class interests. Some of the causes it embraced, such as temperance, religious disestablishment, and Irish home rule, were only tenuously, if at all, connected with the interests of capitalism. Leading liberal thinkers, such as John Stuart Mill, Ritchie, Hobhouse, Keynes and Beveridge, gave only qualified support for capitalism.

The establishment of a capitalist economy was accompanied by the gradual establishment of a liberal democratic system in the United Kingdom, and this may not have been coincidental. Indeed, some Marxists have argued that representative democracy affords the best shell for capitalism. If that is so, then it was hardly surprising that the party of the bourgeoisie should have been in the forefront of the parliamentary reform movement in Britain. However, it should be noted that this cause attracted not only the millowner Bright, but the Whig aristocrat Russell and the landowner Gladstone, and of course the enthusiastic support of liberal tradesmen and skilled workmen.

Of course support for parliamentary reform in the mid-nineteenth century commonly stopped short of support for full representative democracy, and this has provided some support for those commentators who have denied any reciprocal tie of dependence between liberalism and democracy. Arblaster talks of the 'fear of democracy' and argues that 'middle class liberals were fearful, not only for wealth and property, but also for the position and values of their class' and concludes of parliamentary reform 'No issue has so clearly revealed the class character of liberalism as an ideology' (Arblaster, 1964, p. 264). From a different perspective Gray identifies liberalism not with democracy, but with limited government. This, he declares, 'need not be democratic government' and proceeds to argue 'where it is unlimited, democratic government cannot be liberal government since it respects no domain of independence or liberty as being immune to invasion by governmental authority' (Gray, 1986, p. 74).

Such verdicts involve a rather strained interpretation of the evolution of liberalism, and particularly a neglect of its development over the last century. Democracy in the eighteenth century was a remote theoretical model, interpreted by educated Englishmen, if at all, through Thucydides, Plato and Aristotle. Representative democracy in the early nineteenth century was a largely untried system. In these circumstances it is not surprising that middle-class opinion was rather apprehensive about its possible consequences, and it is remarkable that it was advocated at all. Yet it was. Paine, whose political theory has been described as 'vintage liberalism' (Foot and Cramnick, 1987, p. 22) was (as we have seen) a consistent advocate of manhood suffrage. 'The true and only basis of representative government is equality of rights. Every man has a right to one vote' (Paine, 1795, ed. Foot and Cramnick, 1987, p. 459). James Mill not only convinced himself of the case for representative democracy, but also Jeremy Bentham, as the only sure means for promoting the 'greatest happiness of the greatest number', in advance of the Chartist campaign for adult male suffrage. John Stuart Mill argued for the extension of full political rights to women, well before there was any sustained campaign for female suffrage. Commentators have been quick to seize on any shortcomings in the commitment of these writers to democracy: the exclusion of women from James Mill's franchise, and his son's flirtation with plural voting. Yet in so doing they ignore the substance of their support for what was then a radical minority cause.

Of course many Whigs and liberals in the early and mid-nineteenth century did not want to go as far or as fast as these thinkers, but once the logic of the movement for parliamentary reform was accepted and British liberals became finally committed to the theory and practice of representative democracy, their conversion was wholehearted. Indeed, the arrival of 'government by the people' was seen by many liberals as a justification for abandoning former limitations to government intervention. Thus Chamberlain argued in 1885, 'I quite understand the reason for timidity in dealing with this question [poverty] so long as the government was merely the expression of the will of a prejudiced and limited few. ... But now we have a Government of the people by the people ...' (speech at Warrington, quoted in Schultz, 1972, p. 59). Ritchie in 1891 wrote that 'the explicit recognition of popular sovereignty tends to abolish the antithesis between "the Man" and "the State". The State becomes, not "I" indeed but "we" ' (quoted in Schultz, 1972, p. 77). Herbert Samuel in 1902 argued that a reformed state could be entrusted with social reform. 'Now democracy has been substituted for aristocracy as the root principle of the constitution ... the State today is held worthy to be the instrument of the community in many affairs for which the State of yesterday was clearly incompetent' (quoted in Schultz, 1972, p. 81). The acceptance of democracy thus was a critical step towards the New Liberalism. There was an inexorable logic by which liberals progressed from parliamentary reform to representative democracy, to state intervention, and the apparent abandonment of some of the principles associated with earlier liberalism.

The New Liberalism

The 'New Liberalism' which developed from the late nineteenth century has been the subject of intense controversy. For the New Liberals themselves, such as L. T. Hobhouse, who wrote a seminal text on 'Liberalism' in 1911, the New Liberalism developed naturally out of the old, extending and refining familiar liberal principles and concepts. But for some liberals at the time the new ideas seemed more a betrayal than a development of liberalism, a view echoed by modern neo-liberal critics, who identify liberalism with free market economics. For Gray the 'revisionist liberalism' of the late nineteenth and early twentieth centuries was but the culmination of 'anti-liberal elements' which 'began to enter the liberal tradition itself from the mid-1840s in the work of John Stuart Mill' (Gray, 1986, p. 33). For radical and socialist critics on the other hand, the New Liberalism has been dismissed as a forlorn attempt to revive and update an outmoded ideology (Arblaster, 1984, ch. 16).

The origins of the New Liberalism have been variously explained. Intellectually it has been ascribed to the influence of Hegelian idealism on British liberal thinkers (Pearson and Williams, 1984, p. 146). At the level of party politics it has been seen in terms of the need to attract working-class votes, and head off the rising challenge from labour, with both a small and large 'l'. At the level of public policy it has been viewed as a project to modernise the British economy and society and enable Britain to compete more effectively in the world economy and maintain its status as the leading imperial power (Hay, 1983).

To an extent the New Liberalism can be seen, however, as a *post hoc* rationalisation of the substantial growth in government intervention which had been taking place throughout the Victorian period, much of it actively promoted by Liberal governments at national level and committed Liberal supporters at local level. In the debate over the New Liberalism rather too much emphasis has been placed on the welfare reforms of the 1906–14 Liberal government, as if these involved a quite radical departure from previous Liberal practice, when previous Whig and Liberal governments had involved considerable state intervention.

At local level the involvement of Liberals in interventionist policies in the Victorian period is even more apparent. Here there were fewer intellectual inhibitions over collectivist ideas. Enthusiasm for a whole range of publicly inspired civic improvements amounted to a 'municipal gospel'. Radical liberals saw city government as a test-bed for policies which could be applied nationally.

A key figure here was Joseph Chamberlain (1836–1914) who made his name as a radical Liberal mayor of Birmingham, before making a successful transition to the national political scene. His campaign for the 'Unauthorised Programme' in 1885 drew extensively on his own local government experience. 'The experience of the great towns is very encouraging,' he urged.

> By their wise and liberal use of the powers entrusted to them, they have, in the majority of cases, protected the health of the community; they have provided means of recreation and enjoyment and instruction, and they have done a great deal to equalise social advantages . . . You have, in connection with the great municipal corporations, hospitals, schools, museums, free libraries, art galleries, baths, parks. All these things which a generation ago could only have been obtained by the well-to-do, are now, in many large towns, placed at the service of every citizen by the action of the municipalities. (speech at Hull, 1885, quoted in Schultz, 1972, pp. 57–8)

At Warrington in the same year Chamberlain explicitly rejected the principles of *laissez-faire*. The problem of poverty was, he said, one which

> some men would put aside by reference to the eternal laws of supply and demand, to the necessity of freedom and contract, and to the sanctity of every private right of property. But, gentlemen, these phrases are the convenient cant of selfish wealth . . . These are no answers to our questions.

He went on to brush aside allegations that what he was advocating involved socialism.

> Of course it is Socialism. The Poor Law is Socialism. The Education Act is Socialism. The greater part of municipal work is Socialism, and every kindly act of legislation by which the community has sought to discharge its responsibilities and its obligations to the poor is Socialism, but is none the worse for that. (quoted in Schultz, 1972, pp. 58–9)

Chamberlain's subsequent split with Gladstone and later career as a Liberal Unionist member of Tory governments has made his relationship to the liberal tradition somewhat ambivalent and contentious. But as a radical liberal with roots in local government, Chamberlain was only the most prominent of a whole new breed of liberals who were coming to prominence in the party in the late nineteenth century. The radical, reforming approach of the Unauthorised Programme was echoed in the Newcastle programme, and culminated in the social welfare reforms of Asquith, Lloyd George and Churchill.

In this context New Liberal ideas were not some alien transplant from German philosophy. Hegelian idealism was in truth a rather exaggerated influence on New Liberal thought. T. H. Green (1836–82) admittedly derived his 'political obligations' from Kant and Hegel, but not all New Liberals were idealists and not all idealists were liberals. Perhaps the most important of all the New Liberal thinkers, Leonard Hobhouse (1864–1929), was a noted critic of what he termed 'The Metaphysical Theory of the State' (1918). More significant was the influence of earlier British liberals such as Mill, and the developing practice of liberalism at national and more particularly local level. T. H. Green was a local councillor as well as an Oxford philosopher, and well aware of municipal powers and achievements.

The New Liberals were essentially engaged in an extensive project to redefine old liberal concepts and values in line with new political practice. Freedom for Green meant 'a positive power or capacity of doing or enjoying something worth doing or enjoying'. 'The ideal of true freedom is the maximum of power for all members of human society alike to make the best of themselves.' Individual liberty remained the touchstone of liberalism, but the New Liberalism, according to Hobson involved ' a fuller realisation of individual liberty contained in the provision of equal opportunities for self-development' (Hobson, quoted in Eccleshall, 1986, p. 204). Self-development was a key concept which had links with John Stuart Mill and Gladstonian liberalism, but for the New Liberals it could be used to justify state intervention – to remove barriers to self-development. However, 'Liberals must ever insist that each enlargement of the authority and functions of the State must justify itself as an enlargement of personal liberty, interfering with individuals only in order to set free new and larger opportunities' (Hobson, quoted in Eccleshall, 1986, p. 206).

Such caveats were, however, quite consistent with extensive programmes of state action. Another New Liberal, D. G. Ritchie (1853–1903) suggested that 'the means of communication and loco-motion can in every civilised country be easily nationalised or municipalised, where this has not been done already.' Although 'with regard to productive industries there may appear greater difficulty', Ritchie reckoned that the development of 'enormous joint stock companies, worked by salaried managers' would make the 'transition to management by government (central or local) very much more simple and very much more necessary'. The state would 'substitute for the irresponsible company or trust the responsible public corpora-tion' (quoted in Schultz, pp. 75–7).

Hobhouse was prepared to justify extensive interference with the market to secure 'the right to work' and 'the right to a living wage'. There was, he argued, 'a defect in the social system, a hitch in the economic machine'. Individual action is here fruitless. 'The in-dividual workman cannot put the machine straight . . . He does not direct and regulate industry. He is not responsible for its ups and downs, but he has to pay for them' (Hobhouse, 1911 – new edition 1964, pp. 83–4).

Liberal politicians were not always prepared to go as far as these New Liberal ideologues, but the record of the 1906–14 Liberal government included the provision of school meals, old age pensions, health and unemployment insurance, labour exchanges and pro-gressive taxation. There was a readiness to promote state welfare provision, intervene in the operations of the labour market, and secure some modest redistribution of income and wealth (Fraser, 1984, ch. 7). Arguably such measures were the culmination of an inter-ventionist trend which had begun in the early nineteenth century. The academic debate over the degree of influence of the New Liberal thinkers on Liberal policy is rather beside the point. There was, rather, a two-way process in which practice forced some reconsidera-tion of theory, and this in turn helped provide a justification for further reform.

How far was the New Liberalism simulated by the 'rising chal-lenge of labour', about which Liberals were undoubtedly concerned? Some hoped that social reforms would win votes. Others feared they could be an electoral liability. Radical commitments might not win working-class votes, but could easily alienate the middle classes. Rosebery was convinced that the detailed promises contained in the

Newcastle programme had cost the party support (Bernstein, 1986, ch. 2). It was a factor in his Liberal Imperialism and his commitment to the National Efficiency movement which could appeal both to a chauvinistic working class, and progressive businessmen interested in modernisation. In this context social welfare reforms could be dressed up as good for business, and good for the British empire. Later historians have disagreed over the electoral appeal of state welfare. While welfare reforms were advocated by leaders of the organised working class, they were not necessarily popular with working-class voters.

The New Liberalism ultimately failed to prevent the decline of the Liberal Party. Whether this rapid decline into virtual political oblivion was inevitable is an interesting although speculative question on which historians have disagreed (Dangerfield, 1966; Clarke, 1971, ch. 15). However, New Liberal thinking did not share the fate of the party. On the contrary, and rather ironically, the culmination of New Liberal thought can be seen in the social welfare proposals of Beveridge and the economic theory of Keynes which provided the basis of the post-Second World War consensus accepted by the leadership of the Labour and Conservative parties.

Keynes and Beveridge were both large 'L' as well as small 'l' liberals. Beveridge had been strongly influenced by the New Liberal thinking of his youth and had played a role in the establishment of Churchill's Labour Exchanges in the 1906–14 Liberal Government. Keynes had made a major contribution to Lloyd George's election programme in 1929. Although their ideas have been claimed for social democracy, they were essentially in the liberal tradition, particularly the progressive New Liberal tradition. The Beveridge Report was based on the insurance principle, and although far more comprehensive, was in keeping with the spirit of the Lloyd George insurance scheme of 1911. Keynes' economic theory involved government intervention at the macro-economic level, but this removed the necessity for detailed intervention in particular sectors of the economy or industries. Essentially, capitalism would be managed in a way which would continue to allow markets to operate freely at the micro level. Neither Beveridge nor Keynes saw any need for an end to the private ownership of the means of production. It was precisely this kind of state intervention to promote employment and welfare provision but short of socialism which was favoured by earlier New Liberals like Green and Hobhouse (George and Wilding, 1985).

Neo-liberalism

The Keynes–Beveridge post-war consensus was finally shattered, in part by a revival in classical economic liberalism, commonly referred to as 'neo-liberalism', which, although only one letter removed from 'New Liberalism' is far apart on the ideological spectrum. The most obvious feature of neo-liberalism is support for free market principles and opposition to government intervention in the economic and social spheres. The key thinker is Hayek, although a number of other writers have been claimed for this neo-liberal revival with varying degrees of plausibility, including Popper, Talmon, Berlin, Rawls, Nozick, Friedman and Buchanan (Gray, 1986, ch. 5). In Britain, neo-liberal ideas have been advanced by such bodies as the Institute of Economic Affairs, and the Adam Smith Institute, and have been particularly influential within the Thatcher government. Indeed it was suggested by Milton Friedman that Mrs Thatcher was essentially a nineteenth-century liberal. The debate on what has come to be called 'Thatcherism', and its relationship to neo-liberalism will be explored in the context of conservatism (Chapter 5). Here it is only necessary to point out that fashionable neo-liberal thinkers have provoked a considerable reinterpretation of the earlier history of liberalism.

Thus some modern accounts of liberalism by neo-liberals dismiss, ignore or reject a century or more of evolution in British liberal thought and policy, and redefine liberalism exclusively in terms of a rather narrow and one-sided view of classical liberalism (Barry, 1986; Gray, 1986). Friedrich Hayek perhaps started this reinterpretation. He rejected not only the New Liberalism but also a substantial strand of classical liberalism in condemning the 'constructivist rationalism' of the English Utilitarians and others (Hayek, 1975).

Twentieth-century radical and Marxist commentators on liberalism have also tended to elevate the importance of particular thinkers such as Malthus, Cobden and Spencer, and rely on a somewhat selective interpretation of others such as Bentham and Mill, because it fits their general critique. In many ways this provides a valuable corrective to the rosy picture of the liberal tradition provided by liberal sympathisers, but it unfortunately tends to reinforce the one-sided neo-liberal view of liberal ideology. Such critics are rather too ready to accept the claims of the neo-liberals that theirs is the true liberalism, and other brands heresies or aberrations. Arblaster (1984), for example, is dismissive of the New Liberalism (which is described with the addition of a question mark) and clearly regards the neo-liberal revival as more central to liberal philosophy than the development of British liberalism over the last 100 years.

There is surely a problem with a view of liberalism which appears to exclude entirely the liberalism practised by the party of that name in this country over the last century. But it is not just the New Liberalism and its legacy which is rejected, but the radicalism of Paine, and the utilitarianism of Bentham and Mill. Moreover, the emphasis on the economic ideas of the classical economists tends to downplay the importance of the Whig tradition and the liberal Nonconformist conscience to British liberalism. Religious dissent, political reform and a distinctive attitude to international affairs were the driving forces behind Gladstonian liberalism. These were the issues of principle which united and divided politicians, which prompted resignations and party splits, and which inflamed popular passions. Arguments over state intervention involved appeals to economic principles, but tended to be resolved pragmatically. Interpretations of British liberalism wholly or largely in terms of *laissez-faire* economics involve a substantial distortion of history.

Liberalism today

What then is the present position of liberalism in Britain today, and what are its prospects? It was suggested at the beginning of this chapter that all modern British political ideologies could be seen as in some sense 'variants of liberalism'. Moreover, the term 'liberal' is still extensively employed in modern political vocabulary, and can only be invested with some precision by qualifying it. To describe a politician or a writer, or a policy as 'liberal' is profoundly unhelpful, unless some modifying adjective or prefix is employed. Thus there are neo-liberals, market liberals or economic liberals, who favour free market ideas, and are generally regarded as on the right of the political spectrum. Indeed, quite a few combine economic liberalism with distinctively conservative views on social issues and problems. On the other hand, there are progressive or social liberals who are enthusiastic about penal reform, civil liberties, the protection of the rights of minorities, freedom of expression and open government, who are unashamed interventionists in the economic sphere. Those who, like Samuel Brittan, regard themselves as both economic and social liberals are relatively unusual.

Among all these varieties of liberals there remains the British Liberal Party, and its more recent successor the Liberal Democrats, who would still regard themselves as the only true heirs of the liberalism of Gladstone, Mill and Lloyd George, and the only credible vehicle for the promotion and development of liberal ideology.

Liberal Party policy in the post-war period lay comfortably within the New Liberal tradition – welfare capitalism with a strong emphasis on individual rights. Distinctive Liberal policies included early advocacy of UK entry into the EEC, devolution, incomes policies, partnership in industry, electoral reform (sometimes as part of a package of constitutional reform), and a focus on the community (Tivey and Wright, 1989, pp. 83–6). This last element has been closely linked with Liberal successes in local government, where the party has enjoyed a taste of power. At national level it adopted an intermediate position between the two major parties, closer to the Conservatives on trade unionism, and closer to Labour on defence and foreign affairs, where its internationalist stance followed the tradition established by Bright and Gladstone.

Whether the post-war British Liberal Party really did much to extend or develop liberalism may be doubted, however. The party was fertile in policy proposals, without producing any startling new ideas or major thinkers. Neither its electoral successes nor its failures seem to have owed much to liberal ideology. The crucial decisions with which its leadership was faced were tactical rather than ideological: whether to accept Heath's offer of a coalition in 1974, whether to support the Labour government after 1977, how to handle the SDP breakaway from Labour after 1981, and how soon and how fast to promote a merger with the SDP. All these decisions of course had important ideological implications, but they were not ideologically driven.

In fact there was rather more intellectual ferment among the modern Liberal Party's uneasy allies, the SDP, and their post-merger remnants. It could be argued that the dividing line between New Liberalism and Fabian socialism or labourism was always a thin one, (Hobhouse after all talked of liberal socialism in 1911 while Hobson made the transition to Labour following the First World War). It has perhaps grown thinner still as a consequence of revisionist tendencies on the right of the Labour Party in the 1950s, and the SDP breakaway in the 1980s. In this context the Liberal/SDP Alliance and subsequent merger can be seen as the practical expression of an ideological convergence which was already well under way (Behrens, 1989). Thus social democrats like David Marquand could be claimed for liberalism (although Marquand eventually rejoined Labour in 1995). But Liberals reacted rather cautiously to the spate of new social democratic writing and thinking. Bradley (1985) quoted Michael Meadowcroft's warning that 'the SDP is at one and the same time the greatest opportunity and the greatest danger to liberalism for 30 years.' In the end the Liberals effectively swallowed the SDP rather than the other way around, and the modern Liberal Democrats are the clear lineal descendants of the old Liberal Party.

The shifting electoral prospects of the modern successors of the old Liberal Party may be considered only tangentially relevant to the state of liberalism in Britain today. Eccleshall argues, 'There is a sense in which it is not misleading to suggest that the disintegration of the Liberal Party signifies the triumph of liberalism.' He points out that 'liberalism has been vulnerable to ideological pillage from its inception' and concludes 'If liberalism is now partly invisible, this is because so many of its assumptions and ideals have infiltrated political practice and current awareness' (Eccleshall, 1986, p. 56).

There is an obvious sense in which this is true. Many of the specific proposals put forward by liberals in the past, including proposals which seemed once radical or even revolutionary have long been put into practice, and absorbed into British political culture. Moreover, a number of legislative changes in the 1960s, including divorce, homosexual and abortion law reform, and some relaxation of censorship, went a long way towards the implementation of the principles of individual liberty announced by John Stuart Mill in 1859. Subsequent legislation on equal pay, equal opportunities, and race and sex discrimination in the 1970s is also thoroughly consistent with liberal ideology. Such measures have been supported by modern Liberals, but have been advanced by a broad coalition of progressive opinion covering substantial elements in the Labour and Conservative parties. A more recent progressive cause which is even more central to liberal ideology is constitutional reform. Campaigns for civil liberties and more open government, and the considerable impact made by the pressure group Charter '88, are thoroughly in keeping with the liberal tradition, and may be seen as an indication of its modern health and vitality.

Yet at another level it may be doubted how far liberal ideas have really thoroughly permeated modern British society. Much of the liberal legislation on homosexuality, equal opportunities and race and sex discrimination was stimulated by widespread evidence of intolerance, discrimination and persecution, and has provoked a formidable backlash in its turn. Indeed, one fashionable interpretation of the success of 'Thatcherism' is that its neo-conservative or authoritarian populist elements have made palatable its abstruse or repugnant free market elements (Hall and Jacques, 1983; Edgar, 1984). In other words it is its chauvinism, and tough line on immigration, law and order, and defence which have won working-class votes, not its neo-liberal economics. On this interpretation, the progressive liberal orthodoxy of the 1950s and 1960s was essentially an establishment phenomenon. The 'hangers and floggers' attending Conservative Party conferences, and the London dockers who marched in support of Powell were possibly closer to the political views of the masses than the liberal progressive leadership of both major parties.

Others would suggest that the failure of 'progressive liberalism' to achieve a more tolerant, fair and equal society is rooted in the inadequacies of liberal ideology, that the emphasis on civil and political rights, on institutional procedures, and the redress of specific individual grievances, all grounded in individualist liberal philosophy is not enough. Such critics would argue that it is necessary to go beyond liberalism.

Guide to further reading

R. Eccleshall (1986) provides a good reader on liberalism, with a useful introduction – see also his own account of liberalism in Eccleshall *et al.* (1994). J. Gray (1986) gives an accessible, brief, but rather one-sided introduction to liberalism in the Open University series. A. Arblaster (1984) gives a much fuller and broader (if rather hostile) account in his *The Rise and Decline of Western Liberalism*. Stuart Hall provides a brief but closely argued account of 'Variants of Liberalism' from a Marxist perspective in Donald and Hall (eds, 1986). W. H. Greenleaf (1983) has much to say about liberals in the second volume of *The British Political Tradition*, although he is idiosyncratic in his preferences. The New Liberalism is explored from a number of different angles by M. Freeden (1978), P. F. Clarke

(1971) and J. R. Hay (1983). H. J. Schultz (1972) provides a useful reader. Among liberal texts, John Stuart Mill's *On Liberty* (1859) provides the classic defence of free speech and toleration, and much of his other writing is at least worth dipping into (there have been many modern editions, for example, 1962, ed. M. Warnock, or 1971, ed. M. G. Fawcett). L. Hobhouse *Liberalism* (1911, 1964) was written at the height of the New Liberalism.

5

CONSERVATISM

Introduction

The importance of conservative ideas for British politics hardly requires emphasising. In terms of power and influence, conservatism has been the dominant British political creed. Politicians describing themselves as 'Conservative' have been far more successful in elections than those calling themselves liberals, socialists or anything else. Governments largely or wholly composed of members of the Conservative Party have been in office for over three-quarters of the last century. The term 'conservative' has been regularly invoked to justify policies and programmes.

Yet while conservatism has triumphed so conspicuously in Britain its nature remains elusive and contentious. There are most of the usual problems found in interpreting any political ideology in examining conservatism, including conflicting perspectives, and changes over time. A problem which is perhaps less significant is the relationship between British conservatism and conservatism elsewhere, if only because of the markedly insular character of the British variant. Yet there are also some particular difficulties in examining conservatism which are not encountered to the same degree with other ideologies.

One problem specifically associated with conservatism is that it is often denied that it is an ideology at all (Kirk, 1982, p. xiv). Thus for many conservatives, socialism, communism, and possibly fascism might qualify as ideologies, but not conservatism. Conservatism is held to indicate not an elaborate system of thought, but rather an attitude of mind, not the application of some predetermined blueprint, but a common-sense approach to immediate practical problems. Pragmatism is thus opposed to ideology. The Conservative Party is characterised as a pragmatic rather than an ideological party. Consequently, it is asserted, it is a mistake to expect to find consistent principles behind conservatism, which has evolved and changed in accordance with circumstances.

Critics of conservatism sometimes employ a very different terminology to reach a substantially similar conclusion. Conservatism for them is essentially a ruling-class ideology, and it has evolved in accordance with the changing interests of the ruling class (Eccleshall, 1977). Conservative principles are thus rationalisations of class interest, the defence of the status quo and existing property rights, and there is thus little point in seeking any more logical coherence or long-term consistency in conservatism. As one recent trenchant critic has concluded, 'Selfishness is the rationale of their politics, and they have no other rationale' (Honderich, 1990, p. 238).

Both conservatives and their critics have accordingly tended to emphasise the theme of pragmatism. Moreover, reflecting the very considerable success the British Conservative Party has enjoyed in securing outright control or dominance over government in the last hundred years or so, conservatism is presented as essentially a philosophy of government, if indeed it can be viewed as a philosophy at all.

Yet although conservatism now plausibly appears as a philosophy of government or a ruling-class ideology, this was not always the case. For much of the eighteenth century Toryism was the frustrated political expression of the 'outs': malcontents, permanent backwoodsmen and romantic dreamers. In the mid-nineteenth century conservatism was tied to a landed interest which was in manifest decline, and it was liberalism which seemed destined to be established as the ideology of the new emerging ruling class. Even over the last hundred years there have been times, such as 1906, 1945, and even the mid-1960s and 1970s, when the confidence of the Conservative Party has been sufficiently shaken for it to assume briefly a defeatist, oppositional mentality.

However, it has been the remarkable capacity of the Conservative Party to adapt and survive which has enabled it to come back repeatedly from defeat, and re-establish its dominance. This perhaps suggests that the party has carried any ideological baggage lightly. There have been several noted occasions when the Conservative Party, in Disraeli's apt description, has caught its political opponents bathing and stolen their clothes. Even so, it might be doubted whether the British Conservative Party has been notably more adaptable than either the Liberal Party or, in its comparatively shorter history, the Labour Party.

But it is not just its flexibility which makes conservatism a somewhat problematic ideology for systematic exploration. What is also noteworthy about British conservatism is its comparative intellectual poverty, an absence of great texts or authoritative statements of philosophy. Thus conservative ideology has to be substantially inferred from the actions of Conservative governments, from party programmes and the speeches and pronouncements of practising politicians. Moreover, such ideological inspiration which it has sought has often come from outside its own ranks – from the Whig, Edmund Burke, from the radical Liberal Unionist Joseph Chamberlain, from Keynes, and more recently from classical liberalism and neo-liberalism. This seems to confirm the pragmatic nature of conservatism.

Yet, it will be argued here that conservatism is an ideology (at least in the sense outlined in the second chapter). It will be further claimed that although there are considerable tensions within conservatism, in particular the rival libertarian and collectivist traditions of thought identified by Greenleaf (1973), there are nevertheless fairly consistent features of conservative ideology, some of which date back three centuries or more.

Indeed, despite the association of conservatism with pragmatism and flexible adaptation, paradoxically it is possible to argue that conservatism as a political ideology has not changed markedly over the years. The editor of one anthology of conservative thinking has commented, 'An impressive feature of all these expressions of Conservative beliefs is the consistency of outlook which runs from Halifax and Burke to Churchill and Lord Hugh Cecil' (Buck, 1975, p. 26). There is surely some truth in this. While there have been changes certainly in the presentation of conservatism, and more significant changes in policy and strategy, it can be argued that the basic conservative outlook has altered little (Blake, 1985, pp. 359–68). Whereas British liberalism has evolved and changed substantially over the last two centuries, conservatism is a much more static ideology. It is thus possible to illustrate aspects of conservative thinking from quotations drawn almost indiscriminately across three or four centuries.

This is one reason why the historical approach adopted for the examination of liberalism seems less appropriate for conservatism. There is not the same clear pattern of evolution and transformation against a changing historical background; rather there is a continuity of themes over three or more centuries, and it is these themes which will here be explored. However, due weight is also given to the ambiguities and tensions in conservative thinking, and these are particularly apparent in the contested relationship between traditional conservativism, and the ideas associated with the modern Conservative Party. Thus the chapter concludes with a discussion of the New Right, Thatcherism and post-Thatcherism.

The Tory tradition

Just as British liberalism emerged out of the Whig tradition, British conservatism grew out of the Tory tradition. This creates some additional complications in the case of conservatism, for while the term 'Whig' has dropped out of modern political discourse, 'Tory' is still a familiar synonym for 'Conservative'. Here we are essentially concerned with the Tory foundations of modern British conservatism.

Historically Toryism, like Whiggism, dates from the seventeenth century, while its antecedents can be traced back further, whereas conservatism derives from Sir Robert Peel's modernisation of his party, and more specifically from the Tamworth manifesto of 1835. Strictly, the label 'Conservative' should not be used before then, but just as the term 'liberalism' is often extended backwards in time to include earlier thinkers who would not have used or even known the word, so the conservative tradition is frequently and not unreasonably taken to encompass thinkers and ideas which seem to provide the foundations for the subsequent development of conservative ideology. In this context the rather unhistorical use of the term 'Conservative' rather than 'Tory' is useful in claiming for conservatism individuals like Edmund Burke, who was actually a Whig politician in his lifetime, and could not be described as a Tory.

Thus conservatism can be projected backwards before 1835 in a
sense which distinguishes it from Toryism. Some writers would also
project the term 'Tory' forwards after 1835, to denote the older,
traditional ideas and interests within the conservative tradition, but
this has never involved a clear-cut distinction with conservatism,
rather a difference in emphasis. In common parlance a 'Tory' is not
even a particular type of Conservative, but simply a Conservative.

There are some who would deny that modern conservatism has
anything much to do with seventeenth- and eighteenth-century Toryism. It must moreover be admitted that the descriptions Whig and
Tory were pretty loose, and lacking in precision, and moreover
variable over time. Even so, it is possible to make some reasonably
valid generalisations on the values and interests associated with each
political creed. While the Whigs wished to limit royal authority, the
Tories supported the monarchy. The Whigs upheld the right to
religious dissent, while the Tories were the party of the Church of
England. Most important of all perhaps, the Whigs, although led by
aristocratic landowners, were associated with developing commercial
and manufacturing interests, while the Tories were the party of the
landed gentry – small squires rather than great landowners. Here there
are clearly some elements of continuity with the twentieth-century
Conservative Party, for whom the crown and monarchy are still
important symbols, which retains sufficient links with the Church of
England to justify the latter's description as 'the Tory Party at prayer'
despite recent friction beween the party's leaders and some prominent
clerics, and which still has ties of reciprocal dependence with the
landed interest. Behind these interests the Tories stood for traditional
authority and hierarchy in society, although such ideas were less
systematically articulated than their Whig counterparts.

Reaction and gradualism

Tories and conservatives are commonly associated with the right of
the political spectrum and are often pejoratively described as reactionaries. In fact the British right has rarely been reactionary in the
sense of wishing to put the clock back to allow the restoration of
some previous constitutional order or regime, although in the eighteenth century the Tory cause was for a time tainted with, and divided

Period		*Politicians and thinkers*
Late 17th C.	**TORYISM** (Monarchy, Church of England, landed interest) ↓	
18th C.	(Jacobitism? tradition, limitations of reason) ↓	Bolinbroke (Hume) (Burke)
Early 19th century	REACTIONARY TORYISM (Fear of revolution, repression, agricultural protection, romanticism) ↓	Liverpool Castlereagh
1820s	LIBERAL TORYISM ('Liberal' foreign policy, reform, Catholic emancipation) ↓	(Coleridge) Canning Robinson Huskisson
1830s, 1840s	PEELITE CONSERVATISM (Pragmatism, gradualism, acceptance of parliamentary reform, repeal of Corn Laws) ↓	Peel
1860s, 1870s	DISRAELIAN CONSERVATISM ('One-nation', paternalism, patriotism and imperialism, 'Tory democracy') ↓	Disraeli R. Churchill
Mid-1880s to 1930s	UNIONISM (Preservation of Union with Ireland, imperial preference, protection, social reform) ↓	Salisbury J. Chamberlain Balfour Baldwin
1940s to 1960s	POST-WAR ONE-NATION CONSERVATISM (Keynesianism, mixed economy, welfare state, conciliation of trade unions, end of empire, planning) ↓	W. Churchill Macmillan Butler Macleod
1970s, 1980s	'THATCHERISM' (Free market, competition, privatisation, 'traditional Conservative values', strong state, national sovereignty) ↓	Thatcher Joseph (Hayek) (Friedman)
1990s	POST-THATCHERISM	Major

Figure 5.1   The Tory/Conservative tradition

by, Jacobitism (support for the rival claim to the British throne by the Old and Young Pretender).

Thus Bolingbroke (1678–1751), the most important Tory thinker of the eighteenth century, effectively ended his own political career by his rash flight to the court of the Old Pretender in 1714, although subsequently made his peace with the Hanoverians, and devoted his talents to promoting a broad based opposition to the Whig government of Walpole. Yet if he briefly flirted with Jacobitism, Bolingbroke was never a mere reactionary who wished to restore royal absolutism. On the contrary, he lauded the British constitution as 'a mixture of monarchical, aristocratical, and democratical power, blended together into one system' (Bolingbroke, 1735 from extract in Eccleshall, 1990, p. 64).

Since that time British conservatism has not been weakened by divided loyalties to dispossessed regimes. This contrasts with the state of the right in countries like Italy and Spain, but above all France under the Third Republic where the allegiance of the right was divided between two mutually hostile groups of monarchists, Bonapartists, supporters of opportunist adventurers like Boulanger and, later, assorted quasi-fascist groups.

Yet British Tories and conservatives might be described as reactionary in the more literal sense of reacting against claims made by their opponents, as must any group of people whose interests are essentially bound up with the status quo. Thus in the seventeenth century they were reacting against the Puritan assault on the authority of the Church in general and bishops in particular, against the limits the parliamentary opposition to the Stuarts wished to place on royal authority, and against new sources of income and wealth which appeared to threaten their interests.

Eighteenth-century Toryism and nineteenth-century conservatism can be seen more generally as a reaction against the major upheavals and developments in the western world over that period. Here there is a clear contrast with liberalism. Liberalism was a product of the eighteenth-century Enlightenment, the American and French revolutions and, most important of all, of industrial capitalism. Toryism and subsequently conservatism involved a reaction against all these. It was suspicious of the claims made for reason by writers of the Enlightenment, and with the threat this presented to traditional secular and spiritual authority. It was hostile to the language of equal rights expressed by the American rebels and French revolutionaries, and particularly horrified by the claims and conduct of the latter. It was fearful of many of the changes resulting from industrialisation, and the ideas associated with it. Many Tory squires felt threatened by the new wealth and its growing political weight.

Edmund Burke (1729–97) played a leading role in the reaction against some of the major developments of his time, most notably the ideas associated with the Enlightenment and the French revolution. However, in many ways he is a strange figure to be regarded as one of the founding fathers of British conservatism. He was Irish by birth, and for most of his life a prominent Whig politician, regarding himself as a Whig to his death. Like all Whigs he celebrated the glorious revolution of 1688. He also supported the Americans in their war of independence, and was a leading and eloquent critic of George III's party.

What split Burke from his old Whig friends and associates was the French Revolution. Some Whigs, like Fox, greeted this with enthusiasm, and remained broadly sympathetic to it subsequently. Others initially viewed it favourably, and were afterwards disillusioned by the course it took. Burke was horrified from the start, and wrote his *Reflections on the French Revolution* in response (1790, ed. Hill, 1975). At the time this was regarded by his former colleagues as a betrayal of the principles he had formerly stood for. Burke himself was careful to distinguish what he regarded as the essentially conservative ideas behind the English revolution of 1688 from the more radical ideas behind the French revolution.

> The very idea of the fabrication of a new government is enough to fill us with disgust and horror. We wished at the time of the Revolution [i.e. 1688] and do now wish, to derive all we possess as an inheritance from our forefathers. Upon that body and stock of inheritance we have taken care not to inoculate any scion alien to the nature of the original plant. All the reformations we have hitherto made have proceeded upon the principle of reference to antiquity; and I hope, nay I am persuaded, that all those which possibly may be made hereafter will be carefully formed upon analogical precedent, authority and example. (*Reflections on the Revolution in France*, p. 296 of collection of Burke's writing edited by Hill, 1975)

There is much which is significant for an understanding of conservative ideology here. In the plant metaphor there is an explicit recognition of an organic theory of society and the state, which contrasts markedly with the mechanistic and individualistic assumptions behind the Whig/Liberal tradition. It is indeed this organic conception of society that some commentators have seen as the very essence of conservatism (Buck, 1975, p. 26). Burke also shows a marked hostility to the liberal notion that social and political institutions can be remodelled from first principles. There is reference to the importance of inheritance from the past, and reverence for tradition and authority. There is a clear preference for gradualism over radical change. Reforms must be carefully grafted onto the existing political and social system.

A preference for gradual reform, rather than reaction on the one hand or radical change on the other has often been seen as almost a defining characteristic of British conservatism – although there are some significant exceptions, including Disraeli, Joseph Chamberlain (if indeed he properly belongs to conservatism at all) and Mrs Thatcher. What might be considered the mainstream gradualist line is represented by the 'trimmer' Halifax from the seventeenth century, Burke from the eighteenth, Sir Robert Peel from the nineteenth and Michael Oakeshott from the twentieth.

Sir Robert Peel, the founder of the modern Conservative Party, might be considered the best exemplar of conservative gradualism. On three major issues – Catholic Emancipation, Parliamentary Reform and Corn Law Repeal – he long resisted change, but finally conceded it. He helped Wellington carry Catholic Emancipation in 1829 once he became convinced it was necessary. He opposed parliamentary reform, but once the 1832 Reform Act was passed, recognised that the clock could not be put back in the Tamworth Manifesto, which clearly articulated his own gradualist approach to reform (Buck, 1975, pp. 56–8). Finally, after years of defending the Corn Laws which protected British agriculture, he became convinced that their repeal was necessary, and carried it through with Whig support against the majority of his own party in 1846 (speech reproduced in Eccleshall, 1990, pp. 100–102).

Michael Oakeshott, an influential modern defender of conservatism, has written eloquently on what he calls the 'conservative disposition' and more particularly on the conservative attitude to change and innovation. 'To be conservative', he suggests, 'is to prefer the known to the unknown, to prefer the tried to the untried, fact to mystery, the actual to the possible, the limited to the unbounded . . .' Because the conservative enjoys the present he is generally averse to change. 'Consequently, he will find small and slow changes more tolerable than large and sudden; and he will value highly every appearance of continuity.' Proposed innovations should be assessed cautiously: 'Innovation entails certain loss and possible gain, therefore, the onus of proof ... rests with the would-be innovator.' Innovations which appear to grow out of the present, which are in response to some specific defect, which are 'small and limited', and which are slow rather than rapid should be preferred. 'The man of conservative temperament believes that a known good is not lightly to be surrendered for an unknown better' (Oakshott, 1962, pp. 168ff.).

Implicit behind such conservative caution in the face of demands for innovation and change is of course what critics might characterise as some fairly complacent assumptions about the present. Those less able to identify 'known goods' in their own circumstances, or in those of society in general, are more ready to embrace the risks involved in more radical change.

Suspicion of reason

Some commentators have argued that conservatism at bottom involves a relatively pessimistic view of human nature and human potential for individual improvement or social progress. It is a 'philosophy of imperfection' (O'Sullivan, 1976; Quinton, 1978). Compared with liberalism or socialism, less reliance is placed on the reason or the inherent goodness of man, and there is accordingly less optimism about the prospects for improving society. Consequently more emphasis is placed on the importance of leadership, on respect for authority and established institutions, and on the need for a framework of discipline and order. Society needs defending from both internal and external threats. Radical schemes for social and political reform are viewed as inherently suspect and potentially destructive. Existing social arrangements and institutions have stood the test of time and should as far as possible be conserved.

It is not that conservatism is deliberately irrational, as for example fascism unashamedly is. Conservative thinkers emphasise rather the limitations of reason. In some, this reflects religious convictions. The Elizabethan divine, Hooker, criticised those who would erect their own individual judgement against the state or the Church. He was not here criticising reason in general. On the contrary, Hooker believed that human reason was the gift of God. But individual reason is not to be relied upon for certain truth, only 'probable resolutions', and to press private judgement against established authority is thus highly dangerous (Harrison, 1965, pp. 11–25; Quinton, 1978, pp. 23–9). The conservative implications of this attitude are fairly clear.

Others such as the Scottish philosopher David Hume (1711–76) based their suspicions of the claims made for reason on a more general scepticism regarding human knowledge, behaviour and motivation. Certain knowledge of the world is not obtainable. Reason is not the chief inspiration of human behaviour, but rather the slave of the passions. Men act as they do from passion or habit or deference to authority. Thus Hume had a more sceptical view of human potential for rational thought and conduct than some of his intellectual contemporaries both in France and Britain. Unsurprisingly, this led him also to cautious conclusions in matters of politics and government. The established is to be preferred to the untried, and reform undertaken only with care and moderation (Quinton, 1978, pp. 45–51).

Edmund Burke challenged head-on the prevailing rationalist assumptions of his time: 'In this enlightened age I am bold enough to confess that we are generally men of untaught feelings.' He goes on to affirm:

> We are afraid to put men to live and trade each on his private stock of reason, because we suspect that the stock in each man is small, and that the individuals would do better to avail themselves of the general bank and capital of nations and of ages. (1790, ed. Hill, 1975, p. 354)

There could be no more explicit denial of the notion of enlightened self-interest which underpins so much liberal thought. Burke argues that men do not in practice act particularly rationally, and furthermore suggests that most men would be better advised not to rely on their reason. Provocatively he champions what he calls 'prejudice' against what he refers to as 'naked reason'. What he means by prejudice might perhaps be less pejoratively described as instinct or even conscience.

Burke clearly has a conception of human nature which is far

removed from the dispassionate rational calculator assumed by Jeremy Bentham, and it is Bentham who is the explicit target of Benjamin Disraeli in an extravagant diatribe against the age of reason in general, and the British Utilitarians in particular:

> In this country since the peace [i.e. since 1815] there has been an attempt to advocate a reconstruction of society on a purely rational basis. The principle of utility has been powerfully developed . . . There has been an attempt to reconstruct society on a basis of material motives and calculations. It has failed . . . How limited is human reason, the profoundest of enquirers are most conscious. We are not indebted to the reason of man for any of the great achievements which are the landmarks of human action and human progress. It was not reason which beseiged Troy; it was not reason that sent forth the Saracen from the desert to conquer the world; that inspired the crusades; that instituted the monastic orders; it was not reason that produced the Jesuits; above all it was not reason that created the French Revolution. Man is only truly great when he acts from the passions; never irresistible but when he appeals to the imagination. Even Mormon counts more votaries than Bentham. (from *Coningsby*, Everyman edn, 1911, pp. 199–200)

Disraeli's distrust of reason is characteristic of British conservatism, although he is rather untypical in not deriving cautious conclusions from his distrust; on the contrary he appears in this passage to embrace a distinct preference for the heroic over the humdrum and familiar. Perhaps there is an indication here of the psychology behind his later 'leap in the dark' over the Second Reform Act in 1867.

More typically conservative is Michael Oakeshott's attack on 'Rationalism in politics'. The Rationalist, says Oakeshott, 'stands for independence of mind on all occasions, for thought free from obligation to any authority save the authority of "reason".' He is 'the enemy of authority, of prejudice, of the merely traditional, customary or habitual'. This approach applied to politics means that 'to the Rationalist nothing is of value merely because it exists . . . familiarity has no worth'. This means that he regards patching up and repair as a waste of time: 'He always prefers the invention of a new device to making use of a current and well-tried expedient.' Oakeshott goes on to suggest that rationalist politics are 'the politics of perfection' and 'the politics of uniformity'. Oakeshott is here attacking an outlook which is commonly associated with liberals or socialists. Voltaire,

Godwin, Bentham, the Founding Fathers of the American constitution, but most of all Marx and Engels, are castigated for applying a rationalist approach to politics, ultimately derived from what Oakeshott regards as the misguided search for certain knowledge by Bacon and Descartes. Oakeshott does not, however, specifically identify certain political creeds. Rather he seems to regard 'Rationalism' as a deplorable but almost all-pervasive outlook in modern politics. Even Hayek, who himself criticised the constructivist rationalism of such as Voltaire and Bentham is singled out for censure. 'A plan to resist all planning may be better than its opposite, but it belongs to the same style of politics' (Oakeshott, 1962, pp. 1–36).

Human nature

Some commentators would suggest that conservatism not only involves at least considerable reservations about individual intellectual capacities and the potential for rational conduct, but also implies some fairly pessimistic assumptions about human nature. Quintin Hogg has commented that 'man is an imperfect creature with a streak of evil as well as good in his inmost nature' (Hogg, 1947, p. 11). Norman St John-Stevas (1982) has similarly observed that belief in the perfectability of man is a liberal or socialist error – conservatives have on the contrary a consciousness of original sin, although, Stevas goes on to point out, not everyone would give the point a theological formulation.

There is indeed a strong connection between conservative ideology and religious belief. The inherent weakness and wickedness of man has been proclaimed by Christian thinkers down the ages. Man is incapable of redeeming himself through his own efforts. Therefore, ideologies such as liberalism, socialism, and most especially anarchism, which present an optimistic picture of human nature and human potentiality, are at odds with mainstream orthodox Christian faith, which suggests that Christ's intercession is necessary for human salvation. And, just as human beings are too inherently flawed to achieve everlasting salvation through their own unaided efforts, so these same weaknesses prevent spontaneous co-operative social endeavour, and require authority and strong government to keep men in order.

Anthony Quinton, while acknowledging the strength of the conservative religious tradition, has attempted to detach conservative doctrine 'from what is often alleged to be an essential dependence on religious foundations'. He distinguishes between a religious and secular tradition of conservative thought. One tradition, he argues, 'derives its conservative politics to some extent from religious premises, in particular from the moral imperfection of human nature'. Quinton associates Hooker, Clarendon, Johnson, Burke, Coleridge and Newman with this tradition. But Quinton also argues there is a 'secular tradition of conservative thinking' initiated by Halifax, Bolingbroke and Hume, and kept alive more recently by Oakeshott. This emphasises the 'radical intellectual imperfection of the human individual' as well as a 'parallel belief in the moral imperfection of mankind'. But Quinton considers that the latter, although sometimes derived from 'the Christian dogma of original sin' is also shared by many 'secular and even atheistic thinkers, for example Hobbes, Hume and Freud' (Quinton, 1978, pp. 9–16).

It is perhaps unfortunate from Quinton's point of view that he is unable to claim Hobbes for this conservative secular tradition, for it was indeed Thomas Hobbes who painted one of the most celebrated and gloomy pictures of human nature in the raw. Without a common power to keep men in order there would be a continuous war of every man against every man, and life would be 'solitary, poor, nasty, brutish and short'. It was this nightmare vision which required strong government, for Hobbes a government with absolute powers. But although Hobbes' general pessimism about human nature has been widely shared by conservative thinkers, he has been rarely claimed for British conservatism. Quinton disqualifies him on three counts – his absolutism, his rationalism and his individualism (Quinton, 1978, p. 30).

Without Hobbes, Quinton's conservative secular tradition seems relatively insubstantial compared with what must be considered the mainstream Christian tradition. Many conservatives have quite explicitly associated their political principles with their Christian faith. Indeed although all mainstream British political creeds derive some inspiration from Christianity, Anglicanism in particular is highly compatible with conservatism. Not only do they share the same pessimistic assumptions about human nature, they also both involve an acceptance of authority and hierarchy, which might seem a logical corollary of human moral and intellectual deficiencies.

Authority, leadership and Tory democracy

If individual human beings are not rational calculators, and if furthermore the general benevolence of most men and women is at least a doubtful question, then certain implications may be considered to follow. In particular, democracy appears a hazardous enterprise, and the hopes of nineteenth-century liberals like Mill that it could be indefinitely improved through education, naive.

In practice, the conservative has only partially embraced democracy, tempering an acceptance of representative institutions with a strong emphasis on leadership and authority. Earlier, democracy had been viewed with abhorrence. Peel opposed the first Reform Bill, objecting that 'all its tendencies are, to substitute for a mixed form of government, a pure unmitigated democracy' (debate on third reading, quoted in Wright, 1970, p. 119). Salisbury in 1860, reacting to demands for a further extension of the franchise, in similar vein referred to 'the struggle between the English constitution on the one hand, and the democratic forces which are now labouring to subvert it'. He argued that 'Wherever democracy has prevailed, the power of the State has been used in some form or other to plunder the well-to-do classes for the benefit of the poor' (Buck, 1975, p. 104).

Conservatives only moved to a qualified acceptance of democracy when it became clear that it was compatible with maintenance of the existing social order and the defence of property. Thus Disraeli perceived that the working classes could be won for conservatism, and persuaded his party to 'dish the Whigs' by promoting the 1867 Reform Bill (McKenzie and Silver, 1968). His judgement proved defective in the short run, for Gladstone's Liberals gained an emphatic victory in the ensuing 1868 election, but he was vindicated in the longer run, as the Conservatives managed to win and subsequently hold a substantial minority of the working-class vote. Disraeli had earlier toyed with the idea of an alliance between the working classes and the aristocracy against the industrial bourgeoisie. Behind this rather fanciful notion there was a realisation that there was no harmony of interest between industrial workers and their liberal bosses. It was perhaps no accident that Lancashire, the home of 'Manchester liberalism', established a strong tradition of working-class conservatism.

Acceptance of democracy did not mean any real dilution of the characteristically conservative endorsement of authority, hierarchy and the mixed constitution. Beer argues that 'Authoritative leadership is a permanent social necessity for the Tory.' He goes on to suggest that 'parliamentary government and the mass suffrage have been grafted onto and adapted to' a Tory view of the constitution in which all the initiative comes from government. 'Tory democracy gives the voters power. But it is the power of control, not initiation, exercised under government by consent, not by delegation' (Beer, 1982, pp. 94–8). This is very similar to the version of democracy later endorsed by Joseph Schumpeter (1943), in which all the initiative comes from leaders, rather than the masses. Democracy thus involves a constrained competition for the people's vote rather than popular participation in government.

Coupled with all this is the Tory view of an organic society composed of unequal but mutually dependent classes and groups, in which a relatively small group have the attributes, experience and leisure to be qualified to govern. The mass of the people, in this view, are willing to defer to the judgement and experience of this governing class. Bagehot (himself a Liberal) suggested that the 'deference' of the English people was one of the main supports of the English constitution. Lord Randolph Churchill, who coined the term 'Tory democracy', believed it was possible to secure popular support for existing institutions. 'To rally the people round the Throne, and a patriotic people, that is our policy, and that is our faith' (Buck, 1975, p. 102). The assumption is that there is a common national interest which transcends individual or class interests, that all to some degree share the benefits of an ordered society and system of government, that the poorest can be made to appreciate the sanctity of property and existing social arrangements.

To critics of conservatism this is a transparent confidence trick which serves to conceal from subordinate classes their own interests in sweeping reform or revolution. The Tory perspective can thus be summed up in the familiar couplet, 'God bless the squire and his relations, And keep us in our proper stations.' Conservatives would tend to respond that inequality is both natural and inevitable. To preach equality and social justice is to stir up envy, hatred and unhappiness, for the passions aroused can never be satisfied. Moreover, the conservative would argue, everyone, ultimately, has an interest in the sanctity of property.

The defence of property

Conservatives have generally been unequivocal in their defence of property (Nisbet, 1986, pp. 55ff.), an attitude which contrasts strongly not only with that of socialists, but also liberals whose approach to the subject has been ambivalent. Starting from libertarian and egalitarian assumptions, a faith in reason and a distrust of traditional social arrangements, liberals have felt a need to produce elaborate justifications for property, based for example on natural rights, labour, or utility. Sometimes this has led them to justify some forms of property, but not others – there have been particular problems with land and inherited wealth. Conservatives have generally devoted less time and space to the justification of private property, for the simple reason that the issue for them is unproblematic. Existing property rights are part of traditional social arrangements endorsed by conservatives. Inequality in property reflects profound inequalities in abilities and energies. The conservative would concede that the existing distribution of property does not necessarily accord with desert, but would see this as an inevitable consequence of imperfect human social arrangements. Social justice is unobtainable, and attempts to justify interference with existing property rights in the name of social justice threaten the whole institution of private property. The most the conservative is generally prepared to concede is that the possession of property entails obligations and responsibilities.

Thus conservatives have whole-heartedly defended private property, and justified its extremely unequal distribution. Burke argued that 'the characteristic essence of property, formed out of the combined principles of its acquisition and conservation, is to be unequal.' Great concentrations of property 'form a natural rampart about the lesser properties in all their gradations'. Inherited property is also strongly defended: 'The power of perpetuating our property in our families is one of the most valuable and interesting circumstances belonging to it, and that which tends the most to the perpetuation of society itself' (1790, ed. Hill, 1975, pp. 316–17).

Modern conservatives have been as committed to the defence of property. Oakeshott associates the possession of private property with freedom, and goes on to suggest that private ownership of the means of production, essentially capitalism, is also necessary for liberty. 'The freedom which separates a man from slavery is nothing but a

freedom to choose and to move among autonomous, independent
organizations, firms, puchasers of labour, and this implies private
property in resources other than personal capacity' (Oakeshott, 1962,
p. 46). Scruton (1980, p. 99) talks of 'man's absolute and ineradicable
need of private property'. This, he says, 'represents the common
intuition of every labouring person'. Against the classical liberal or
the modern neo-liberal, Scruton is prepared to justify state regulation
of private property and market forces, but at the same time he
strongly attacks deliberate state intervention to achieve the redistribution of property through progressive taxation, wealth and inheritance
taxes (p. 108).

The problem with property for conservatives has been more one of
strategy rather than of principle – how to persuade the majority with
little or no property to accept the existing distribution of property.
Conservatism was initially associated with a particular form of
property – land – and indeed there still lingers among some conservatives a distrust of other forms of wealth (Nisbet, 1986, p. 63).
Towards the end of the nineteenth century the British Conservative
Party became the party not just of landed property but of property in
general, as the manufacturing interest increasingly deserted the Liberals, alienated by radicalism and Irish Home Rule. Yet a wider base of
popular support was required for electoral survival.

Various strategies were employed in practice, including social
reform and imperialism, but there has also been, particularly recently,
a deliberate attempt to widen and extend property ownership. It was
Eden who used the phrase 'property owning democracy' and post-war
governments in particular have sought to promote home ownership,
and more recently wider share ownership. Earlier, conservatives at
both central and local level had supported public housing, and had
been content to encourage home ownership through tax relief. More
recently the party has encouraged and subsequently compelled the
sale of council houses, and actively discouraged further council house
building. The result has been to turn owner-occupation into the
majority form of housing tenure. Some tax concessions, but more
notably the privatisation of major nationalised industries on favourable terms for small investors, has enabled Mrs Thatcher to claim that
there are now more share owners than trade unionists. Thus the
ownership of property, both in the tangible sense of bricks and
mortar, and in the more symbolic participation in capitalism, has been

significantly extended, although its uneven distribution remains substantially unchanged.

Paternalism and collectivism

Until perhaps recently, the defence of private property has not
generally for conservatives entailed an unqualified defence also of the
free market. Indeed it might appear that 'self-help' and '*laissez-faire*'
were inappropriate injunctions for the many people who, according to
conservative views of human nature and intellectual capacity, were
generally incapable of perceiving their own rational self-interest, and
could not be relied upon to be particularly enlightened in its pursuit.
On the contrary, it seemed clear to many Tories that such people
needed help and guidance, and sometimes also firm control. The
authority of the state was thus required to provide a framework of
order and discipline, but also support for those unable or incapable of
helping themselves. Moreover, others who were fortunately placed in
terms of natural endowments or wealth had an obligation to provide
that help, guidance and control. Society was more than a mere
aggregate of individuals. It was rather an organic whole, necessarily
involving ties of mutual dependence, which in turn suggested social
duties and responsibilities as well as individual rights. This was the
basis for what has been termed 'Tory paternalism'.

Disraeli is the Conservative pre-eminently associated with paternalism. In his novel *Sybil* there is a strong attack not only on the 1832
Reform Act but also, and more importantly on the whole system of
capitalist values which Disraeli associated with industrialisation:

> If a spirit of rapacious covetousness, desecrating all the humanities of
> life, has been the besetting sin of England for the last century and a
> half, since the passing of the Reform Act the altar of Mammon has
> blazed with triple worship. To acquire, to accumulate, to plunder each
> other by virtue of philosophic phrases, to propose an Utopia to consist
> only of WEALTH and TOIL, this has been the breathless business of
> enfranchised England for the last twelve years. (from *Sybil*, p. 56 of
> 1980 Penguin edn)

Here Disraeli is assaulting all the ideas and slogans associated with
the Whig/Liberal tradition of thought, but particularly those of
laissez-faire economics. Behind such wholesale condemnations of
new values and interests lay a nostalgia for a vanished past which

perhaps only existed in Disraeli's romantic imagination – an ordered society of mutual dependence, where privilege entailed obligations to those less fortunate and where social divisions and class conflict did not exist. For Disraeli liked to think that somehow social conflict could be healed. In another often quoted passage from *Sybil* he talks of the Victorian England of his day in terms of two nations of the rich and the poor.

> Two nations; between whom there is no intercourse and no sympathy; who are as ignorant of each other's habits, thoughts and feelings, as if they were dwellers in different zones, or inhabitants of different planets; who are formed by different breeding, are fed by different food, are ordered by different manners, and are not governed by the same laws. (*op. cit.* p. 96)

Disraeli was thus fully aware of the depth of social divisions in the England of his day, but like later Conservatives who adopted the 'one-nation' slogan, hoped that somehow they could be transcended and one nation made of two.

The Conservative Party has always claimed to stand above class and for the nation as a whole. For political opponents, particularly for socialists, this is a transparent 'con trick' – a capitalist society necessarily involves class conflict, and conservatives mask this social reality in their own interests (Honderich, 1990, chs 6 and 7). And indeed Disraeli himself sometimes reveals an element of class interest in his concern for social reform, for example in a comment in 1848 'the palace is not safe, when the cottage is not happy' (quoted in Beer, 1982, p. 267). Even so, Conservative politicians have had little difficulty in convincing themselves of the idea of a conservatism standing for the nation and against sectional interests, and it has had a potent appeal.

It should be noted, however, that this paternalism did not then necessarily imply state action. Disraeli's biographer has claimed, 'He had a genuine hatred of centralization, bureaucracy and every mani-festation of the Benthamite state' (Blake, 1966, p. 282). For Disraeli the state was almost the last rather than the first resort. He was well aware that for numbers of the poor 'self-help' was a futile injunction, but anticipated that the help they required should be forthcoming from the traditional aristocracy, from the Church, and from voluntary activity of all kinds. In *Sybil* his targets were the uncaring landowners who neglected their tenants and the new capitalists who exploited

their workforce, and these are contrasted with examples of philan-
thropic aristocrats and caring industrialists. In his political speeches
he took much the same line. At Shrewsbury in 1843 he blamed
current political evils on the development of property divorced from
duty. Much of this of course runs directly counter to the notion of
rational self-interest and self-help, but hardly suggests that Disraeli
saw the state as the principal vehicle for the alleviation of social
distress.

Arguably he became more committed to state action subsequently.
In his 1872 speech to the National Union he described the 'elevation
of the condition of the people' as the third great object of the Tory
Party, although the speech was longer on rhetoric than specifics.
While much has been made of Disraeli's commitment to social
reform both before and after he became Prime Minister (Beer, 1982,
ch. 9), recent historians have exposed the myth that there was any
clear consistent programme of social reform behind his administration's legislative record (Smith, 1967, p. 202). Disraeli's modern
biographer, Lord Blake, apparently anxious to re-establish his subject's conservative credentials in a Thatcherite era, has observed, 'His
policies have been much misinterpreted, no least by those who
unplausibly regard him as an ancestor of the welfare state – a sort of
arch wet' (*Guardian*, 4/10/82).

The commitment of Disraeli's immediate successors to social
reform is still more questionable. Randolph Churchill's enthusiasm
for Tory democracy and reform involved more rhetoric than solid
reality, but his early resignation in any case removed any prospect
that Salisbury's government would pursue the social question. Even
the adhesion of the radical Liberal Unionist, Joseph Chamberlain,
made little difference to what has been described as a period of
'Conservative inertia' (Beer, 1982, p. 271). Indeed by 1894 Chamberlain had so far moderated his earlier radicalism to complain that 'the
resolutions of the TUC . . . amount to universal confiscation in order
to create a Collectivist State' (quoted in Adelman, 1970,
p. 107).

Protection and Tory collectivism

In so far as some conservatives wished to interfere with market
forces, it was less in the interests of social reform than economic

protection and industrial reorganisation. In the early nineteenth century the Tories were the party of protection. After the split over
Repeal of the Corn Laws in 1846 the bulk of the party remained
protectionist until reluctantly persuaded that the cause was no longer
practical politics. Later in the nineteenth century the demand for 'fair
trade' as opposed to 'free trade' was articulated. In 1903 Joseph
Chamberlain turned the issue into a veritable crusade with his
demand for imperial protection. It was this issue on which Baldwin's
1923 government was defeated at the polls, and it was the Conservative protectionists whose views eventually prevailed in the
National governments of the 1930s. Neville Chamberlain as Chancellor of the Exchequer was to boast that his Import Duties Bill
provided the government with 'a lever as has never been possessed
before by any government for inducing or, if you like, forcing
industry to set its house in order' (quoted in Beer, 1982, p. 293).

Protection necessarily involves state action of a sort, but the term
'collectivism' implies rather more state intervention. For modern
Conservatives collectivism has acquired strong negative connotations,
becoming closely associated with socialism, but it was not always so.
Thus Gilmour carefully describes Neville Chamberlain's state-
interventionist policies to rationalise industry in the 1930s as 'collectivist . . . rather than socialist' (Gilmour, 1978, p. 36). Yet Chamberlain's Tory collectivism involved managed capitalism rather than
socialism, a point which might also be made about Michael Heseltine's more recent enthusiasm for state intervention.

But it was the conservatism of the period after the Second World
War which can be most plausibly associated with collectivism.
Macmillan had once provocatively declared that Toryism had always
been a kind of paternal socialism. He preached an interventionist
'Middle Way' between *laissez-faire* capitalism and socialist state
planning. The wartime Tory Reform Group urged the acceptance of
social reform and more specifically the Beveridge Report which was
declared the 'very essence of Toryism' (quoted in Beer, 1982,
p. 307). In opposition from 1945–51 the commitment to social reform
was firmed up. Butler, the architect of the 1944 Education Act
declared in 1947 'We are not frightened at the use of the State. A
good Tory has never in history been afraid of the use of the State.'
This sweeping and surely inaccurate verdict was endorsed by
Anthony Eden: 'We are not the political children of the *laissez-faire*

school. We opposed them decade after decade' (both quoted in Beer, 1982, p. 271).

The rhetoric of these modern day heirs of Disraeli was rather more matched by reality than that of the great Victorian politician. The Welfare State established by the coalition and Labour governments was maintained and even in certain respects enhanced. A policy of compromise and accommodation was applied to labour and the trade unions. Most remarkably perhaps, after the initial denationalisation of steel and road haulage, other state-owned industries were maintained. Overall, the role of government coninued to expand, and public expenditure continued to rise. Indeed, Macmillan accepted the resignation of his entire Treasury team in 1958 rather than the cuts in spending which they demanded. The commitment to full employment policies was maintained, through orthodox Keynesian demand management policies, by successive Tory chancellors. When such policies did not succeed in correcting such deep-seated problems as low growth, balance of payments deficits and weak sterling, Macmillan's government moved towards more intervention rather than free market solutions. The National Economic Development Council signalled a new interest in long-term economic planning, and the National Incomes Commission institutionalised the new Conservative concern with incomes policy. This was perhaps the high-water mark of Tory collectivism.

As with liberal critics of the New Liberalism, there are some conservatives who would regard this whole approach as a monstrous aberration, a departure from true conservatism. A few who participated in these governments, such as, most notably, Lord Joseph (1976), have since recanted, and declared they only discovered true conservatism subsequently. Others such as Sir Ian Gilmour (1978) have continued to claim that Butler and Macmillan represent the mainstream Tory tradition, and that it is the free market neo-liberal nostrums of the New Right which are heretical.

There are indeed some interpretations of conservatism, particularly S. H. Beer's (1982), which have seen the post-war one-nation conservatism as the culmination of a Tory collectivist tradition, but this has always involved a rather selective interpretation of conservative history. Beer emphasises some periods and some individuals, and ignores others. Salisbury, who presided over Conservative Party fortunes longer than Disraeli, and who has some claims to be considered an important conservative thinker, is not even mentioned by Beer, who dismisses his period of dominance as a period of 'Conservative inertia'. Rather more convincing is Greenleaf's (1973) portrayal of a continuing tension within conservatism between its libertarian and collectivist strands. Greenleaf regards both strands as part of an authentic conservative tradition.

Arguably, however, both the libertarian and collectivist strands of conservatism require a strong state and an emphasis on leadership and authority which would be anathema to many liberals and socialists (Gamble, 1988). The need for leadership has been a perennial Tory theme, from Bolingbroke in the eighteenth century, through Carlyle and Disraeli in the nineteenth century, to Churchill and Mrs Thatcher in the twentieth century. Respect for authority is a key message in the thought of Burke and Salisbury. The free economy advocated by the modern New Right is widely perceived as requiring a strong state. Government might abdicate some of its functions, but not its power and authority. Government indeed has to be strong to provide the conditions for the market to operate. It has to be strong to resist pressures and claims upon it from powerful sectional interests including both producer and consumer groups.

Patriotism and imperialism

Reverence for the authority of the state chimed in easily with conservative nationalism and imperialism. Yet until the later nineteenth century conservatism had no monopoly of patriotic sentiment. Indeed, nationalism was closely associated with liberalism, and the Whig/Liberal Prime Minister Palmerston had been notably successful in exploiting patriotic feeling in his own and his party's interest. By the end of the century, however, Gladstone's Irish policy and his internationalism, and subsequent Liberal divisions over the Boer War, coupled with Disraeli's assiduous promotion of imperialism and the national interest, associated conservatism with patriotism. This proved a highly successful electoral strategy, particularly with the newly enfranchised working classes. Beer observes, 'In imperialism . . . the party had found a cause with a mighty appeal to the voter.' He goes on to note that 'only from the election of 1886 . . . did the party win those majorities of the popular vote which eluded even Disraeli' and concludes that imperialism had made Tory social reform redundant (Beer, 1982, p. 272).

McKenzie and Silver (1968) clearly document Conservative Party literature addressed to the electorate which exploited nationalist and imperialist sentiment from the 1880s to the 1960s. Liberals, radicals and socialists were constantly accused of being unpatriotic and undermining English and imperial interests. Thus the Liberal government in 1895 was accused of being 'a weak, vacillating, craven Ministry . . . which dares not defend British interests effectively, and which will submit to be kicked and kicked and kicked until at last the spirit of the English people is aroused in its majesty' (quoted in McKenzie and Silver, p. 53). In 1900 the radicals were associated with 'a Small England, a Shrunken England, a Degraded England, a Submissive England' (quoted op cit., p. 56). By 1910 socialists were associated with radicals in a Conservative pamphlet which claimed 'If you fight for radical socialism you fight for a divided nation . . . a divided Kingdom – the union sold! a British Isle no more, Ireland breeds treason at the Empire's core' (quoted pp. 63–4). In 1924 the Labour government was accused of putting 'the foreigner first' and preferring 'the Bolshevisks to our own people' (p. 65). In 1951 it was argued 'Socialists sneered and still sneer at what they call "Imperialism" . . . The Conservative Party, by long tradition and settled belief, is the Party of the Empire' (p. 68).

While such language is not found in more erudite statements of party philosophy, it could be argued that it is perhaps a better guide to the popular appeal and interpretation of conservatism. Of course nationalist sentiment is by no means confined to the Conservative Party. The musical halls, the press, and later the electronic media have helped created a popular nationalist culture which has also coloured British liberalism and labourism (Schwarz in Donald and Hall, 1986, p. 177). But it was the Conservative Party which most successfully exploited the patriotic theme, reinforcing claims to stand above narrow class interests and for the nation as a whole. 'Being Conservative is only another way of being British' claimed Quintin Hogg (quoted by McKenzie and Silver, 1968, p. 18).

Baldwin and Churchill in their different ways were particularly skilful in associating themselves and their party with British values and interests. The more internationalist climate in the post-Second World War era, coupled with the decline in the British empire and British power, for a time made patriotic rhetoric appear somewhat outmoded. Under Macmillan and then Heath the Conservatives pursued entry into the European Community, and appeared to have converted their party to the European ideal. However, Enoch Powell's English nationalism, expressed in his opposition to black immigration, the EEC and concessions to the opposition in Ulster, although scorned by the establishment, and rejected by Heath, showed that chauvinism still had popular appeal, not least from elements of the working class. This has been further demonstrated by Mrs Thatcher. While the Falklands has been the most dramatic illustration of this renewed conservative nationalism, the emphatic assertion of British interests has been a consistent theme in defence and foreign policy since 1979.

Conservatism and Thatcherism

No examination of British conservatism would be complete without some discussion of what has come to be called 'Thatcherism'. Unlike socialism or even liberalism, British conservatism has not previously been much concerned with doctrinal disputes. Such disputes as have occurred within conservatism have been more tactical than theoretical. Indeed, as has been noticed, ideas have not been systematically elaborated. Conservatism has thus evolved as a broad church, with, inevitably, some internal tensions, but with little in the way of doctrinal purity to advance and defend. There is nothing remotely resembling Labour's celebrated 'Clause 4', for example, to serve as an article of conservative faith, and thus no foundation for major doctrinal splits.

Arguably, this changed after Mrs Thatcher became leader of the Conservative Party in 1975. Both admirers and critics suggested that her leadership entailed a sharp break with the mainstream Tory tradition. It was widely alleged that her brand of conservatism had more in common with nineteenth-century liberalism, historically the antithesis of Toryism (Milton Friedman, interview in the *Observer*, 26/9/82). This perception was given some substance by Mrs Thatcher's own early speeches as Leader of the Opposition, where she extolled Victorian virtues of self-reliance, attacked collectivism and dismissively referred to 'bourgeois guilt', a phrase widely interpreted as a criticism of Tory paternalism as much as socialism. She also acknowledged the influence of two celebrated neo-liberals, Friedman and Hayek, and, behind them, the virtual founder of classical economics, Adam Smith (Thatcher, 1977).

Even while Mrs Thatcher was still in opposition, the liberal
rhetoric disturbed both critics and some admirers within the Conservative Party. Sir Ian Gilmour, later to become a victim of one of
Mrs Thatcher's first Cabinet sackings, carefully distinguished between conservatism and liberalism in his book *Inside Right* (1978).
William Waldegrave (1978), later a member of Thatcher's and
Major's governments, attacked neo-liberalism, and reasserted a conservative tradition involving the acceptance of state power. Several
contributors to a generally sympathetic volume of *Conservative
Essays* edited by Maurice Cowling (1978) were expressly critical of
liberal ideas. Peregrine Worsthorne referred dismissively to 'Some
libertarian mishmash drawn from the writings of Adam Smith, John
Stuart Mill, and the warmed up milk of nineteenth-century liberalism'
(Cowling, 1978, p. 149) Roger Scruton, another contributor, went on
to produce his own elucidation of conservatism, in which liberalism
was subjected to rather more scornful criticism than Marxism
(Scruton, 1980).

The divisions within the Conservative Party under Mrs Thatcher
were early popularised as a distinction between 'Wets' and 'Drys',
which does not necessarily equate with a distinction between conservatism and liberalism. In so far as the labels relate to theory rather
than style, the 'Drys' were associated with fashionable monetarist
ideas, the 'Wets' with the apparently discredited Keynesianism
(Keegan, 1984). 'Monetarism' was never a very helpful label to
describe the new conservative ideas, however. Monetarist policies
were initiated by the previous Labour Government, and were not
distinctively Thatcherite. Moreover, it soon became clear that there
were fundamental problems in attempting to control the money
supply, and subsequently the Thatcher government quietly abandoned
monetarism.

The term 'monetarism' to describe the approach of the new
government soon gave way to the labels 'Thatcherism', and the 'New
Right'. Neither label was ideal. 'Thatcherism' attributed too much to
Mrs Thatcher personally. 'The New Right' has a broader, international connotation, but raises further problems of definition and
interpretation.

The radical and Marxist left provided an early influential analysis
of Thatcherism, which was seen as combining some traditional conservative elements – patriotism, law and order, authority and strong
government – summed up by the term 'authoritarian populism',

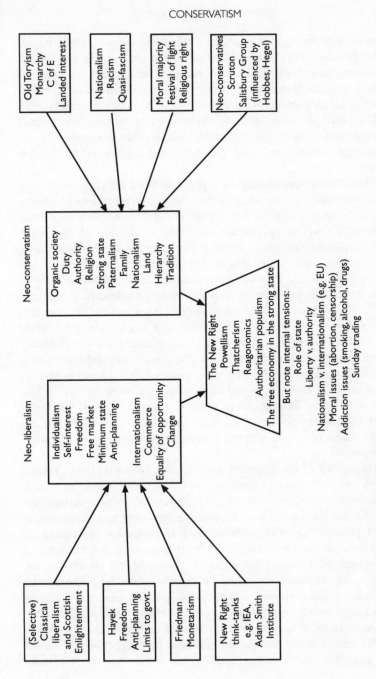

Figure 5.2 The New Right and Thatcherism

coupled with free market economics (Hall and Jacques, 1983; Edgar, 1984; Gamble, 1988). Most British-oriented texts on the New Right have emphasised the latter, and have presented the phenomenon largely in terms of economic theory (Bosanquet, 1983; Green, 1987). Yet this arguably underplays the significance of moral, authoritarian and patriotic elements to New Right thinking even in the British context, and certainly neglects their considerable importance in the right-wing republicanism of Reagan and Gingrich in the United States.

Thus Thatcherism and the New Right drew on both neo-liberal and neo-conservative elements (Levitas, 1986). Although neo-liberalism and neo-conservatism sprang from very different roots they both involved a reaction against the dominant orthodoxies of the recent past: neo-liberalism against Keynesianism and the Welfare State, neo-conservatism against the progressive liberal permissiveness of the 1960s. To a degree they were compatible. Both implied hostility to trade unionism, bureaucracy and corporatist tendencies in government. Yet there were also tensions. For example, on the environment neo-conservatives tended to be right-wing conservationists, while neo-liberals sought to remove controls on planning and development which interfered with market forces. There were also differences on a host of moral issues such as abortion, censorship and Sunday trading. However, the most important divisions were over foreign policy and particularly Europe. Thus some Conservatives saw the European Community in terms of their own free market convictions, while others perceived a threat to national sovereignty and national interests.

The record of the Thatcher governments (Riddell, 1983; Young, 1989) showed strong elements of both neo-liberal and neo-conservative thinking. The massive privatisation programme, the introduction of compulsory competitive tendering and deregulation, the legislation on trade unions, and the changes introduced or threatened in the Universities, the legal profession and the medical profession, all reflected the influence of neo-liberal economics. By contrast, the Falklands War, Mrs Thatcher's approach to Europe, firm controls on immigration, tough penal policies and the National Curriculum in education were hardly inspired by free market ideas, and were more in keeping with traditional conservatism.

The extent of the ideological shift can be exaggerated, however. The neo-conservative authoritarian streak in Thatcherism involved a change in emphasis from the liberal progressive attitudes of Macmillan, Butler, Macleod, Boyle and Heath, but reflected the attitudes and demands which regularly surfaced from the rank and file at Conservative Party conferences throughout the post-war period. Also, the libertarian strand in conservatism was not new, as Greenleaf (1973) has demonstrated. Even in the supposed heyday of Tory collectivism there were strong pressures for competition. The Conservatives were re-elected to the slogan 'Set the People Free' in 1951, and proceeded to dismantle rationing and controls, denationalise steel and road haulage, establish commercial television, and later commercial radio, relax rent controls, and abolish resale price maintenance. The sale of council houses, sometimes regarded as quintessential Thatcherism, was Conservative policy in the 1950s. Here Mrs Thatcher differed from her predecessors in her more ruthless application of policy.

The forced sale of council houses at substantial discounts, and the privatisation of the former national industries perhaps had as much to do with pragmatic political objectives as free market ideas. The extension of home ownership and share ownership gave more voters a stake in property and popular capitalism, increasing the natural conservative constituency in the country, while reducing Labour's traditional constituency of council tenants, public sector employees and trade unionists. It can be seen in terms of the politics of statecraft, the construction of new coalitions of interests (Bulpitt, 1987). Mrs Thatcher, like Disraeli over a century before, was making a bid for the skilled working-class vote.

At another level it can be argued that Thatcherism was a response to altered circumstances. In the earlier post-war period it seemed that commitment to the welfare state and full employment was necessary to win elections. By the 1970s both the economic assumptions behind those commitments and their political rationale were seen as questionable. Faith in Keynesian demand management was undermined by the performance of the economy, while a growing proportion of the electorate seemed disillusioned with both the benefits of the Welfare State and its mounting cost, with adverse consequences for taxation and take-home pay. Thatcherism thus involved a response to the new mood.

There is clearly something in such analysis, although in her third term Mrs Thatcher's government pursued policies which seemed to have a clearer ideological than electoral rationale. The introduction of

the Poll Tax, the reform of the Health Service, the privatisation
of water, and the almost exclusive reliance on high interest rates to
combat inflation seemed to owe more to neo-liberal economic theory,
than to any electoral calculations.

Moreover, ideas were clearly important to Mrs Thatcher and those
who surrounded her. Mrs Thatcher argued that the Conservatives
needed an ideology to counter socialism. She spurned the traditional
civil service sources of policy advice, consulting New Right think-
tanks such as the Institute of Economic Affairs and the Adam Smith
Institute, and, with Keith Joseph, founding the Centre for Policy
Studies. There was moreover a demonstrable link between ideas and
policy. For example, public choice theory provided the intellectual
justification for the Poll Tax and the introduction of executive
agencies into the civil service.

Even so, Thatcherism perhaps always involved more political style
rather than ideological substance. Conviction politics replaced the
habitual search for compromise and consensus. Mrs Thatcher had
sufficient self-confidence to scorn requirements of internal party
balance, and eschew caution. If there was an element of Thatcherism
which ran counter to traditional conservatism it was not so much the
neo-liberal economics, as the pace of change. However Thatcherism
is defined, it cannot be equated with gradualism. There are few
precedents in Britain for Mrs Thatcher's brand of right-wing
radicalism.

Seen in perspective Thatcherism appears as neither an aberration
nor a transformation in British conservatism, but a period which is
generally consistent with the broad Tory tradition, yet showing a few
unusual features. Mrs Thatcher's legacy is likely to remain controversial, and prone to regular reassessment. Inevitably such re-
appraisals will subtly influence the future development of
conservatism, which, in the absence of any doctrinal purity, has
always set considerable store on past leaders as role models.

Conservatism and post-Thatcherism

The circumstances of Mrs Thatcher's fall in 1990 sparked off some
speculation over the future direction of British conservatism. Yet it
was always unlikely that there would be a strong and immediate
reaction in the Conservative Party against the policies pursued since

1979. Too many leading Conservatives were implicated in Thatcherism to make total repudiation a credible option. Moreover, the victory of John Major, Mrs Thatcher's chosen successor, first in the leadership election of 1990, and then in the General Election of 1992, apparently confirmed that the Thatcherite legacy was safe.

Indeed, although there has been a marked change in political style there have been few discernable differences in policy and ideas. The Poll Tax, incautiously described as the flagship of Thatcherism, was an early casualty, but this had become a political necessity. Otherwise the Major government energetically pursued the changes in education and health begun under Mrs Thatcher, and extended competition in public services. There was no slackening in the privatisation programme. The politically contentious breakup of British Rail was forced through, while the government was only diverted from its intention to privatise the Royal Mail (which Mrs Thatcher had avoided) by the lack of a sufficient parliamentary majority. Major's only significant innovation has been the Citizen's Charter, hailed by some as a new deal for the public services, but viewed by critics as essentially cosmetic.

Yet if the record in government shows a continuation of Thatcherism, the future prospects for conservatism are more problematic. The Party both in Parliament and the country is more divided than it has been perhaps since the split over protection in the early twentieth century. The way in which Mrs Thatcher was brought down left a legacy of bitterness and internal recriminations. Differences over policies and ideas were intensified by personal and faction rivalries, to the extent that dissecting the fault lines in modern conservatism has already become something of an academic industry.

In part these differences only mirror old tensions, between, for example, the libertarian and collectivist strands in conservatism identified by Greenleaf, or the familiar distinction between radicals and consolidators. Yet they are further complicated by the intensifying disagreement over Europe, which itself derives from one of the unresolved contradictions of Thatcherism. The European Community (now Union) on the one hand seemed to embody the free market capitalist values dear to Mrs Thatcher, which is why she enthusiastically signed the Single European Act. Yet it also was associated with bureaucratic and corporatist tendencies which she opposed. More seriously, intensifying pressures towards closer political union apparently threatened Britain's national sovereignty and independence, a

core conservative value. Mrs Thatcher's personal schizophrenia over
Europe reflected the tensions between the neo-liberal and neo-
conservative elements in her own political philosophy, and this
schizophrenia has been bequeathed to her party. Although John Major
gave early indications that he was more sympathetic towards the
European ideal, his tone became increasingly Euro-sceptic as he
sought to appease the increasingly bitter internal party factions.

The divisions over Europe are, however, perhaps a symptom rather
than a cause of a deeper malaise within conservatism. Dwindling
popularity has promoted doubts and introspection. Conservatism is
moreover increasingly on the defensive. Under Mrs Thatcher it
offered a radical challenge to the Butskellite consensus of the post-
war era. The very success of that challenge has now transformed
conservatives into defenders of a new status quo, increasingly subject
to criticism, particularly on the management of the reformed Health
Service and the privatised utilities. Moreover, Conservatives are
obliged to defend a chequered economic record. Two recessions,
culminating in the effective forced devaluation of Black Wednesday,
have undermined their claims to economic competence. Tax rises
after 1992, coupled with the collapse of the housing market, have
alienated a substantial section of the middle classes which have
always provided the Conservatives with their core electoral support.

Of course, it is also true that some of the problems with which
Conservative governments have been grappling reflect changes both
in British society and the wider world – demographic change, the
breakdown of traditional families and communities, technological
change and unemployment, resource depletion and pollution and the
changing relationships between the developed and the developing
worlds. In such circumstances it is unsurprising that New Right
prescriptions have failed to produce magic solutions. Yet the free
market was the 'big idea' which Thatcherism apparently offered to
transform the British economy and society, and this big idea has
ultimately proved no more successful than the Keynesianism it
superseded. Moreover, over two decades of free market orthodoxy,
some of the familiar problems of market failure are being rediscovered.

While some Conservatives still believe that competition and the
free market have not been pursued sufficiently vigorously, others
justify state intervention and public services, and incline back towards the one-nation conservatism of the the Butskellite consensus.

In part this is an argument inspired by conflicting ideological convictions, in part a pragmatic search for the best means to rebuild political support. It is unlikely that these differences will be resolved in the immediate future. However, conservatism is a political creed which has showed considerable flexibility over a long history, and it would be unwise to bet against its capacity to adapt and survive.

Guide to further reading

It is difficult to recommend a single volume which encapsulates the essence of British conservative thinking. O'Sullivan (1976) and Nisbet (1986) both offer interesting interpretations of conservatism in an international context. Scruton (1980, 1983) provides a provocative and idiosyncratic account from his own neo-conservative perspective. Honderich (1990) provides a sledgehammer demolition. Interesting views on British Tory/Conservative thought are contained in Beer (1982) and Greenleaf (1973, 1983). Perhaps the most reliable introduction to conservative ideas, however, is the anthology, with introduction and notes, by Eccleshall (1990). Other useful anthologies include those edited by Buck (1975) and Blake's one-volume history of the Conservative Party (1985) also gives a valuable insight into conservative thought at different periods.

On specific periods, Quinton (1978) is useful on the seventeenth- and eighteenth-century foundations of conservative thinking, while Barnes in Seldon and Ball (1994) discusses twentieth-century conservative ideas. The literature on Thatcherism is extensive and daunting. Hall and Jaques (1983), Gamble (1988), Young (1989), Kavanagh (1990), Adonis and Hames (1994) are all interesting. Kavanagh and Seldon (1994) have edited a useful collection of essays on Major.

Classic conservative texts include Burke's *Reflections on the Revolution in France* (various editions, e.g. Hill, 1975) and Oakeshott's elegant collection of essays *Rationalism in Politics* (1962). An insight into Disraeli's ideas can be gathered from his novels *Sybil* (1845) and *Coningsby* (1844), although a more balanced account of the contribution of the mature Disraeli to conservatism might be derived from his biography by Blake (1966).

6

LABOURISM AND SOCIALISM

Introduction

Socialism only developed as a coherent ideology in the nineteenth century, although forerunners can be identified earlier. Essentially, socialism involved a reaction against, and a radical alternative to, industrial capitalism. In terms of class interests, socialism can be seen as the political ideology of the new urban working class, effectively created by industrialisation, just as conservatism was, initially, the ideology of the landed interest and liberalism the ideology of the bourgeoisie, or manufacturing interest. While conservatism involved a defence of the status quo or a return to the recent past, and liberalism provided a justification and support for an ongoing industrial transformation, socialism developed as a radical or revolutionary ideology requiring a fundamental transformation of existing society, and its underlying assumptions and values.

Thus socialists sought a radical overhaul of existing property relations, involving the transfer of the private ownership of the means of production to social ownership, and a massive redistribution of income and wealth in favour of the working classes. This involved also a rejection of the free market values and competition lauded by liberals in favour of planning and co-operation. Most socialists instinctively felt that it should be possible to improve on the unplanned outcome of market forces under capitalism, with its periodic booms and slumps, involving unused capacity and human misery.

But although socialism in some ways was the very antithesis of liberalism, it can also be said to have grown out of liberalism. Both were products of the modern world – of the rise of science, industrialisation and associated political upheavals. Socialism thus shared with liberalism a post-Enlightenment rationalism, and optimism over progress. It adopted much of the liberal political programme, most notably for a reform and extension of the franchise, and the establishment of civil rights. Moreover, it embodied many liberal values, such as the familiar revolutionary triad, liberty, equality and fraternity, although giving them a markedly different interpretation.

Beyond this it is difficult to generalise, as the nature and definition of socialism is problematic and controversial. Many of those who regard themselves as socialists would vehemently deny the claims of others to the same description. Thus the socialist credentials of the British Labour Party are contestable. Some critics would deny that Labour has ever been a socialist party, and employ instead the term 'labourism' to describe the party's ideology (Miliband, 1972; Saville, 1988). Others accuse the party of abandoning socialism. However, Labour politicians, like those elsewhere who have chosen the parliamentary road to socialism, have often rejected the claims of others, such as Soviet and Chinese Communists, to be true socialists. Some of the differences between socialists over both ultimate objectives and the means of achieving objectives are explored in the next two sections of this chapter.

Thereafter, the focus is primarily on the British experience of socialism, which is distinctive. Some strands of thought which were strong in other countries, such as Marxism and anarcho-syndicalism, have been relatively weak in Britain. Moreover, in many other countries different strands of left or socialist thought are represented in contending political parties: Communists, anarchists, socialists, social democrats. However, in Britain there has never been a significant left-wing or socialist rival to Labour. Thus although socialism is the most international of political ideologies, British socialism is almost *sui generis* – of its own kind. Even at the elite level there is a parochial flavour to much British socialist thought. It is British thinkers, such as Robert Owen, William Morris, the Webbs, R. H. Tawney, G. D. H. Cole, George Orwell and Anthony Crosland, who are cited as significant influences. This is still more evident at the popular level. The British Labour Party, the Labour movement and associated Labour and socialist institutions developed in their own highly individual ways.

Thus this chapter seeks to explain the development of this British variant of socialism, with sections exploring the specific experience of the British working class, the relative weakness of Marxism, the importance of trade unionism, and the contrasting contributions of ethical socialists and Fabians to the development of Labour thought. Labour thinking inevitably involved some rationalisation of Labour practice, and so some brief reference must be made to the experience of Labour governments, and the predominance of parliamentarism and centralised state socialism over alternatives such as guild socialism or local socialism.

This chapter then explores the struggles over the Labour Party's ideology from the 1950s to the present day, particularly over internal party democracy and the role of trade unions on the one hand and the symbolic issue of clause four of the Labour Party constitution on the other. Some have seen reforms attempted or achieved by the party's leaders from Gaitskell to Blair as a necessary updating of the party's socialist message, while others have seen them as a betrayal of fundamental socialist values. This returns the debate once more to the meaning of socialism.

Yet the future of socialism in Britain is clearly related to the future of socialism worldwide. The rapid collapse of the Soviet form of socialism in Russia and eastern Europe from 1989 has cast a long shadow over socialists everywhere, even those among the most vociferous critics of Soviet communism. The implications are discussed briefly in a final section.

Socialist values

Socialism is pre-eminently an ideology of equality, and it is the centrality of this value which marks it off from conservatism with its emphasis on hierarchy, leadership and natural inequality, and from liberalism, where a commitment to formal legal and political equality has not been extended to economic and social equality. Socialism involved from the beginning a fundamental critique of existing inequality under capitalism and a programme for a significant redistribution and equalisation of income, wealth and power.

Yet socialists have not always agreed over what this commitment to equality should involve in practice. For a few it has involved the total abolition of personal private property, a solution anticipated by Plato for the Guardians of his ideal state, and by some religious communities. For many socialists it is, however, only the private ownership of the means of production which needs to be replaced by common ownership. The application of this principle has aroused acute debate. It has sometimes been interpreted by mainstream British socialists as public ownership of the 'commanding heights' of the economy. There have also been considerable differences over exactly what common ownership entails in practice – for example, state ownership or workers' control.

Revisionist socialists, now often described as social democrats, have argued that the promotion of equality no longer requires wholesale public ownership. According to this analysis, progressive taxation coupled with state welfare benefits will help to produce a more egalitarian society, although there is no very clear conception of how much inequality can be tolerated, or how far it is practical or desirable to push equality.

While both advocates and critics acknowledge that socialism is in some sense about equality, the importance attached to liberty is rather more contestable. As Tawney (1964, p. 164) suggests, 'Liberty and equality have usually in England been considered antithetic', and indeed conservatives and liberals have often accused socialists of sacrificing liberty to equality. Socialists have generally strenuously denied this, maintaining that equality is a condition of liberty. Equality does not mean uniformity, but rather frees individuals to develop their full and different potentials. The socialist commitment to liberty has been strongly re-emphasised by modern British Labour Party politicians (Hattersley, 1987).

Socialists, like some New Liberals, tend to see freedom in what has been termed a positive rather than a negative sense – freedom *to* enjoy something which is valued, rather than freedom *from* restraint and coercion. 'Liberty implies the ability to act, not merely to resist' (Tawney, 1964, p. 165). Critics have pointed to some inherent dangers in the notion of positive liberty, suggesting it may be used to justify coercion for people's own good (Berlin, 1967). Some indeed would argue that socialism inevitably involves loss of liberty. Neo-liberals like Hayek identify freedom with the market order. While a command economy clearly conflicts with freedom in the market, Hayek also argues that any state intervention or planning, even of the milder kind associated with moderate parliamentary socialism, contributes to 'The Road to Serfdom'.

By contrast, socialists have generally argued that the freedom celebrated by classical liberals and neo-liberals is fairly meaningless in the context of severe economic and social deprivation and a culture which inevitably reflects the values of the dominant class. Most socialists see human behaviour as essentially socially determined, the product of its environment, an assumption which cuts across a basic tenet of classical liberalism, that individuals know and pursue their own interests. For socialists, people's expressed interests are not necessarily their real interests, plausibly in view of assumptions concerning the social determination of attitudes and behaviour. Thus freedom in a capitalist society is largely illusory for the majority, not only because choice is in practice severely constrained, but also because people do not necessarily recognise what is in their own best interest.

The third term in the revolutionary triad – fraternity – has been less emphasised and analysed, but it is both important and problematic for socialism. Behind the notion of the 'brotherhood of man' lies an affirmation of the inherent worth of all humanity, regardless of class, nation, colour, creed, or (despite the somewhat sexist terminology) gender. Moreover, fraternity focuses specifically on the inter-relations between human beings rather than the individual, and on the value and importance of social interaction and community. There is an implicit assumption that human beings have the capacity to live peacefully and co-operatively with each other.

This conception of man as essentially a social and, potentially at least, a selfless animal contrasts markedly with both conservative notions of a fatal flaw or evil streak in human nature and the competitive, self-seeking individualism which underpins liberalism. It is important because it is upon this optimistic assumption concerning human nature that the feasibility of socialism essentially depends. It is also clearly problematic. Conservatives and liberals regard the socialist view of human nature as naive and unrealistic. Conservatives would claim it was invalidated by the abundant evidence of man's inhumanity to man over many centuries, liberals assume a need for individual rewards and incentives. Most socialists would reply that violent, competitive and acquisitive behaviour is socially determined – it is learned rather than natural. A socialist society would foster different values and behaviour.

Evolutionary and revolutionary socialism

If there are some differences among socialists over ultimate objectives, there are greater differences over how these objectives are to be
achieved, not surprisingly as socialism, unlike liberalism and conservatism, involved a radical alternative model of social and economic organisation for which there were initially no examples.
Socialism, moreover, implied a massive redistribution of income and
wealth, and it was difficult to envisage the beneficiaries of the
existing social and political system voluntarily relinquishing their
property and power. Thus the means of transition to socialism was
always a crucial issue.

A fundamental distinction can be drawn between those favouring
an evolutionary, gradualist route to socialism, relying on rational or
moral persuasion, and those who, enthusiastically or reluctantly,
endorse revolution. Evolutionary socialism has always been the
dominant strain in Britain, although ideas and analysis have sometimes been borrowed and adapted from the alternative revolutionary
tradition.

Revolutionary socialism had been in part inspired by the example
of the French revolution, which, although not essentially socialist,
had shown that an existing ruling class could be overthrown, and thus
provided a precedent and inspiration for further attempts to secure the
transformation of society through insurrection. The French socialist
Blanqui (1805–81) was the leading advocate and practitioner of the
insurrectionary road to socialism, although others argued that a
socialist revolution did not necessarily involve an armed uprising and
violence.

But many socialists rejected the revolutionary route to socialism. It
is worth emphasising that the legacy of the French revolution was
somewhat ambivalent. It had disappointed many early enthusiasts
both in France and in other countries, for it had 'destroyed its own
children', and culminated in dictatorship. Thus for many it was not an
example to be followed but a failure and a warning. This was perhaps
particularly so for early British socialists, who hoped to build
socialism peacefully, from the bottom up, sometimes through ambitious attempts to establish small-scale model socialist communities,
but more usually through practical experiments in mutual aid and
self-help for working people, such as consumer and producer co-

operatives, friendly societies and trade unions, and through the encouragement of education.

Yet it could be argued that attempts to build socialism from the bottom up substantially ignored the problem of power. Such initiatives could not, in isolation, produce that fundamental transformation of society, and fundamental redistribution of income and wealth which socialists sought. Marx and Engels thus attacked this form of socialism as 'utopian', as there was no realistic strategy for its achievement.

Marx is clearly associated with the revolutionary route to socialism, although his conception of a revolution and the way it would be achieved was very different from Blanqui's. Marx's approach was based on an analysis of underlying trends in the historical evolution of societies. Key elements in this historical evolution were classes, defined in terms of their relations with the means of production. In a capitalist society the crucial division was between the owners of capital, and the industrial proletariat who owned only their own labour. The dynamics of capitalism required the exploitation of the proletariat by the capitalists in pursuit of profit. This fundamental conflict of interest could not be resolved, and indeed it was bound to be intensified, as competition between capitalists would increase the exploitation and misery of the workforce. For Marx, a successful working-class revolution would be the inevitable consequence of the intensification of class conflict in a capitalist society.

Needless to say, it was Marx's revolutionary socialism which provided the inspiration for the Russian revolution, and numerous other revolutions since, although neither the background circumstances, nor the actual course of these revolutions, have closely reflected Marx's analysis. Lenin, in particular, provided his own gloss on Marx, extending the notion of a temporary dictatorship of the proletariat, and developing the concept of democratic centralism to establish an authoritarian, highly centralised state socialism.

In the meantime an alternative evolutionary, parliamentary route to socialism seemed increasingly plausible, with the extension of the franchise to the working class in Britain and other liberal capitalist countries from the second half of the nineteenth century onwards. The parliamentary route involved the formation of new working-class socialist parties, competition for votes and parliamentary seats, and ultimately the capture of the apparatus of the state through a parliamentary majority. Thus power could be won, and socialism established, through peaceful and democratic struggle. Indeed, for many, socialism seemed the natural corollary of democracy. Political equality would lead inexorably to social equality.

But although socialist parties were to enjoy considerable electoral success in western Europe, progress towards socialism has been, for many socialist supporters, disappointing. Sometimes this has been ascribed to betrayal by the parliamentary leadership – a familiar complaint on the left. Indeed, it can be argued that there are endemic pressures to accommodation and compromise within the parliamentary system (Michels, 1962).

Yet it could equally be argued that compromises with socialist objectives were necessary to win working-class votes, and thus were an inescapable consequence of the electoral strategy. It was too readily assumed, both by early socialists and some of their opponents, that political democracy would lead rapidly to a major redistribution of income and wealth in favour of the masses. The extent to which the values of liberal capitalism were embedded in society as a whole was not appreciated, and the task of converting the working class to fundamentally different values in a hostile climate, was correspondingly underestimated (Coates, 1980).

Some would further argue that the parliamentary route to socialism inevitably involves a 'top down', elitist, or paternalist approach, and results in a centralised state socialism which is the antithesis of the participative, co-operative values which were the essence of early socialist ideals.

Attitudes to the state have varied markedly among socialists. At one end of the spectrum are anarchists who would totally reject the authority of the centralised state, at the other end those who would, like Sidney Webb, identify the growth of state authority with socialism. Many socialists have argued, with Marx, that the existing state apparatus in a capitalist society inevitably reflects a narrow class interest and involves coercion, and thus must be replaced by new institutions. But while Marx suggested that the state would 'wither away' after the revolution, Lenin and his successors developed a strong centralised state which showed few signs of withering. Western parliamentary socialists, while abhorring the Leninist state, have still tended to see socialism in terms of centralised state economic planning and collectivist state welfare provision. More decentralised, participative forms of socialism have been less evident.

Associated with this debate over the state there has also been within Britain as elsewhere a debate over the relative merits of parliamentary and extra-parliamentary (particularly industrial) action as a means to achieve social and political change. The trade unionism which was established in Britain from the second half of the nineteenth century onwards was predominantly legalistic, respectable, and limited to immediate practical objectives concerned with pay and conditions. But it was always possible to conceive of the use of industrial muscle to achieve wider economic and political ends. Syndicalists rejected parliamentarism in favour of such industrial action. Workers could thus use their power to seize control of industry. In theory this could be wholly non-violent. Disciplined strikes by workers in key industries, or a general strike, would immobilise the country and lead to a peaceful revolution. In practice it was likely that such industrial action would lead to violence. Moreover, syndicalists have had a clear class-conflict view of politics, so that syndicalism belongs more properly in the revolutionary rather than the evolutionary strand of socialism.

It should already be clear that radically different strategies for achieving socialism mask underlying differences over the analysis of existing society. Marxism involves a materialist interpretation of history, which suggests that political power and political development reflect economic and technological factors. Marxist economics assumes in turn that inter-class relations are inevitably exploitative, that there is a fundamental and irreconcilable conflict of interest between capital and labour in a capitalist society. Other socialists, including most British socialists, have eschewed the language of class conflict. Free enterprise or *laissez-faire* capitalism is condemned as immoral and inefficient, with the implicit assumption that socialism is ultimately in the general or national interest rather than a class interest. It follows that even dominant interests in existing society may be persuaded of the benefits of socialism, a notion which to the Marxist is simply naive.

The rise of the industrial working class in nineteenth-century Britain

As the first industrialising nation, Britain was the first country in which something like a modern industrial working class emerged. Previously there were labouring classes, but not a working class conscious of its identity and collective interest. Industrialisation involved a new concentration of workers, both in workplaces and in fast growing urban settlements. This facilitated the communication of ideas and organisation, and made the working class a factor in politics which could no longer be ignored.

There was certainly plenty of evidence of discontent among the labouring classes in Britain in the early stages of the industrial revolution. There was some revolutionary Jacobinism among tradesmen and artisans in the late eighteenth and early nineteenth centuries. There were the Luddite riots of 1811–13, involving machine breaking – an understandable reaction against the immediate impact of industrialisation on the employment and living standards of skilled workers. There were mass meetings and demonstrations, such as that broken up at Spa Field Manchester in 1819 by cavalry. There were revolutionary plots, culminating in the 1822 Cato Street conspiracy. E. P. Thompson (1980) has woven all these and other strands together to produce a convincing picture of an emerging radical working-class consciousness, a picture perhaps reinforced by the trade union activity of the 1830s and still more by Chartism, a broadly based working-class movement with radical political objectives, including the vote for all adult males, but involving a variety of ideas and strategies. Whether this expanding working class, increasingly conscious of its common interest, posed a real danger to the existing social order is debatable, although certainly some of the political establishment feared an intensifying class conflict and revolution.

Working-class radicalism did not necessarily involve socialism, but socialist ideas were advanced in the first half of the nineteenth century. Some such as William Thompson (1775–1833) and Thomas Hodgskin (1783–1869) had derived socialist conclusions from Ricardo's labour theory of value. The most influential British socialist in the first half of the nineteenth century was, however, Robert Owen (1771–1858).

Owen had demonstrated at New Lanark that it was possible to make money by enlightened capitalism, and at his more ambitious

American model community, New Harmony, that it was equally possible to lose a fortune. But even in his early years he was more than just an enlightened philanthropist. His work at New Lanark reflected a conviction which is characteristic of socialism, that people are moulded, for good or ill, by their environment. Such a view contradicted the conventional religious notion of personal moral responsibility, and indeed Owen's irreligion soon lost him the respectful reputation he had briefly enjoyed in parliamentary circles. But as his influence with the political establishment declined, his reputation among the radical working class rose, and Owen was strongly associated with an ambitious spread of trade unions in the 1830s and the establishment of the co-operative movement in the 1840s (Owen, edited by Claeys, 1991).

Owen's legacy was considerable and controversial. Marx and Engels attacked him in the Communist Manifesto, grouping him with Saint-Simon (1760–1825) and Fourier (1772–1837) as a utopian socialist. The charge reflects his involvement in the move to establish model socialist communities cut off from the rest of the world and also the lack of a clear strategy to achieve socialism. Owen eschewed revolution, while his support for trade unionism and the co-operative movement could be comfortably accommodated within Victorian working-class self-help. Yet in some ways the label 'utopian' seems unfair for a man who immersed himself in working-class politics and causes, and Engels later delivered another more generous verdict: 'Every social movement, every real advance in England on behalf of the workers links itself to the name of Robert Owen' (Marx and Engels, 1962, vol. 2, p. 127).

Owen died in 1858, and from the 1850s both socialism and working-class militancy, following the collapse of Chartism, made little headway. British working-class leaders largely accepted the gradualist reformist parliamentary culture. Political and social reforms in the nineteenth century seemingly confirmed the existing system's capacity for change. Religious and other cleavages which cut across class divisions helped blunt social conflict. The benefits of early industrialisation and, more arguably, imperialism, improved living standards among elements of the working class particularly from the mid-nineteenth century onwards, when skilled craftsmen organised themselves into effective unions, which secured real improvements in pay and conditions and widened differentials with other workers, creating an aristocracy of labour (Gray, 1981). All this reduced hostility to the economic system, to the extent that accommodation within capitalism rather than its wholesale transformation was increasingly sought by leaders of the organised labour movement, many of whom saw no reason to go beyond radical liberalism in their political demands (Pelling, 1965, p. 6).

Thus in marked contrast with developments in France and Germany, socialist ideas were only weakly articulated in Britain in the period after 1848, and there was virtually no organised socialist activity before the 1880s (Pelling, 1965, pp. 13–15), by which time socialist ideas and socialist parties were already established with a mass following in several other European countries. Even after distinct socialist organisations emerged in Britain from the 1880s onwards, and ultimately a separate Labour Party, the influence of radical liberal thinking remained strong. Bentham, Mill, Hobhouse, Hobson and later Keynes and Beveridge, all arguably had a bigger influence on the character and development of British socialist thought than many thinkers with more authentic socialist credentials. British socialism thus substantially grew out of radical liberalism, and has long continued to bear the marks of its origins.

Marxism and the British labour movement

The failure of British workers to develop a stronger class consciousness and a revolutionary social and political programme was sadly noted by two celebrated foreign observers of the British social and political scene in the second half of the nineteenth century. Marx and Engels spent the bulk of their working lives in England, studied conditions in England extensively and involved themselves in British working-class politics. Moreover, Britain, as the most advanced capitalist country in their day, might appear the prime candidate for a Marxist-style socialist revolution. Despite all this, Marxist ideas have had less influence on the development of socialist thought in Britain than in Germany, France, Italy, Russia, China and many other countries where the ground for their reception might seem far less fertile.

Indeed, although the British authorities kept a watchful eye on the socialist agitator in their midst, they seem to have concluded that he was not particularly dangerous. Grant Duff, a Liberal MP who arranged a meeting with Marx at the suggestion of Queen Victoria's eldest daughter, enjoyed three hours' civilised conversation with him and concluded, 'It will not be Marx who, whether he wishes it or not, will turn the world upside down' (McLellan, 1976, p. 445). While this was not among the more accurate historical prophecies ever made, it would have been less wide of the mark if applied exclusively to Britain.

The relatively weak influence of Marxist ideas in Britain can be largely attributed to factors already explored: political stability and a tradition of gradualism, a blurred and fluid class system, the existence in Owenism of a distinct native strand of socialism, the relative prosperity of sections of the working class, the extension of the franchise and the reforms apparently secured through parliamentarism, the acceptance of trade unionism by the political establishment, and the consequent movement of labour leaders towards accommodation within the existing economic and political system.

Several accounts have also stressed personal factors, particularly the eccentric and abrasive personality of Britain's leading native Marxist in the late nineteenth and early twentieth centuries. H. M. Hyndman (1842–1921) was a former Tory imperialist who managed to upset his mentors, Marx and Engels, and quarrel with most other leading socialists of his day (Pelling, 1965, pp. 18–32; Pierson, 1973, pp. 60–75; Callaghan, 1990, ch. 2). He was an able polemicist, but might have had more influence had he been less scathing about the theory and practice of trade unionism. His Social Democratic Federation (SDF), the oldest and in some ways the strongest of the three socialist organisations which combined with trade unions to form the Labour Representation Committee in 1900, left the Committee within a year, and subsequently had only a marginal influence on the development of socialist ideas in Britain.

Of course the spread of Marxist ideas in Britain was not just dependent on Hyndman. Marx's theories were familiar in British socialist circles, although not always fully understood or appreciated. William Morris (1834–96), while enjoying the historical parts of *Capital* confessed that he 'suffered agonies of confusion of the brain over reading the pure economics of that great work' (Morris, ed. Briggs, 1962, p. 34). George Bernard Shaw (1856–1950) tried to convert his fellow Fabians to Marxist economics, but was soon persuaded to repudiate Marx in favour of the then orthodox economics of Jevons (1835–82) (Foote, 1986, p. 25). In general, early British socialism was eclectic, and Marx was only one influence among many.

Nor did that situation change much subsequently. The Bolshevik revolution of 1917 renewed interest in Marxist ideas both inside and outside the Labour Party (Callaghan, 1990, ch. 7). However, the emergence of the Communist Party of Great Britain in 1920 from older small socialist groups, and the refusal of the Labour Party to allow the new body to affiliate to it, emphasised the split between revolutionary and evolutionary socialism, in Britain as elsewhere. The hardening division between western-style parliamentary socialism (represented by the Second International) and Soviet-style communism (represented by the Third International) rendered Marxist analysis suspect in Labour circles. Moreover, the electoral progress of the Labour Party in the 1920s apparently confirmed the faith of the leadership in parliamentarism and constitutionalism.

Later, the economic crisis and collapse of the Labour government in 1931 led some British socialists like Strachey (1901–63) to question gradualism and embrace Marxism, and rendered the alternative Soviet model of socialism more attractive, even to the high priests of British evolutionary socialism, Sidney and Beatrice Webb. Marxism and Russian-style communism were intellectually fashionable throughout the 1930s, but even so their influence on the leadership of the Labour Party and the bulk of the working class was fairly negligible (Pimlott, 1977).

After 1945, the Cold War and growing economic prosperity in the west again rendered Marxist analysis suspect or seemingly irrelevant. Strachey repudiated his earlier Marxist views (Foote, 1986, p. 210). Tony Crosland (1956, p. 2) was briefly dismissive. 'In my view Marx has little to offer the contemporary socialist either in respect of practical policy, or of the correct analysis of our society, or even of the right conceptual tools or framework.'

After the revisionist heyday of the 1950s Marxism again became more fashionable in left-wing academic circles, and was articulated by a number of fringe-left groups and parties. Sophisticated Marxist analysis had some impact on thinking within the Labour Party, and at another level in the 1980s there were some highly publicised attempts at infiltration of constituency parties and trade unions by organisations such as the Militant Tendency, and its more fundamentalist Marxism. Even so, it may still be argued that the real influence of

Marxist ideas on the Labour Party both in the parliamentary party and
the country remained relatively weak (Coates, 1980, p. 163).

Trade unionism and labourism

The failure of revolutionary socialism to have much impact in Britain
might be ascribed in part to the strength and character of British trade
unionism. Trade unionism and socialism share a concern to advance
the interests of the working class. They place a similar emphasis on
collective values, but otherwise do not necessarily coincide in terms
of ultimate objectives or strategy. Trade unions exist to promote the
interests of their members, largely in terms of pay and conditions,
through collective bargaining, backed by sanctions, including ultimately the withdrawal of labour. They do not necessarily seek, as
socialists do, a fundamental transformation of the economic and
social system. Indeed, free collective bargaining implies some accommodation within a capitalist system. Moreover, pursuit of immediate
interests in the workplace is not necessarily compatible with the
collective interests of the working class as a whole, particularly if that
is taken to include those not currently part of the paid labour force:
children, the old, sick, disabled and unemployed, and unwaged
women.

The craft unions for skilled workers which developed in Britain
from the mid-nineteenth century onwards were particularly respectable and moderate in their methods and objectives. These constituted
something of a labour aristocracy (Gray, 1981) which had profited
sufficiently from the existing economic system to resist the attractions
of socialism. Socialist ideas were more prevalent among the leaders
of groups of semi-skilled and unskilled workers, who became effectively organised for industrial purposes later in the century (Callaghan,
1990, ch. 4). Even so, the bulk of trade unionists seemed indifferent
or hostile to socialism by the turn of the century and many retained
strong links with radical liberalism.

Thus trade unionism certainly did not imply socialism. Nor did it
even involve necessarily separate labour parliamentary representation. Unions are essentially concerned with industrial rather than
political action, and there is no imperative requirement for them to
seek direct involvement in the parliamentary arena. Until the late
nineteenth and early twentieth centuries most trade unionists pre-

ferred to concentrate on the immediate issues of wages and conditions, avoiding wider political activity. In so far as they sought political influence, they were content with the two established political parties, which, from self-interest, were increasingly sensitive to labour pressure.

Several factors caused a change in outlook, including the reluctance of the established parties to endorse working-class candidates, some bitter industrial disputes in the early 1890s, and most significantly, growing anxieties about the legal position of trade unions, following a series of disquieting cases in the courts (Pelling, 1965, p. 200). These doubts were not sufficient to impel more than a minority of unions to come together with three socialist societies to establish the Labour Representation Committee (LRC) in 1900. It was the impact of a particular court case in 1901, concerning a strike against the Taff Vale Railway Company, which persuaded most unions of the need for parliamentary representation to look after their interests (Pelling, 1965, pp. 213ff.). Affiliations to the infant Labour Representation Committee trebled. Subsequently, the commitment of the vast bulk of the trade union movement to what was soon renamed the Labour Party was never in serious doubt.

Yet the commitment remained initially (and arguably always essentially) to labour representation rather than socialism. As Ernest Bevin graphically described it, the Labour Party emerged from the bowels of the trade union movement. What the trade unions wanted was a party to advance and defend the interests of unions in particular, and the working class more generally.

There were of course already some reciprocal ties between trade unionism and socialism. Some individual trade union leaders and activists were socialists, and the unions who joined the LRC were plainly prepared to enter an alliance with established socialist organisations, even if they were not initially prepared to commit the new party to socialist goals. Some socialists on the other hand had given considerable encouragement and support to the New Unionism from the 1880s.

But there were, all the same, considerable mutual suspicions. Hyndman's general hostility to what he saw as the limitations of trade union action led him soon to withdraw his SDF from the LRC, while the Fabians were patronising and disparaging about both the unions and the working classes (Adelman, 1986, p. 10). It is scarcely surprising that some trade unionists were in turn critical of middle-class intellectual socialists whose commitment to trade unionism and the labour movement seemed at best doubtful.

Yet the 'contentious alliance' (Minkin, 1991) between the trade unions and the Labour Party survived and thrived. The relationship remained sufficiently close for them to be regarded as wings of a single labour movement, with the parliamentary party representing the movement in the political sphere and the TUC representing the movement in the industrial sphere. While there was always some latent potential for ideological conflict between the two wings of the movement, this was minimised by the general compatibility between British trade unionism and the mainstream British interpretation of socialism. Both were essentially moderate, reformist and gradualist. Both were content to work legally within the existing state apparatus.

Indeed, one perhaps surprising consequence of the major role of trade unions in the British Labour Party was to establish the primacy of parliamentary rather than industrial action as the strategy for the achievement of socialism. Once the TUC decided to back parliamentary representation, it committed the trade union movement wholeheartedly to parliamentarism. There were of course trade union leaders who were attracted to anarcho-syndicalist ideas and industrial action to achieve political objectives both before and after the First World War, but these were a minority within the trade union and labour movement. When a General Strike did occur in Britain 1926, the moderate, non-revolutionary character of both wings of the labour movement was clearly demonstrated. The unions showed an impressive collective solidarity in obedience to the strike call, but neither the TUC General Council nor the Labour parliamentary leadership was remotely interested in the strike as a political weapon. Instead, the purely industrial character of the dispute was emphasised. The outcome confirmed to both the Labour parliamentary and trade unionist leadership the futility of industrial action for political purposes, and reinforced parliamentarism (Miliband, 1972, p. 151).

Indeed, after the failure of the General Strike in 1926 the trade unions became more committed than ever to the Labour Party. Yet although the unions supplied the bulk of the Labour Party's finance, the majority of places on the National Executive Committee and through their affiliated membership the overwhelming majority of votes at the Labour Party Conference, this power was seldom used to embarrass the parliamentary leadership at least until the 1960s, despite repeated Conservative claims that the party was effectively controlled by the unions (McKenzie, 1963).

Yet if the unions did not effectively control the parliamentary party, trade union attitudes and values strongly coloured the party's interpretation of socialism. Even after the Labour Party was formally committed to socialist objectives in 1918 some would argue that the ideology of the Labour Party remained essentially 'labourist' rather than socialist (Miliband, 1972, p. 61; Saville, 1988). The term 'labourism' implies an ideology which articulates the felt interests of labour, or the working class. To a very considerable extent the Labour Party was successful in establishing itself as the party of the working class, convincing the bulk of manual workers that Labour represented their interests (although a significant minority continued to vote Tory). However, it does not follow that most of the working class were necessarily converted to socialism.

Indeed, it might be argued that 'labourism' represents what Parkin (1972, p. 81) has described as a 'subordinate value system' promoting accommodation with the established social and political order, as opposed to a 'radical value system' providing a direct challenge to that order. Thus workers wanted a party which would protect their trade union bargaining rights, raise their standard of living and provide certain benefits such as cheap public housing and free health care, but not necessarily a party which would challenge the whole basis of the economic and social system.

The Labour Party and socialism

If Labour began essentially as a trade union party, it has always contained socialists, and since 1918 at least has been committed to socialist objectives. Yet the extent and nature of the Labour Party's socialism has been contentious since its origins. In marked contrast with some continental socialist parties which began as revolutionary socialist and became reformist over time, Labour began as a trade unionist reformist party which moved in the direction of socialism. However, for reasons already discussed it was most unlikely that the brand of socialism embraced would owe anything of significance to Marx. In fact the socialism of the Labour Party was to be a blend of the ethical socialism particularly associated with the Independent

Labour Party (ILP) and the gradualist and social scientific outlook of the Fabians.

Ethical socialism was in large part the product of a religious or quasi-religious outlook. Indeed, there has been a significant strand of Christian socialism within Britain, from Kingsley (1819–75) and Maurice (1805–72) in the nineteenth century, through Tawney (1880–1962) and Cripps (1889–1952) in the early and mid-twentieth century, until more recently John Smith and Tony Blair. Some of these Christian socialists were Anglicans and others Roman Catholics, but there were particularly strong links between Nonconformism, especially Methodism, and the British labour movement.

Yet for many, socialism was not derived from religion, but almost a religion itself, and religious language and imagery was a pervasive element of much turn-of-the-century socialist propaganda. This was particularly true of the Independent Labour Party, founded by Keir Hardie in 1893, and one of the three socialist organisations which in 1900 joined with the trade unions to form the Labour Representation Committee. Hardie (1856–1915), who became the new party's first leader, contrasted the 'glorious Gospel of Socialism' with 'the gospel of selfishness'. Religious imagery was common among socialists of the period (Greenleaf, 1983, vol. 2, p. 414; Callaghan, 1990, p. 67). The Glasiers published a book entitled the *Religion of Socialism* in 1890, and John Glasier subsequently referred to the 'sacrament of socialism' (quoted in Foote, 1986, p. 34). Such language came easily to working people brought up in an atmosphere of Christian evangelism in Nonconformist chapels, and served the same function of conversion to the faith, whether Christian or socialist.

The religious atmosphere of meetings of the ILP and some other socialist groups may not have persisted, but a moralistic strain has been a feature of British labourist and socialist ideology down to the present day. Arguably it has brought a fervour and commitment to the socialist case which has been a potent factor in winning and retaining mass support. The ethical socialists were consciously articulating a new morality involving unselfish, co-operative behaviour, which made certain assumptions about human nature and potential, and involved a direct challenge to the self-interested individualist assumptions behind classical economics and *laissez-faire* liberalism.

One aspect of this ethical approach was a universalism which emphasised the brotherhood of man, and rejected conflict and division. Hardie explicitly rejected the Marxist doctrine of the class war, and in this he has been followed by the mainstream British socialist tradition. Thus the most influential British socialist writer, R. H. Tawney, pinned his hopes on education and the development of a new social consciousness.

The main weakness of ethical socialism was a certain intellectual fuzziness at its core. A thorough-going Marxist analysis was implicitly rejected, but there was little in the way of a convincing alternative theoretical foundation for socialism. Ethical socialism was long on commitment and evangelical fervour, but short on economic and social analysis. Foote's verdict (1986, p. 37) is brutal: 'It was basically a withdrawal from the world, and as such, it was impossible to translate into the practical politics of government.' There is something in this. Their socialist vision could win converts, and thus help win power, but offered little guidance in using power. Millennial visions of the future were not much help in coping with the pressing problems of the present.

This deficiency was in part supplied by another very different strand in British socialism, the Fabians, who were in many respects the antithesis of the ILP. If the imagery and rhetoric of the ILP was moralistic and quasi-religious, the Fabians prided themselves on their rational and scientific approach to economic and social issues (Greenleaf, 1983, vol. 2, p. 392). While the ILP recruited working-class activists and aspired to become a mass party, the Fabians began as a small group of middle-class intellectuals, with ambivalent attitudes to working-class politics.

The Fabian Society had been founded in 1884. It was named after the Roman General, Fabius Maximus Cunctator, who defeated Hannibal by patient delaying tactics (effectively refusing to fight him), and it adopted the emblem of the tortoise on its early publications. Both name and emblem were symbolic of a commitment to gradualist, non-revolutionary socialism. Beyond that there was no party line, and the early Fabians contained a diversity of ideas and a rare array of intellectual talent, including two authors who were to establish a world reputation, Shaw and Wells, a celebrated children's writer, Edith Nesbit, an important if neglected social scientist, Graham Wallas, the neo-Malthusian, Annie Besant and the psychologist, Havelock Ellis. It was, however, Beatrice and Sidney Webb who were to become most closely identified with Fabian socialism (Greenleaf, 1983, vol. 2, p. 381).

Some would deny that Fabian socialism involved socialism at all. If the objective of the common ownership of the means of production is regarded as the litmus test for socialists, then Sidney Webb (1859–1947), who drafted Clause 4 of the Labour Party's constitution in 1918, was a socialist. Those who would deny the label 'socialist' to the Fabians have focused on their gradualist parliamentarian strategy for achieving socialism rather than their objectives.

The Webbs believed, like Marx, in the inevitable triumph of socialism, but whereas Marx saw this as the result of class conflict and revolution, the Webbs viewed it as the irresistible end-product of the steady growth of state intervention in society, the 'inevitability of gradualness'. Lovingly, Sidney Webb chronicled all the activities once 'abandoned to private enterprise', now controlled or regulated by the state. While many continental socialists saw the existing state apparatus as the enemy, Webb tended to assume that the advance of the state was synonymous with the advance of socialism. Critics have suggested that Webb was far too ready to claim for socialism every trivial extension of state intervention, and to assume that socialism and collectivism were one and the same.

The Webbs believed the trend towards collectivism was irreversible, because state provision was manifestly more efficient than private provision. Good government was essentially a matter of applying the appropriate expertise, based on scientific research and professional training (Greenleaf, 1983, vol. 2, pp. 397ff.). The Webbs themselves were indefatigable researchers. They saw their socialism as essentially dispassionate, rational and scientific.

By the same token it was also paternalist and elitist. The Fabians were imbued with middle-class attitudes, and despite their early involvement in the Labour Party, initially had little faith in trade unions or the working class. Socialism was to be applied from the top down for the benefit of the working class, rather than won by pressure from below. Their vision of socialism involved scientific administration by disinterested, properly trained and qualified civil servants, and owed more to the British utilitarian tradition than to continental socialism. It was to be achieved by rational persuasion – the Webbs hoped their ideas would permeate society, including particularly the current political establishment, and they pressed their recommendations on leading Liberal and Conservative politicians, at least in the period before 1914.

This rational, scientific and paternalist socialism was very different from the evangelical and populist socialism of the ILP. Even so, the ideas of the ethical and Fabian socialists were not incompatible. Both had their roots in strands of liberalism – the Fabians in utilitarianism, the ILP in Nonconformist radicalism. Both wished to transcend the radical liberal tradition and the labourism associated with trade unionism. Yet both at the same time rejected the class war, and Marxism. Both were parliamentarist, and, despite the millennial rhetoric employed by the ethical socialists, essentially gradualist. Their role within the Labour Party was, until 1918 at least, complementary rather than competitive. The ILP was the recruiting agent, trying to win the working class for socialism, the Fabians were more an intellectual think-tank, carrying out policy-oriented research.

After 1918, and the establishment of a national organisation for the Labour Party, with individual membership, the ILP lost its distinctive role in recruitment, and became effectively a party within a party. With the influx of the 'Red Clydesiders' in the 1920s they also became more revolutionary, at least in terms of rhetoric. The resulting tension between a reformist parliamentary leadership and an increasingly critical and radical-left ILP led ultimately to disaffiliation from the Labour Party in 1932. The ILP's influence was subsequently marginal.

By contrast, the Fabian Society, eclectic and undoctrinaire, has continued to provide a forum for ideas and a research capacity for the Labour Party until the present day. This has been its strength. Its weakness might be that very eclecticism which has made it receptive to new ideas and research agendas. Thus it has never developed a coherent economic and social theory to provide an intellectual alternative to Marxism. Nor has it even evolved much in the way of lower order partial theories which might be of practical benefit to Labour governments. Thus while the Fabians cannot be accused of neglecting economics they have not produced a distinctive brand of Fabian economics, but rather have drawn extensively from fashionable and largely non-socialist economists, unsurprisingly leading to prescriptions which have tended to reflect the professional consensus of the day. Ultimately the Fabians have been no more successful than the ILP in supplying an intellectually coherent alternative form of socialism to Marxism.

State socialism and alternatives to state socialism

The ideology of the Labour Party was the product, then, of four main influences: radical liberalism, trade unionism, Fabianism and ethical socialism (associated initially largely with the ILP). In terms of sheer numbers, organisational strength and financial support trade unionism was by far the most significant of these contributory elements. Yet, as has been noticed, on wider political issues the trade union wing of the labour movement was generally content to defer to the leadership of the parliamentary party, and at this level other influences predominated. Thus the dominant figures in Labour's early history, Keir Hardie, its first leader, Ramsay MacDonald, its first Prime Minister and Philip Snowden, its first Chancellor of the Exchequer, all came up via the ILP, although Hardie and MacDonald had also been members of the Fabians, whose influence reached a peak after 1918, when Sidney Webb helped to write the new party constitution, and joined the Labour governments of 1924 and 1929–31. Nor should the influence of radical liberalism be underestimated. MacDonald's early links with liberalism through the 'Rainbow Circle' were reinforced by his association with anti-war Liberals after 1914, many of whom subsequently joined Labour, together with other progressive Liberals, despairing of the fortunes of their former party. Significantly, ex-Liberals figured prominently in MacDonald's governments.

It has already been noted that socialists disagree as much over means as ends, and the British Labour Party has attracted perhaps more criticism over its strategy than its values. The circumstances in which the Labour Party was founded involved a clear commitment to electoralism and parliamentarism. It was also implicitly assumed that electoral success would secure real power, and effective control of the state, enabling progression towards socialism. In contrast with Marxism, syndicalism and anarchism, the socialism of the Labour Party assumed that the state was benign (Barker, 1978, p. 48). Indeed, Labour accepted without question most of the apparatus of the British state. Socialism was to be achieved by acquiring, through the ballot box, control of Westminster and Whitehall, winning and using the power of the state. This implied a centralised state socialism, imposed from the top downwards.

How far there was ever a realistic alternative to this centralised state socialist model is debatable. The roots of early British socialism lay in grassroots working-class self-help. The socialism of Robert

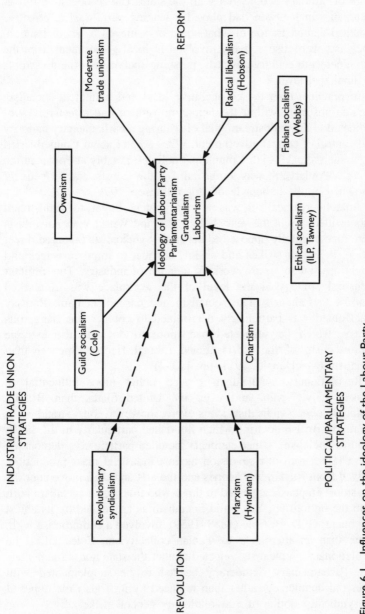

Figure 6.1   Influences on the ideology of the Labour Party

Owen and, later, William Morris, was bound up with the life and work of ordinary people, not with the state. The co-operative movement, in which Owen had played a leading part, was an effective practical demonstration of what could be achieved by mutual action. Socialists were also actively involved in local government from the late nineteenth century onwards, pursuing socialism at the grassroots or municipal level.

In practice, both the co-operative ideal and municipal socialism became absorbed within the labour movement and effectively subordinated to the mainstream goal of securing a parliamentary majority and control of central government. When some Labour Councils tried to pursue radical socialist municipal policies, notably at Poplar in the 1920s, 'Poplarism' was outlawed by the courts and effectively disowned by the Labour leadership (Branson, 1979).

Anarcho-syndicalism was a more potent threat to mainstream Labour ideology in the years before the First World War. Anarchists were fundamentally opposed to the state. Syndicalists favoured direct action, including strikes and sit-ins, not just to improve wages and conditions but to secure workers' control of industry. This militant industrial strategy at the level of the workplace was in marked contrast to Labour's state socialism and parliamentarism. Ramsay MacDonald was particularly determined to counter this dangerous heresy, which he suggested had more to do with the extreme libertarianism of the old-fashioned Liberal Herbert Spencer than socialism (MacDonald, 1911, pp. 123–4).

Revolutionary syndicalism proved rather more influential in France, Italy, Spain, and even the United States than Britain. Watered-down syndicalist ideas were, however, one strand in a peculiarly British doctrine which flourished particularly in the 1920s – Guild Socialism. Other elements included participative democracy and a rather romantic revulsion against industrial mass production, derived from Ruskin and Morris and the arts and craft movement. Its grassroots emphasis appealed to those who favoured a socialism built from the bottom up. Yet Guild Socialism as articulated by its ablest proponent, G. D. H. Cole (1889–1959), involved a compromise with, rather than an alternative to, Fabian collectivism. Cole, unlike the revolutionary syndicalists, rejected neither the state nor parliamentarism. Parliamentary democracy needed to be supplemented with industrial democracy rather than replaced by it. Thus Cole opposed the syndicalist notion of a revolutionary general strike.

Labour in power? MacDonaldism

One reason why these rival socialist currents of thought ultimately made little headway after the First World War was because of Labour's apparent progress under Ramsay MacDonald. The party's rapid advance in terms of parliamentary representation seemed to confirm the wisdom of the Westminster-centred electoral strategy. Labour overtook the Liberals in 1922 to become the second largest party in Parliament, the official opposition, and alternative government in waiting. Unexpectedly soon, they exchanged opposition for office. In 1924 and again from 1929–31 MacDonald headed minority Labour governments.

Yet it was questionable how far office involved real power, particularly if that was interpreted in terms of the ability to secure a socialist transformation of the British economy and society. Of course, Labour was constrained by the lack of an overall parliamentary majority, and this alone ruled out radical socialist reforms. Yet there were few signs of radical intentions. MacDonald and his colleagues were keen to reassure the political establishment of their moderation. They were firmly committed to a gradualist, one-step-at-a-time approach. Their socialism remained an article of faith, but it was a distant aspiration. For the present they had to operate the existing capitalist system by tried and trusted methods.

It was Labour's misfortune to be in office from 1929 when the whole western economic system was in the grip of a mounting crisis, in which such tried and trusted methods proved lacking. From a Labour perspective the crisis was a crisis of capitalism. Theoretically the remedy was socialism, but there was no mandate for socialism, and in any case the time scale implicit in a long-term gradualist transition to socialism rendered it irrelevant as an immediate response to the crisis. Thus the Labour government was helpless in the face of rising unemployment and a growing financial crisis, and in August 1931 finally broke up in disagreement over the spending cuts demanded by business and finance (Skidelsky, 1967; Marquand, 1977).

To the consternation of his party, MacDonald then agreed to stay on as Prime Minister to head a (largely Conservative) national government. On the left this outcome was variously interpreted as the consequence of long-premeditated treachery by MacDonald, a palace plot, and a banker's ramp. Labour's whole parliamentary strategy

appeared to be in ruins. The party was decimated at the ensuing
General Election.

For some socialists 1931 confirmed Communist criticism of
Labour and parliamentarism, and led to a revival of interest in the
Soviet route to socialism, ironically at a time when the Stalinist
tyranny was at its worst, culminating in purges and show trials.
Others, like the majority of the ILP, rejected both communism and
Labour's gradualist parliamentarism, seeking an alternative 'revolu-
tionary' route to socialism, which was never too well defined (Brock-
way, 1977).

Yet such defections ultimately had little impact on the Labour
movement, for whom MacDonald and his associates were convenient
scapegoats. Thus MacDonald's treachery only demonstrated to his
embittered former supporters that he had never really been a socialist.
In truth MacDonald's ideas were only too typical of the socialism of
the Labour Party, which combined the cautious rational pragmatism
of the Fabians and the millennial socialism of the early ILP. The
Labour split in 1931 was not essentially ideological. The divisions in
the Labour Cabinet were over details rather than questions of philosophy and broad strategy. Purged of MacDonald and his associates,
the new party leadership remained committed to his version of
socialism and his gradualist parliamentary strategy – 'MacDonaldism
without MacDonald' as Miliband (1972) described it.

Labour in power – the Attlee government

The Second World War and Labour's role in the coalition government from 1940–5 helped to revive the party's fortunes, and rendered
socialist ideas more acceptable. The war involved state planning of
output, partly presided over by Labour politicians. Alliance with the
Soviet Union also helped to make central planning more fashionable.
Moreover, war both accustomed people to high levels of state activity
and state spending and taught them to look to the state to meet
peacetime needs. Thus hopes for post-war reconstruction and social
reform assumed a large measure of state direction and control. All
this was highly consistent with the ideas of the Labour Party, which
was thus well placed to realise public hopes and expectations after
1945, when it won a landslide electoral victory and, for the first time,
a substantial parliamentary majority.

Herbert Morrison's identification of socialism with the work of the Labour government has a grain of truth if applied specifically to the socialism of the Labour Party. Both at the time and for a generation afterwards it was the record of the 1945–51 Attlee government which seemed to embody what the Labour Party meant by socialism. Labour's performance in office gives a clear indication of how leading Labour politicians interpreted socialism – both what it was and what it was not.

Labour's continuing commitment to a reformist parliamentary strategy rather than the alternative Soviet approach was clear from its foreign policy, in which it showed strong support for NATO and the American alliance in the developing Cold War with the Communist world. It was indeed foreign policy which provoked early left-wing disquiet with the Attlee government, and which was a major factor in the subsequent Bevanite split in the 1950s.

However, socialism is essentially about domestic economic and social policy rather than foreign policy. There were four principal planks to the Attlee government's domestic policy: the establishment of a welfare state, nationalisation of key industries to promote a mixed economy, Keynesian economic planning and the promotion of industrial harmony through partnership with the trade unions. Taken together, they provided the basis of a post-war settlement and a new political consensus which was to last into the 1970s. Yet while all of these planks involved state intervention and interference with market forces they involved not the replacement of the capitalist economy by a socialist planned economy, but a modification of capitalism and a qualified acceptance of it.

This was most obviously true of the adoption of Keynesian economic theories, which became a key ingredient of the Labour Party's post-war thought, although Labour politicians such as Bevin and Dalton and a younger generation of Labour thinkers, headed by Evan Durbin, Douglas Jay and Hugh Gaitskell, had advocated the ideas of Keynes rather earlier (Foote, 1986). Acceptance of Keynesian economic theory was thoroughly consistent with Labour's gradualist state socialism. Keynes himself was a committed Liberal, never a socialist. Although critical of many aspects of capitalism, he was in the last resort and essentially a defender of the capitalist system. Keynesian macro-economic planning involved governments attempting to influence aggregate demand through fiscal and monetary policy. In so far as this was successful it apparently removed the

necessity for Government intervention at the micro level, to determine the output of particular industries. Keynesianism appealed to
Labour as it involved planning of a sort. Moreover, for a long time it
successfully delivered full employment, a goal which had eluded
inter-war governments. Yet Keynesian planning was effectively a
substitute for, rather than a step towards, full socialist planning as it
had previously been understood.

The establishment of a welfare state providing a system of social
security 'from the cradle to the grave' drew rather more on socialist
values, but it built on reforms achieved by Liberals and Conservatives
and on proposals developed under the wartime coalition government.
The new system of national insurance in particular derived from the
1942 report of William Beveridge, a life-long Liberal whose commitment to individual responsibility was embodied in the insurance
principle. However, Bevan's National Health Service, funded largely
from taxation and initially free to all users, was rather more socialist
in inspiration.

The further incorporation of trade unions into the political establishment was facilitated by a Labour government with strong organisational links with the trade union movement. Yet this was a process
which had been begun as early as the First World War (Middlemas,
1979), and had been promoted by Churchill's coalition government.
Whether the arrival of trade union leaders like Ernie Bevin into the
heart of government heralded a socialist revolution is, however, to be
doubted. It involved, rather, the high point of a trade unionist or
labourist ideology. The trade union movement and individual trade
union leaders acquired power and influence on the tacit understanding
that this would be exercised moderately, in the national interest. Thus
trade unions co-operated in wage restraint policies, as they were to do
again in the 1960s and 1970s.

The Labour government's nationalisation policies derived more
obviously from socialist inspiration, and specifically from Clause 4 of
the Party's constitution with its celebrated commitment to the 'common ownership of the means of production, distribution and ex-
change'. Even so, pragmatic rather than ideological arguments were
advanced for the nationalisation of specific industries. More to the
point, the government made clear that its nationalisation programme
was in effect limited to the 'commanding heights' of the economy –
mainly the fuel and transport industries. Finally, and most significantly to syndicalists, under the guidance of Herbert Morrison

nationalisation took the form of wholly state-owned public corporations, run by appointed managers rather than the workers. Critics
described it as state capitalism rather than socialism. While a significant section of the economy was now publicly owned, giving
added credence to the notion of a mixed rather than a capitalist
economy, such critics argued that it was still run in the interests of
capital rather than labour.

Yet, despite such sniping from the left, the package of policies
pursued by Labour retained a large measure of public support,
demonstrating that Labour's version of socialism was compatible
with parliamentary democracy. The achievement was also fairly
durable, lasting substantially for a generation. To that extent the old
Fabian belief in permeation did not prove so wide of the mark.
Labour's values were effectively incorporated into a cross-party
consensus, variously described, but sometimes called social democratic.

Even so, the Attlee government's very success left an awkward
legacy for the Labour Party. From the perspective of the leadership,
Labour's programme was essentially completed by the 1945–51
government. It was not the first instalment of a socialist transformation of Britain's economy and society, but the culmination and final
end-product of that mixture of radical liberalism, trade unionism and
fabianism which was the essence of British socialism. Attlee, Bevin
and Morrison had fulfilled their strictly limited socialist revolution,
leaving their successors with little more to do than defend that
achievement.

A problem which only became apparent later was the extent to
which the Attlee government's socialist achievement rested on its
least socialist element, Keynesian economic theory. The apparent
breakdown of Keynesian analysis and prescription in the 1970s not
only challenged much of Labour's case for government economic
intervention and a mixed economy, but also undermined the viability
of the Welfare State.

Revisionism, pragmatism and fundamentalism

Theoretical justification for Labour's policies lagged somewhat
behind practice. Although several Labour politicians and thinkers
such as Morrison himself, Dalton, and from a younger generation

Evan Durbin and Douglas Jay contributed to the evolution of Labour
ideas in the 1930s and 1940s (Foote, 1986, ch. 9), it was only after
Labour was once more in opposition from 1951 that a comprehensive
attempt was made to update the party's ideology to bring it more in
line with what a Labour government had actually tried to do. The
most significant contribution to this reappraisal was Tony Crosland's
The Future of Socialism (1956).

The Future of Socialism sharpened, although it did not inaugurate,
a developing ideological schism within the Labour Party between a
revisionist socialism (or social democracy) and what might be characterised as fundamentalist socialism. The schism effectively began
with Bevan's resignation from the Attlee government in 1951 over
the introduction of health service charges, developed into a personalised division between the supporters of Bevan and those of his arch
rival of the right, Hugh Gaitskell, and survived the deaths of both the
leading protagonists to become a long-running and deep-seated
struggle between left and right factions for the soul of the party from
the 1960s through to the 1980s.

'Revisionism' is a term widely employed, especially by Marxists,
to describe efforts to update, moderate or water down socialism. Yet
it is not a wholly suitable term to describe the updating of a party
ideology which had never been revolutionary. Moreover, if Crosland
was a revisionist he was clearly not revising or rejecting the work of
the Attlee government. On the contrary, his attempt to redefine
socialism could almost be interpreted as a *post hoc* rationalisation
for that government's achievements. Yet Crosland's ideas clearly
had something in common with those of revisionist socialists in
other countries, and to that extent the label 'revisionist' is not
inappropriate.

From a left-wing perspective, Crosland's book involved a rejection
of socialism and an acceptance of a modified capitalism. Crosland, by
contrast, believed he was redefining rather than abandoning socialism. Capitalism in its old nineteenth-century sense no longer existed,
he argued. It had been transformed out of all recognition by progressive taxation, welfare reforms and state enterprise, but above all
by the divorce of ownership from effective control of industry. Thus
the ownership of the means of production was no longer critical.
What was required was professional management, coupled with
effective influence and control in the public interest. This was
compatible with various forms of ownership – Crosland's own

preference was for a pluralistic diversity of forms, a genuinely mixed economy. Socialism was essentially not about the ownership of industry but about the pursuit of equality, through universal social benefits, progressive taxation and the redistribution of the product of economic growth.

Although this revisionist socialism was substantially compatible with Labour's past record in office, it was rather less compatible with the party's explicit commitment to common ownership in Clause 4 of its constitution which implied a more fundamentalist socialism. Modernisers believed that this commitment to common ownership or nationalisation alienated voters, so that after Labour lost its third successive General Election in 1959 the party leader, Hugh Gaitskell, embarked on a campaign to drop Clause 4 as part of a process of updating the party's message and appeal. Also canvassed was a loosening of the party's trade union links and even a change of the party name, which indicates that Gaitskellism involved something other than old-style labourism (Jenkins, 1991).

Gaitskell's attempt to change the party failed. Yet his old supporters continued to act as a faction within the party through to the 1980s, when some of them broke away to form the Social Democratic Party (SDP). Retrospectively it could be said that they always stood for social democracy rather than socialism within the Labour Party, although Crosland for one continued to proclaim his socialism until his death in 1977.

The left was fighting an essentially defensive battle initially which did not involve any elaborate ideological reformulation, although it subsequently gained some inspiration from a variety of sources, including the academic Marxist New Left, and various radical social movements – most notably the peace movement and the women's movement. In the 1970s the left renewed its attempt to commit the party, in line with Clause 4, to an extensive further programme of nationalisation, including the banking and building industries. An influential attempt to provide an updated intellectual foundation for the Labour left's programme was provided in Stuart Holland's *The Socialist Challenge* (1975).

The most bitter conflicts between the Labour left and right were not, however, ostensibly over rival interpretations of socialism, but over party organisation, and over defence and foreign policy issues. Disputes over party organisation did reflect different assumptions over party democracy, but ultimately were about means rather than ends – essentially the power to control the party agenda and leadership. Bitter divisions over nuclear disarmament in part stemmed from a strong moralistic and quasi-pacifist tradition which Labour inherited from the Liberals, although behind the issue of the bomb were also differences over the western alliance which reflected contrasting assumptions about the objectives of the superpowers, the United States and the Soviet Union. Yet the most bitter issue dividing left and right in the 1970s and early 1980s was the European Community. It was not initially so, when supporters and opponents of EC membership could be found on both wings of the party. Subsequently, Europe became the crucial test of allegiance, with the social democratic right championing membership and the socialist left demanding withdrawal.

Between the left and right were those who sought balance and compromise in the interests of party unity. All major parties involve coalitions of different interests and tendencies, with inevitable tensions within them. As a 'broad church', the Labour movement has always contained a range of interests and tendencies, including social reformers, both moderate and militant trade unionists, and various kinds of socialists. Moreover, Labour could only achieve power in Britain's parliamentary system if it could retain the commitment of both its socialist left and reformist right. Arguably, the preservation of some ambiguity over ultimate values and objectives was necessary to keep different factions happy. Thus Labour leaders Wilson, Callaghan, and in the last analysis, Foot, all tried to preserve a pragmatic balance between left and right.

Critics argued that Harold Wilson, in his 1964–70 and 1974–6 Labour governments, was more concerned with day-to-day party management and presentation than longer term socialist objectives. Wilson's death in 1995 assisted a more positive reappraisal, already under way, of the achievements of his governments, which secured a significant expansion in educational opportunities, and presided over modest progress towards a more equal and tolerant society (Pimlott, 1992). Even so they did little to advance or further define British socialism, involving essentially an increasingly desperate defence of the consensus largely established by the Attlee government – a defence made more difficult by the breakdown of the Keynesian assumptions on which that consensus substantially rested. Thus once more economics was Labour's 'Achilles' heel'.

Democratic socialism and social democracy

Although the tension between the contrasting ideological projects of
the Labour left and right had always been a source of tension and
sometimes open conflict it was only in the 1980s that a substantial
breakaway threatened to destroy Labour's fragile unity. The breach
was prefaced and apparently provoked by a swing to the left within
Labour. This was symbolised by the election of the old Bevanite and
unilateralist, Michael Foot, as leader, but also involved changes to the
party's constitution, including the introduction of an electoral college
for future leadership elections and mandatory reselection procedures
for sitting MPs, and a policy commitment to withdraw Britain from
the EEC (Kogan and Kogan, 1982). Four former Labour Cabinet
ministers, Roy Jenkins, Shirley Williams, Bill Rodgers and David
Owen, then set up a new party, the Social Democratic Party (SDP),
which was soon joined by another two dozen Labour MPs (Bradley,
1981; Stephenson, 1982; Jenkins, 1991).

The split naturally entailed some redefinition of ideological position both among those who broke away from the Labour Party and
those who remained. 'Social democrat' had for some time been a
convenient label for describing reformist or revisionist socialists,
although ironically it had once been the preferred name for revolutionary Marxists. 'Democratic socialism' became an umbrella term
for the Labour left. Such semantic nuances came to loom large.

A common accusation against the SDP was that they were attempting to construct not an essentially new party, but a Mark II Labour
Party. Indeed, they claimed to be the true heirs of Attlee and
Gaitskell, and adopted the name of the Labour thinker, Tawney, to
describe their newly created rival to the Fabian Society. Their leaders
alleged that they had not left the Labour Party, but that the Labour
Party had left them, implying a marked ideological shift to the left by
Labour. The SDP programme involved, critics alleged, a new yesterday – support for the EEC and NATO, modified Keynesianism, the
Welfare State and incomes policy. The only essentially new policy
proposal was constitutional reform, particularly electoral reform, a
commitment which owed much to their new allies, the Liberals.
Although there was a considerable intellectual ferment, including a
spate of new books by prominent social democrats defining and
redefining their ideological position, the only potentially important

new idea was the social market (Williams, 1981; Owen, 1981; Marquand, 1988).

The SDP failed to make good their claim to old mainstream Attlee-type socialism, as most Labour 'moderates' in Parliament, and the vast bulk of Labour councillors, active members and trade unionists declined to join them. The new members they attracted were largely 'political virgins' – not previously closely identified with any old political party, and indeed enthusiastic about a wholly new party with a new style and approach. Yet the SDP leaders' preoccupation with past battles within the Labour Party bedevilled any project to establish a new party with a new philosophy and programme. As a result of their failure either to capture the 'moderate' Labour faction or to forge a new political ideology, the SDP was eventually obliged to choose between submerging their identity within the Liberals, or political extinction.

New Labour?

The left's apparent triumph within the Labour Party, which had provoked the SDP breakaway, proved short-lived (Seyd, 1987). There has been some subsequent debate as to whether the formation of the SDP assisted or delayed the return of the Labour Party to 'moderate' consensus politics (Healey, 1989; Jenkins, 1991; Hattersley, 1995). The point is somewhat academic. It seems clear that a more potent influence on Labour has been Mrs Thatcher's brand of conservatism. Four successive Conservative Party election victories from 1979 have altered the political landscape and compelled some rethinking of Labour's philosophy and commitments. The party could no longer simply defend the Attlee inheritance. They could seek to restore it, or jettison parts no longer considered relevant, or forge new policy proposals. Preservation of the status quo was no longer an option. Realisation of this compelled not only an extensive policy review, but some ideological reassessment, beginning under the leadership of Kinnock after the 1987 election, and continued by first Smith and then Blair (Shaw, 1994).

Thus Labour has now abandoned virtually all the commitments which led to the establishment of the SDP. The 1983 manifesto commitment to withdraw from the European Community was among the first casualties of this new realism. Since then Labour has become positively enthusiastic about Europe. Following the 1987 defeat, the commitment to nuclear disarmament, with which Kinnock had been closely associated, was quietly abandoned. After the more unexpected 1992 defeat, Labour has sought to avoid any commitment to raise spending and taxation. More fundamental to the party's ideology has been a rethinking of the relationship with the trade unions, and, most significant of all, a rewriting of Clause 4 of the party constitution.

While the importance of the union link has been reaffirmed, in practice the Labour leadership has increasingly distanced itself from the unions. It is now clear that the bulk of the Conservative union reforms will not be reversed. Moreover, organisational reforms, including the end (in theory at least) of the block vote, and a reduction in the weighting of trade union votes at Labour Conferences are likely to reduce union influence over party policy.

This accentuates a trend away from Labour's past identification with trade unions and the manual working class which has been under way for over half a century. Thus most of the parliamentary party and even the bulk of constituency activists have long ceased to be of the working class (Hindess, 1971). Secondly, and partly perhaps reflecting these social changes within the party, the policies pursued by Labour have not always appeared to benefit the working class. For example, the expansion of higher education in particular can be interpreted as an enormous boon to the middle class paid for out of the taxes of the community as a whole, including increasingly the working class. Moreover, in recent years Labour has been represented as more interested in promoting equal opportunities for women, blacks or gays, than defending the interests of their traditional working-class clientele. Such perceptions may be exaggerated, but underline the extent to which the Labour Party is no longer automatically seen by many white, and predominantly male, manual workers as 'their' party.

Moreover, the manual working class is itself relatively smaller, and more divided – for example, between public and private sector employees, between council tenants and owner-occupiers, and on gender and ethnic grounds. Some workers have become relatively affluent consumers and property owners, while others have lost jobs and seen their living standards eroded. Such changes have weakened working-class solidarity. As the working class appears less homogeneous it is not surprising that there is less of a common working class culture.

Thus the Labour Party needs to widen its social base to survive. Labour began as an explicitly class party, with a programme pitched deliberately at the working class, although of course it always enjoyed some middle-class support and active involvement. The reduction in size and the fragmentation of the old manual working class means that Labour has to broaden its appeal. This suggests the need for some ideological revision, away from labourism. The implications for socialism are unclear.

'New Labour' is in one sense little more than a rhetorical flourish or a marketing ploy. It is not a new party. Even the most controversial changes – the rewriting of Clause 4 and the reform of the union link – are more to do with presentation than substance. Labour was never really committed to wholesale public ownership, and the unions have never really exercised the power over the parliamentary party which the constitution apparently gave them. Thus the reforms are more to do with the abandonment of what are perceived as electoral liabilities. Labour's proclaimed ideology has been adjusted to accord more closely with Labour practice.

Two themes associated with the new Labour leadership do require some notice, however – Christian socialism and community. Tony Blair, like his immediate predecessor John Smith, is a practising Christian who derives his socialist convictions from his Christianity, drawing on a long tradition of Christian socialism within the Labour Party which has been less in evidence in recent years. That tradition has involved strengths and weaknesses (see above). While the moral conviction and sincere commitment of Christian socialists have added powerfully to the party's appeal, the implications for analysis and policy prescription are less clear. Moreover, there is an additional problem today which did not exist when Christian socialism was at its most influential, before the First World War. Then Britain was still substantially a Christian country. This is no longer so. Christian imagery no longer has the same resonance for the majority, and may be positively alienating for those attached to other faiths.

Blair has also laid considerable emphasis on the concept of community, which links closely with the socialist values of fraternity, solidarity and co-operation, and contrasts with the extreme individualism associated with the New Right. It also suggests an inclusive concern for all members of the community, rather than the divisive politics of class, which fits comfortably within the mainstream tradition of British socialism, and broadens Labour's electoral appeal.

Finally, it implies a concern with the small scale and a more decentralised, participative approach to socialism, which is useful for a party trying to avoid its past association with bureaucratic centralised state socialism. Communitarianism has become intellectually fashionable on both sides of the Atlantic (Etzioni, 1995), and the manifold positive associations of the term 'community' makes it an appealing addition to the vocabulary of politicians. However, in the hands of both philosophers and politicians it remains imprecise, evoking almost any kind or size of human organisation or association. Its common use as an all-purpose sanitising term, promiscuously available across the political spectrum, renders 'community' a somewhat insubstantial foundation on which to base a remodelled socialist philosophy.

Broadly consistent with both Christian socialism and community is another fashionable term which Blair has more recently proclaimed – the stakeholder economy. The immediate media interpretation was that this was New Labour's big idea, to counter the free market ideology of Thatcherite Conservatism. Conservative critics denounce 'stakeholding' as a code for a return to corporatism, trade union power, and traditional socialism. By contrast some of the left saw it as a further indication of an accommodation with capitalism and a betrayal of traditional socialist ideas. To some a 'stakeholder economy' sounded too similar to the Conservative slogan 'shareholder economy'. Others confessed to total mystification. A key text which provided some of the inspiration for Blair's adoption of 'stakeholding' was a surprise best seller of 1995, Will Hutton's book *The State We're In*. Hutton himself was quick to welcome Blair's endorsement, and spell out some of the implications (e.g. *Guardian* 17/1/96 and 22/1/96). At one level, attention was drawn to several established 'stakeholder companies' in the United Kingdom, such as British Telecom. At another level British capitalism was compared unfavourably with that in Japan and countries in western Europe, where economic activity was not dominated exclusively by pursuit of short-term profits. However, it remains to be seen whether 'stakeholding' will prove to be just another ephemeral fashionable term in political debate, or whether it can be fleshed out to provide a coherent ideological foundation for New Labour's programme.

British socialism and the wider world

It was noted at the outset of this chapter that although socialism is an overtly international ideology, British socialism is peculiarly insular. The ideology of the Labour Party can only really be understood by reference to key formative events and dates: 1900, 1918, 1926, 1931, 1945. Its internal debates were influenced by British politicians and thinkers.

Yet inevitably the wider world has impinged considerably on Labour's development – the politics of empire, two world wars, the inter-war slump and post-war boom, the Cold War, European integration, decolonisation and the rise of the third world. The tacit assumption that it is possible to build a kind of socialism in one country has been undermined by the increasing significance of multinational corporations and the communications revolution which have assisted globalisation.

However, the external development with the most profound and far-reaching implications for British socialism was perhaps the collapse of Soviet communism, even though it was acknowledged on both sides that the ideology of the Labour Party had nothing to do with Bolshevism or Soviet communism. British Labour politicians were loud in their denunciations of Moscow, and Moscow repaid the compliment by describing Labour as at best bourgeois revisionists and at worst social fascists. Thus the collapse of communism would seem only to justify and strengthen the alternative western parliamentary approach to socialism.

Yet it has not worked out quite like that. Whatever its deficiencies in the eyes of western socialists, Soviet communism represented an apparently flourishing alternative to western capitalism – living proof that it was possible to organise an economy on different lines (Hobsbawm, 1994b). Its collapse has removed the alternative, and the constant threat it presented to capitalism. Socialism everywhere has suffered a psychological defeat, while a triumphalist capitalism no longer feels obliged to make concessions to the interests of labour. The events of 1989 confirmed the supremacy of the free market and discredited planning.

Yet while socialists are now operating in a 'sceptical age' (R. Miliband, 1994), Dahrendorf's assumption (1990) that socialism in all its variants is dead seems at least premature, although much depends on how socialism is defined. If it is perceived essentially as the ideology of the underdog, socialism of some sort will persist as long as there are poor, underprivileged and oppressed people. If it is interpreted in terms of public ownership its prospects are more doubtful, although the case for more effective social control of the means of life and work is already being reasserted. If it is understood more loosely to involve state intervention and a degree of planning, this seems inevitable. A paradox of the New Right has been its apparent inability to diminish the state it abhors. Even privatisation has not allowed the state to withdraw from the relevant policy areas. Yet the extent of state intervention in Britain under Thatcher and Major should make socialists more wary of any automatic equation between state intervention and socialism.

What is questionable is the notion of socialism in one country, whether pursued by Stalinists, Maoists, or insular-minded Labour politicians. It is now much more difficult to immunise a whole society from global economic, cultural and political pressures. Capitalism is global and socialists must perforce think globally. In theory socialism has always been international, its concern the human race. In practice socialists, and British socialists perhaps especially, have often been insular and even chauvinist. To survive in the modern world socialism has to become what it has always professed to be – international.

Guide to further reading

Some suggestions for further reading on socialism in general are included at the end of the next chapter. Here the emphasis is on British socialism. A good starting-point is Bernard Crick's (1987) useful, if idiosyncratic, brief introduction to socialism which includes some short extracts from British texts. Anthony Wright (1983) has introduced and edited a one-volume reader on British socialism. Those wishing to sample British socialist thinkers further will find it relatively easy to obtain writings by Robert Owen, William Morris, R. H. Tawney, C. A. R. Crosland, and others mentioned in the text. Two recent commentaries on the development of British socialist thought can be recommended, Geoffrey Foote (1986) and John Callaghan (1990).

From the massive literature on specific aspects and periods the following are worth a mention (in rough order of subject matter):

E. P. Thompson's (1980) classic but controversial account of the rise of the English working class in the early nineteenth century, S. Pierson (1973) on Marxism and British socialism, H. Pelling (1965) on the early history of the Labour Party, R. Miliband (1972) on parliamentary socialism, J. Saville (1988) on labourism, C. A. R. Crosland (1956) for his key revisionist text, L. Minkin (1991) on the labour–trade union link, P. Seyd (1987) on the rise and fall of the left, E. Shaw (1994) on developments in the Labour Party since 1979, D. Miliband (1994) for a wide-ranging selection of essays on issues facing the modern left and R. Miliband (1994) for his final testament, published posthumously.

7
THE FAR LEFT AND THE FAR RIGHT

Introduction

So far this book has concentrated on what might be regarded as
mainstream political ideologies which have attracted sufficient support in Britain to influence government and public policy. This
chapter is concerned with political creeds such as communism,
anarchism and fascism which in Britain at least have only secured a
minority following, with a generally negligible impact on policy.
Outside the prevailing consensus, they are widely perceived as
extremist ideologies – out on the political fringe of the far left and the
far right. However, it should be noted that the term 'extremism' like
'moderation' are relative terms, and they tend to reflect the perspective of those using them. Moreover, while all of the creeds
discussed in this chapter are associated with the British political
fringe, they have in other countries at various times been influential
or dominant ideologies.

A conventional left–right political spectrum places communists,
Trotskyists, and perhaps anarchists on the extreme left, and fascists
on the extreme right at opposite ends of the political spectrum. The
seating in a continental legislature would serve to emphasise
the point, with communists and their allies on the far left, beyond the
socialists, and fascists or neo-fascists on the far right, beyond
conservatives. Their proximity both on the conventional political
spectrum and in actual party seating arrangements suggests some

affinity between communists and socialists on the one hand, and between fascists and traditional nationalists or conservatives on the other. This has sometimes been borne out in practice on the European continent, with examples of 'popular front' left-wing coalition governments containing communists and socialists, and parliamentary alliances between fascists and the traditional right which helped bring both Mussolini and Hitler to power.

In Britain the relative insignificance of communists and fascists in parliamentary terms at least has ruled out the need for any formal collaboration; rather, the relationship has involved allegations of penetration and hidden influence. In this fashion, the Communist Party and various Trotskyist groups have from time to time sought to join or infiltrate the Labour Party, which in turn has had to counter a series of 'red scares' launched by its opponents which have tried to associate Labour with communism. Fascist attempts to infiltrate the Conservatives have apparently been less systematic and less successful, although a number of individual members of extreme right groups have later been active in the party.

Yet there is a view that the far left and the far right have more affinity with each other than those who are apparently closer on the political spectrum. This is a view articulated in its most sophisticated form in the theory of totalitarianism, which was particularly fashionable in America at the height of the cold war. Fascism and communism were seen as opposite sides of the same coin. Both were ideologies which required the total subordination of the individual to the state, where no independent organisations such as churches, unions, or other political parties were allowed to operate freely. The implied contrast was with pluralism, involving a diversity of associations freely interacting. The theory of totalitarianism was developed by Popper (1962), Talmon (1960) and Arendt (1967). Although it was held to be a peculiarly twentieth-century phenomenon, influences were discerned in the ideas of Plato, Rousseau and Hegel among others. The fiction of Orwell, Huxley and Kafka provided convincing and awful warnings of the nature of totalitarian society.

Yet the notion of totalitarianism is now less intellectually fashionable. There is less confidence in the freedom and individuality fostered by western pluralist democracies, so that the simple contrast between pluralism and totalitarianism is seen in less stark and complacent terms. Ideology, once viewed as the particular preserve of totalitarian systems, is now seen as all-pervasive. There is also a greater appreciation of the differences between Soviet-style communism and fascism. The most obvious and most fundamental distinction is that the fascists, despite their radical rhetoric, did nothing to demolish the capitalist economic system.

However, it is not necessary to swallow the theory of totalitarianism to detect some similarities between the far left and the far right both in general and more specifically in the British context. Both are outsiders, against the political system, and against the prevailing political culture. Both have therefore been seen, not surprisingly, as subversive by mainstream parties which broadly share that prevailing political culture. Both have presented the other as the real enemy, but to a degree both need each other as bogeymen and targets. And in Britain both have exaggerated the significance of the other: communism was widely proclaimed in the 1930s as 'the only alternative to fascism', and the far right routinely blamed 'communist subversion' for Britain's real or imagined ills.

Another interesting similarity in the British context is that both the ideologies of the far left, particularly the orthodox communist variant (Callaghan, 1987, p. 28), and British fascism (Payne in Laqueur, 1979, p. 309), are substantially imported creeds, with little specifically British intellectual contribution. In turn, their 'alien' nature severely reduced their prospects of making serious headway in British politics. In France, for example, both far right and far left could tap into a deep well of popular consciousness: the right into monarchism, Bonapartism, Catholicism and the values and traditions of the army; the left into the revolutions of 1789 and 1848, the Paris Commune of 1870–1, and the values and symbols of republicanism. France was a deeply divided society which was more receptive to sharply polarised political ideologies – to both communism and a variety of fascist or quasi-fascist movements. In Britain it is possible to dispute the nature and extent of political consensus, but the broad apparent agreement on the core institutions and values associated with the political system would seem to make things very difficult for parties and movements outside that political consensus.

The far left

The 'far left' is a convenient umbrella term for describing a number of communist, left-wing socialist, and anarchist groups, which broadly share a commitment to revolutionary rather than evolutionary socialism. It is this which distinguishes the far left, conceptually at least, from mainstream British socialism and labourism. However, the term 'revolution' is variously employed, and different groups on the left have various perceptions of both the nature of revolution, and the manner in which it might be achieved.

In many other western countries, such as France, Italy, Spain and Germany mass communist, revolutionary socialist or anarchist parties were established in the course of the twentieth century. In Britain no such party or movement has come near to achieving comparable success. The Communist Party of Great Britain reached its high watermark in 1945, with the election of two MPs, who both lost their seats in 1950. The Independent Labour Party, after it had disaffiliated from the main Labour Party was still represented by a handful of MPs in 1935 and 1945. Richard Acland's Commonwealth Party secured some brief success in the unusual circumstances of a wartime electoral truce between the major parties. More recently no separate left-wing party has come remotely close to electing a single MP.

The extent to which the relative weakness of the far left in Britain can be simply ascribed to unhelpful circumstances and the prevailing liberal democratic consensus is a question which has already been touched upon. At the same time, the far left has arguably contributed to its own impotence. In the first place, the far left in Britain has long been riddled with internal dissension. Relative insignificance has never seemingly inhibited the far left from indulging in frequent splits, purges, fierce doctrinal disputes and vituperative personality conflicts, which have sapped energies and diverted attention away from more positive work. Secondly, an obsession with Leninist doctrinal orthodoxy, shown not only by the Communist Party, but by some of its various Trotskyist and Maoist rivals, has inhibited the development of a Marxist-based analysis more relevant to British politics and society (Callaghan, 1987). The same doctrinal orthodoxy has also made it more difficult for established left groups to respond to new political currents in British society, such as feminism, environmentalism and black consciousness. Thirdly, despite the participation in the left of a number of colourful personalities, no outstanding British socialist thinker or political leader emerged on the non-Labour left to provide the focus for a mass movement. Significantly, the far left has always had to rely on left Labour politicians, such as Cripps, Bevan and Benn, to provide leadership and inspiration for broad left crusades.

The strategy of far left groups has been born out of impotence, ranging from the pursuit of formal affiliation with the Labour Party, through various forms of informal infiltration or 'entryism', to establishing a totally separate and rival party organisation in competition with Labour. The Communists campaigned intermittently for formal affiliation with Labour, and at times deliberately pursued entryist tactics, while at other periods have eschewed any connection with Labour's 'social fascists' or 'bourgeois reformists'. Trotskyist groups have sometimes worked openly within the Labour Party (International Marxist Group, and until 1965, International Socialists). Sometimes they have sought to infiltrate secretly into the Labour Party (Socialist Labour League, Revolutionary Socialist League and the Militant Tendency). Sometimes they have formally withdrawn from the Labour Party to establish their independence, and perhaps a separate political party (Workers' Revolutionary Party, Socialist Workers' Party). None of these strategies has been attended with any marked success, although Militant infiltration of some Constituency Labour Parties became the subject of some concern within the Labour Party and considerable media hype outside it in the mid-1980s.

Communism

The Communist Party of Great Britain was founded in 1920, and involved a fusion of earlier Marxist groups, such as the British Socialist Party (formerly Hyndman's Social Democratic Federation) and the Socialist Labour Party. There was thus an indigenous strand of Marxism which might have been drawn upon, but in practice the Russian Revolution, and Lenin's interpretation of Marx and Engels, became the paramount influences on the British party (Challinor, 1977). It was Lenin's ideas which became the new orthodoxy – soviets or workers' councils, rather than bourgeois parliamentarism, the leading role of the Communist Party, and 'democratic centralism'. All other approaches to socialism were condemned, their exponents regarded as apologists for capitalism, or even 'social fascists'. The Soviet Communist leadership required total allegiance to the principles of Leninism. Not only were earlier British Marxists virtually forgotten, but other western Marxists were ignored, and the writings of Marx and Engels only known and understood through the prism of orthodox Leninism. It was assumed that the apparently successful

Russian experience could be transplanted to British soil, and little attempt was made to interpret and apply Marxist theory to British or, indeed, western European circumstances. From the foundation of the party through to the 1960s it was considered that the Soviet leadership was almost beyond criticism, and the British Communist leadership loyally followed the Moscow line through every sharp policy reversal on doctrine, on relations with other parties such as Labour, and on foreign affairs.

The almost slavish loyalty to Moscow through the period of the purges and show trials of the 1930s, the Nazi–Soviet pact of 1939 and the post-war Russian domination of eastern Europe coincided with the relatively most successful period of British communism. The financial and political crisis of 1931 seemed to confirm prophecies of the imminent collapse of capitalism, and the impotence and unreliability of Labour. Visitors to the Soviet Union reported enthusiastically on the new civilisation in the making, while reports of the purges were dismissed as exaggerated or discounted as anti-Soviet propaganda. The threat of fascism, and active communist involvement to counter that threat, notably in Spain, led some to conclude that only the communists could be relied upon to oppose the fascist menace. While the Nazi–Soviet pact inevitably led to some disillusionment, this was soon forgotten when Stalin's Russia was invaded by Germany, and instantly became a valued ally.

Thus communism was intellectually fashionable through the 1930s and until the end of the war. It was in this period that membership expanded to a peak of around 64,000 in 1942 (Callaghan, 1987, p. 48). Yet the influence of the party was never just confined to its formal membership. At one level this was the time when a number of young establishment intellectuals were recruited to work as undercover agents for the party, a role which some continued to perform with a remarkable dedication for the rest of their lives. At another level it was in this period also that the party became influential in a number of trade unions, and won some wider sympathy and support within the labour movement. Indeed, Callaghan (1987, p. 45) suggests that in the late 1930s the party preferred to keep potential recruits in the Labour Party to boost prospects for Communist affiliation and left unity campaigns. Such tactics helped reinforce Labour fears of Communist 'fellow travellers' within the party.

Yet the Labour and trade union leadership remained sternly resistant to both this persistent open courtship and undercover infiltration by the Communists, who despite their converts among intellectuals, made little real headway among the British working class. Thus the Communists were a nuisance rather than a serious rival to Labour.

Moreover, despite the impressive intellectual support the Communist Party attracted at this time, its doctrinal orthodoxy ensured that it produced little or nothing in the way of new political thought (Newton, 1969, ch. 2). In fact some of the writers who joined the party seemed to have sought from it not intellectual stimulation, but the kind of certainty and consolation that others have sought from religions, and it is perhaps no accident that some later turned from communism to Christianity.

Therefore, although there was a British Communist Party, there was not, until perhaps more recently, a distinctively British communism. It is true that the party apparently endorsed the parliamentary road to socialism from 1951, but opponents were unimpressed, perhaps rightly in view of the British party leadership's endorsement of the Russian suppression of the Hungarian revolution of 1956, and their reluctance to accept the growing criticism of Stalinism which was beginning to emerge from Moscow itself. Hungary, and disillusion with the Stalinist record did, however, lead to a considerable exodus from the party, and belatedly provoked some reappraisal among those who remained. In 1968, in sharp contrast with the earlier reaction to the invasion of Hungary, the Soviet invasion of Czechoslovakia was condemned. Following the example of some other western Communist parties, notably the Italians, the Communist Party of Great Britain moved away from their earlier slavish adherence to the Moscow line towards Euro-Communism.

The party's new approach was most clearly exemplified in the pages of the party's journal *Marxism Today*, which under the editorship of Martin Jacques from the late 1970s through the 1980s provided a vehicle for some wide-ranging new analysis and ideas from those inside and outside the party. This did not please some of the hardliners who still controlled the party's daily newspaper, the *Morning Star*, and there were some dark mutterings over the 'designer Marxism' of the monthly journal. Yet increasingly a new realism reigned which involved a recognition of the party's political impotence, and pointed towards a new role as intellectual think-tank for the labour movement. Indeed, the party's openness to new ideas belatedly won it some grudging admiration across the political spectrum. In 1989 the party produced a 'Manifesto for New Times' which considered the implications of the far-reaching changes which had taken place in the British economy and society in the 1980s, and which commanded some respectful interest outside the party's ranks.

The supreme irony is, however, that British communism jettisoned the narrow orthodoxies of Lenin and Stalin, and discovered a rich diversity in Marxist-inspired theory some fifty years too late, on the eve of the decisive repudiation of Soviet-style communism over much of eastern Europe, which for much of the world implied a repudiation of Marxism also. It also meant the end of the subsidies from Moscow which had enabled the Communist Party to support publishing ventures which otherwise might not have been viable. With the Moscow model which had sustained it over most of its history discredited, the Communist Party of Great Britain decided to follow the example of some other former Communist parties and changed its name to the Democratic Left in 1991. It also resolved to concentrate on political debate rather than contesting elections. However, a minority opposed these decisions, and four candidates stood for election under the party's old name in 1992. Yet while it is still not clear whether the formal obituary of the Communist Party can now be written, the ideology which it represented for most of its history seems dead beyond recall.

Trotskyism and revolutionary socialism

By no means all British revolutionary socialists supported the Communist Party. Indeed, some on the far left were bitter critics of the Soviet road to socialism, and others who revered Lenin deplored Stalin. In particular, there were a number of revolutionary socialist groups who derived their inspiration principally from Leon Trotsky (1879–1940).

Trotsky's own early life as a charismatic revolutionary, his major role and independent stature in the Russian revolution, his subsequent quarrel with Stalin, exile and eventual brutal murder by a Stalinist agent, would perhaps have been enough to secure his sanctification by those communist sympathisers who felt that the Russian Revolution had somehow taken a wrong turning. However, Trotsky's own lucid writing, coupled with the brilliant advocacy of his biographer, Isaac

Deutscher (3 volumes, 1954, 1959, 1963), have helped to preserve the Trotsky cult long after his death. Thus Trotsky has continued to provide inspiration for those who have rejected the example of Stalinist and post-Stalinist Russia. In Britain there was not just one, but several distinct brands of Trotskyism, embodied in different groups and parties on the far left.

As Callaghan (1987) points out, however, Trotskyism has generally been as narrow and doctrinaire an ideology as orthodox communism. Trotsky, while repudiating Stalin, endorsed Lenin, who had, before his own death, already effectively established an authoritarian political system which stifled dissent. Hence Trotskyism generally involved the uncritical acceptance of Leninism, and some of the British Trotskyist groups showed a dogmatic doctrinal orthodoxy which rejected any deviation from the true Leninist faith as heresy, although others have followed Trotsky's earlier criticism of 'democratic centralism', supporting more internal party democracy. Trotsky personally was associated with the theory of 'permanent revolution', involving a series of upheavals operating across state boundaries on a global scale, and he rejected Stalin's alternative scenario for 'socialism in one country'.

The most dogmatic of the British strands of Trotskyism was displayed by the various groups dominated by Gerry Healy from the late 1940s through to the 1980s, including particularly the Socialist Labour League (SLL) and the Workers' Revolutionary Party. Any who challenged Healy's own line and his supremacy were expelled in periodic purges. Some success was enjoyed in pursuing entryist tactics towards the Labour Party, but according to Callaghan (1987, p. 80) the SLL was already declining when the ambitious decision to turn it into an independent political party was taken in 1973. Repeated forecasts of the imminent collapse of capitalism were invalidated by events, and the party finally collapsed into division and disarray, amid charges of sexual misbehaviour by its septuagenarian leader which provided a field-day for the popular press.

More intellectually respectable and less exclusive variants of Trotskyism were the International Socialists, who were transformed after 1977 into the Socialist Workers' Party and who put their faith in trade union militancy which was then growing, and the relatively small but influential International Marxist Group. Both had some success in exploiting industrial disputes and single issue campaigns over nuclear disarmament, Vietnam and Northern Ireland, but both, despite their proletarian rhetoric, made relatively little impression on the industrial working class.

The Trotskyist group which achieved the greatest media attention and a degree of notoriety was none of the above, but Ted Grant's Revolutionary Socialist League, and, more particularly, the newspaper *Militant* founded in 1964, which officially had no links with the parent organisation, although the links have been clearly established (Callaghan, 1987, p. 196). Relying on the fiction that there was no organisation behind *Militant* and that it was just a loose network of newspaper promoters and sellers, the Militant Tendency was successful in dominating the Labour Party Young Socialists in the 1980s and also in infiltrating a number of Labour constituency parties, leading to the selection of Militant-backed Labour Party parliamentary candidates, some of whom became MPs, and the virtual takeover of the Liverpool Labour group. Alarm within the Labour Party coupled with adverse media publicity led to the expulsion first of *Militant*'s editorial board, then of members suspected of Militant connections both in Liverpool and elsewhere. After a prolonged struggle the MPs associated with the Tendency were finally deselected, and the last of them lost their seats in 1992.

Doctrinally, the Militant Tendency was dogmatic, narrow, and particularly resistant to new currents of thought on the left. Thus Militant showed little interest in feminism, ethnic minorities, local economic development or decentralisation. To judge from the experience of Militant in power in Liverpool, their approach to office was akin to old-style municipal socialism or labourism, with the emphasis on mass housing, bureaucratically administered, as the main solution to the problem of urban decay.

The future of Trotskyism in any form as a distinct strand of political thinking now seems problematic. International developments, particularly the changes in Russia and eastern Europe, would seem to threaten its viability. Significantly, the repudiation of Stalin and authoritarian dictatorship has not led to a rehabilitation of Trotsky, who, in the context of the democratic movement, seems an irrelevant figure in the east. Logically, this would seem to indicate that Trotskyism as it has been practised since the 1930s has no future in the west either, but Trotskyist groups have been adept in the past in explaining the renewed relevance of their creed in altered circumstances, and in detecting propitious signs of revolutionary potential in superficially unpromising situations. No doubt their intellectual ingenuity will be sufficient to sustain a small but limited following, and replenish defections through new converts. The Socialist Workers' Party in particular continues to survive, and, within the limited context of the far left, thrive.

Anarchism

Anarchists are opposed to all manifestations of the power of the central state, favouring instead the voluntary association of people in decentralised communities. Thus anarchism has always involved a strong individualist and libertarian streak which is at odds with much thinking on the socialist left, and which has proved attractive to some on the right, particularly in the United States, where strands of anarchism have become intellectually fashionable among some free market defenders of capitalism. However, most anarchist thinking has been as hostile to concentrations of economic power as political power, and as opposed to marked inequalities of income and wealth as among socialists and communists. Indeed, anarchism has been widely regarded as part of the socialist movement. It was, for example, the anarchist socialist, Proudhon (1809–65) who replied to his own question 'What is property?' with the celebrated answer 'Property is theft'. Thus most anarchists firmly belong to the left, and indeed the far left.

Anarchism has had a strong popular support following in some countries, most notably in Russia until the Bolshevik Revolution, and Spain before and during the Civil War of 1936–9. However, as one British anarchist has sadly admitted, 'English anarchism has never been anything else than a chorus of voices crying in the wilderness' although the same author adds the qualifying observation 'some of the voices have been remarkable' (Woodcock, 1963, p. 414). Indeed, Britain has contributed markedly to anarchist thinking. William Godwin (1756–1836) is often considered to be the father of anarchism, while prominent British socialists such as Robert Owen and William Morris have sometimes been claimed for anarchism. More recently, writers such as Herbert Read have been avowed anarchists, while others including George Orwell have displayed anarchist sympathies. Yet despite such intellectual advocacy, there has never been a significant anarchist movement in Britain. The most that can be claimed is that anarchist ideas have fed into other movements, such as syndicalism and guild socialism.

One reason for anarchism's lack of popular appeal has perhaps been its association in the public mind with nihilism and violence. The negative images of Conrad's novel *The Secret Agent*, the lurid media portrayal of the sinister 'Peter the Painter' in the seige of Sidney Street, and more recently the activities of the 'angry brigade' in Germany have contributed to a stereotype of the anarchist as a bomb-throwing fanatic. While a few anarchists have indulged in mindless violence, such behaviour is far from typical of anarchism in general. The anarchist ideal involves individuals freely co-operating in harmonious peaceful communities. Some of the leading anarchists have been pacifists, opposed to all forms of violence on principle. Kropotkin (1842–1921), perhaps the greatest of the anarchists, was widely perceived as a gentle, almost saint-like, figure.

Indeed, the objections commonly made to anarchism relate more to practicalities than to ultimate objectives. Critics on the right suggest that anarchists are hopelessly optimistic about the capacity of human beings to live peacefully together without some coercive authority to keep them in order – human beings are simply not good enough for anarchism to be feasible. Critics on the left focus on the deficiencies of anarchist politics. While anarchists abominate power they have no realistic strategy for dealing with the realities of power in existing society. Suspicious of the power inherent in all organisations, anarchists are loathe to organise themselves. Thus anarchists are perceived by some others on the left as escapist utopians.

There is another reason why anarchism has been particularly marginal to British politics. The appeal of anarchism depends on a recognition of the essentially coercive and oppressive nature of the state and political authority. However, the state has not generally been seen as oppressive in British political culture. Where it has been, for example in Northern Ireland, there have been other causes to enlist energies. Across most of the political spectrum the state has been perceived as neutral or benign, which hardly provides fertile soil for an ideology which is fundamentally anti-state.

However, anarchism, although out of the British political mainstream, has not been without influence. Anarchist groups in Britain have contributed to the politics of protest in recent years, combining with others on the left to oppose nuclear weapons, government policy in Northern Ireland and the Poll Tax. Anarchists have also participated in the Green movement, and their ideas have been influential in developing decentralised community-based strategies. At the intellectual level fashionable post-modernist ideas are more compatible with anarchism than mainstream political ideologies. Even so, it seems unlikely that anarchism will ever become a significant political force in Britain.

The far left and the Labour left

It has not been possible in this discussion of the far left to avoid frequent references to the Labour Party, itself an indication of the essential weakness of the non-Labour left. Unlike many socialist parties on the continent, Labour did not split into separate revolutionary and reformist parties in the 1920s, and subsequent defections, such as that of the Independent Labour Party in the 1930s, have only served to show how difficult it is for a non-Labour socialist party to survive in Britain.

Socialists have therefore frequently had to choose between compromising their ideas and aspirations by working within the broad Labour coalition, or preserving their ideological purity in fighting for one of a variety of forlorn prospects outside it. Some have oscillated between these alternatives, depending on the prospects for the left within the Labour Party. At times, such as the early 1960s, 1970s and 1980s, the Labour Party appeared to be moving decisively to the left, and attracted unattached socialists as well as deliberate infiltrators. At other times, for example during the later 1960s and 1970s, some socialists gave up Labour in despair, and joined non-Labour socialist groups and parties, or devoted their energies to single-issue campaigns. The dilemma for socialists is unlikely to be resolved without massive changes to the whole party system and political culture. By the mid-1990s those seeking a left-wing version of socialism could find little grounds for hope within Blair's New Labour, but, as always, no realistic alternative outside it, although in January 1996 Arthur Scargill optimistically launched his own Socialist Labour Party. It remains to be seen whether this latest in a long line of breakaway left-wing parties will prove any more enduring and successful than its predecessors.

For many socialists the question of whether to work inside or outside, through or against, the Labour Party is essentially tactical.

Most of the left strands of thought which can be found outside the Labour Party can also be found inside it. Some of these strands are inconsistent with Labour's general commitment to parliamentarism and constitutionalism, and from time to time the Labour leadership has been sufficiently concerned to mount purges and expulsions. At other times, the party has been content to enlist their energies and turn a blind eye to their heresies. Revolutionary groups themselves have alternated between strategies of undercover infiltration and open competition.

The far right

If there has been little scope for the far left outside the Labour Party, there has arguably been even less scope for the far right outside the Conservative Party. This partly reflects Conservative success in containing potential splits or defections, and partly the familiar, and of course not unconnected point, about the strength of the prevailing political culture, with its commitment to parliamentarism and moderation. As with the Labour Party, there have been periodic howls of anguish from Conservatives at betrayals by the leadership – for example in 1846 over Corn Law repeal, in 1911 over curbing the power of the Lords, in the 1930s over India and in 1956 over the retreat from Suez. But the 'diehards' rarely persisted with their opposition, and in any case, there was nowhere else to go. More significantly, there were few of the conditions which supported far-right movements in other countries. Thus, after the decline of Jacobitism in the eighteenth century, there were no supporters of dispossessed regimes to provide a focus for right-wing opposition – no monarchist party. Nor were there dispossessed aristocrats or great landowners thirsting for revenge against the liberal bourgeoisie, nor a substantial rural peasantry opposed to economic and social change. There was no sizeable professional standing army which might have provided the source and potential muscle for right-wing disaffection. During the nineteenth century and the first half of the twentieth century a degree of complacency about Britain's great power status reduced the scope for the kind of fanatical assertive right-wing nationalism which seems to have been fed in some countries by defeat and humiliation. Even the dismantling of the British empire, although it provoked some anger and dismay on the right, was relatively peaceful, and did not lead to a substantial influx of former settlers, angry and bitter at their dispossession and betrayal, to form the nucleus of a far-right opposition.

Britain never had flourishing right-wing nationalist, legitimist, agrarian, religious, or simply reactionary parties. Cynics might argue that they were hardly needed, as all these tendencies could be contained within the Conservative Party. Although there is perhaps some truth in this, it is also the case that the Conservative Party has only survived and thrived because it has never allowed itself for long to be dominated by a particular right-wing tendency or reactionary faction. Right-wing groups, such as the League of Empire Loyalists in the 1950s and more recently the Monday Club, have operated on the fringes of the party, but have either not sought, or not obtained, substantial popular support. On the other hand, disaffected Conservative politicians such as Enoch Powell have sometimes attracted an extra-parliamentary following, but this has rarely if ever been translated into an organisational form which could challenge the party.

Divisions among Conservatives during the Thatcher period, and more particularly since her fall in 1990, have challenged assumptions concerning the inherent unity and loyalty of the party. Yet the growth of factionalism has at no time threatened a breakaway, either from the left during Mrs Thatcher's long premiership, nor from the right subsequently. There was never any real prospect of the Euro-sceptic rebels who lost the party whip from 1994–5 attempting to form a separate party to compete with the Conservatives. Similarly, Redwood's challenge to Major in 1995 involved a battle for the soul of the party but did not portend separation.

Thus in the absence of other challengers, the only real far-right alternative to conservatism which has been presented to the British electorate over the last fifty years or so has been some brand of fascism or quasi-fascism.

Fascism and the far right

Most European countries between the wars experienced strong fascist or quasi-fascist movements, and in some there have been some distant echoes of fascism in the post-war era. In Britain, fascist and overtly racist political parties have had little impact. Mosley's British Union of Fascists attracted some publicity in the early 1930s, but never posed a serious threat, and was in manifest decline well before the Second World War. In the post-war period, although Mosley himself made spasmodic attempts at a political comeback, it was new parties, such as the National Front and the British National Party, which inherited his constituency, and his appeal, based on a mix of patriotism, racism and violence, but with even less success.

Fascism was always a rather strange amalgam of ideas, and it is perhaps easier to describe what it was against rather than what it was for. Essentially a product of the twentieth century, fascism was a comparative latecomer to the political scene, and thus to a degree involved a reaction against earlier political beliefs and ideologies. Indeed, 'the essential anti-character of its ideology and appeal' (Linz, p. 15, in Lacqueur, 1979) has been widely noted. Fascism certainly can be seen as a reaction against the rationalism, individualism, liberalism, parliamentarism and democracy which constituted the mainstream west European and British political tradition. Other antagonisms implied strange contradictions which were part of the essence of fascism. To an extent it involved a reaction against industrialisation and urbanisation, and the whole modern world. At the same time, fascism was also clearly a product of that same modern world, and fascist leaders proved adroit at exploiting modern methods of communication, using twentieth-century technology to promote traditional symbols and values. Fascist and Nazi government involved the same strange blend of traditional values and modern technology.

Fascism also managed, remarkably, to be both revolutionary and reactionary, anti-bourgeois and anti-communist. One influence was the anti-democratic and anti-Marxist elitism of Pareto and Michels. From the start, fascists were virulently anti-communist, and assisted in strike-breaking, an activity which attracted financial and other support from industrialists, but both fascism and nazism also involved anti-capitalist socialist rhetoric, drawing particularly on anarcho-syndicalist ideas, and it was this apparently revolutionary social programme which appealed to at least a sizeable minority of indus-trial workers in Italy and Germany.

For some, fascism promised a middle way between communism and capitalism – a new economic and social order which would transcend old divisions. Instead of class conflict and dissension it offered unity, order and discipline. There were elements in fascism

which could appeal to the idealism of the young, and those disenchanted with the messy compromises, wheeling and dealing associated with old-style parliamentary politics. Corporatist ideas, as
developed by Mussolini in Italy, were seen as the antithesis of
parliamentarism, party political games and industrial conflict. Yet at
the same time, the other face of fascism, the glorification of physical
force, and the use of violence and intimidation, were present from the
beginning. Other omnipresent features were of course the cult of
leadership, authority and quasi-military organisation, extreme nationalism and racism.

Some commentators have sought to differentiate between fascism
in opposition and fascism in power, between fascism and nazism, and
between fascist movements in different countries and continents.
Even so, there remains a fairly strong family resemblance between all
these various manifestations of fascism. In the case of Britain,
Mussolini's original model was fairly faithfully imitated both by his
various admirers in the 1920s, and by Mosley's British Union of
Fascists in its early years. Later, Nazism, with its greater emphasis
on anti-Semitism and biological racism, became a more potent
influence.

It is difficult to interpret fascist ideology wholly or substantially in
terms of class interests, although some Marxists have interpreted it as
the product and rationalisation of a particular phase of capitalism. In
fact fascism seems to have drawn some support from a wide range of
classes and groups within society – from traditional elite groups, from
the middle classes, from both industrial and agricultural workers, and
from intellectuals. Some interpretations draw on psychology rather
than sociology – for example, fascist sympathies are related to
patterns of upbringing and an 'authoritarian personality'. The notion
seems inherently plausible, and suggests the possibility of relating
other ideologies to personality. Even so, its explanatory potential
appears limited, as it fails to demonstrate why fascism flourished in
some countries and made little impact on others. Political explanations rather than socio-economic or psychological explanations seem
to have most mileage in them. Thus fascism flourished in countries
which suffered military defeat, national humiliation, political instability and recurrent political crises. The relative absence of such factors
in Britain is a partial explanation of the relative weakness of British
fascism.

Fascism in Britain – Oswald Mosley

Nevertheless, interest in, and support for, fascist ideas was far from negligible in Britain in the 1920s and early 1930s. It was the supposedly more positive aspects of Mussolini's fascism – economic progress, corporatism, order and discipline – which aroused some respectful attention in British political circles. The less savoury aspects of his regime (which did not then include anti-Semitism) were played down or ignored. There were, however, some native nationalist and racist groups which responded more enthusiastically to fascism. A British fascist group was established as early as 1923, in direct emulation of Mussolini's example, and this moved from anti-communism and strike-breaking to a full fascist programme by 1930. There were also a number of right-wing anti-communist nationalist groups with quasi-fascist ideas, including the British Empire Union and the National Citizens' Union and some smaller breakaway fascist movements, such as the National Fascisti, and the Imperial Fascist League, the last of which was strongly anti-Semitic (Benewick, 1972, ch. 2; Thurlow, 1987, ch. 3).

It was, however, none of these, but Oswald Mosley's British Union of Fascists, founded in 1932, which came to be seen as the embodiment of British fascism, and either absorbed or rendered irrelevant other groups. Mosley himself had some claims to be regarded as a heavyweight politician and thinker (Skidelsky, 1990), but although he clearly possessed some charisma, his intellectual qualities and originality have perhaps been exaggerated (Leach, 1995, ch. 5). He had begun his career as a Conservative MP. Then, after a brief spell as an independent, he had transferred his allegiance to Labour, going on to become a minister in MacDonald's 1929 Labour government. When his quasi-Keynesian ideas for fighting unemployment were rejected by the government, and then, more narrowly, by the Labour Party, he resigned, and went on to form his own New Party, with some support and wider sympathy from MPs, prominent figures and intellectuals across the political spectrum. Defeat in 1931 in by-elections and the General Election turned Mosley rapidly away from conventional parliamentary politics towards a fascist ideology, closely modelled on Mussolini's example (Benewick, 1972, ch. 7), and the New Party was soon converted into the British Union of Fascists (Benewick, 1972, ch. 3).

In the process Mosley lost most of his early respectable political and intellectual support. Partly perhaps in compensation he increasingly exploited anti-Semitism in poor working-class areas, notably the East End of London (Benewick, 1972, p. 152; Thurlow, 1987, pp. 104ff.). Anti-Semitism was derived more from Nazism than fascism, and rapidly, along with virulent nationalism and violence, became central to Mosley's appeal. This, however, was already fading by the late 1930s, as his movement's models and exemplars appeared increasingly a threat to Britain's interests. After a spell of internment during the war (Thurlow, 1987, ch. 9), Mosley re-emerged to set up a new organisation in 1948, the Union Movement, with a remoulded 'Euro-fascist' ideology (Taylor, 1982, p. 8). He drew some support from the same London East End areas where he had been popular before the war, yet his involvement in British politics became increasingly sporadic. Although he attempted to exploit hostility to immigration in the 1950s and early 1960s, it was new far-right groups with new leaders which then secured some publicity and support for racist programmes.

The far right in modern Britain

The far right in Britain has been as susceptible to splits and bitter personal and doctrinal feuds as the far left. In the post-war period a handful of potential führers, Colin Jordan, John Bean, John Tyndall and Martin Webster, have competed for dominance of a succession of far-right organisations, which have periodically merged, splintered and reassembled. In the 1950s the most prominent group on the far right was the League of Empire Loyalists. From this two virulently racist splinter groups emerged: the White Defence League, led by Jordan, and the National Labour Party, led by John Bean and John Tyndall. These came together to form the British National Party in 1960, which subsequently split in 1962 when Jordan and Tyndall left to form the National Socialist Movement. This soon divided again when the two leaders quarrelled over the woman who briefly became Jordan's wife, and Tyndall with Martin Webster founded the Greater Britain Movement in 1964. In 1967 the British National Party and League of Empire Loyalists merged with some of the fragments of other groups to form the National Front, which soon came under the dominance of Tyndall and Webster. However, in 1980 Tyndall broke with Webster, and left to establish his own New National Front, and in 1982 the British National Party. Of these groups and parties the most important in electoral terms were the National Front in the 1970s, and subsequently the British National Party in the 1980s and 1990s.

Whereas Mosley had openly proclaimed his fascist beliefs, some of the post-war extreme right groups and leaders were more cautious in admitting fascist sympathies. The National Front certainly included supporters and even leading figures whose nationalism and racism did not necessarily extend to a full acceptance of or even acquaintance with fascist or Nazi ideology. But some of its more prominent figures had clear Nazi associations (and Nazism was perhaps now a more significant influence than fascism, in so far as the two creeds can be effectively distinguished). Taylor (1982, p. 77) claims that the National Front ideology corresponded closely with the ideas in Hitler's *Mein Kampf*, and details thirteen common features. He goes on to suggest, however, that the National Front restricted its full fascist or Nazi ideology to an 'inner circle' of 'insiders', while resting its more general populist appeal substantially to the race and immigration issue.

The National Front for a time successfully exploited racial tension and opposition to immigration, achieving some media prominence and even, apparently, electoral support. It secured 16 per cent of the total vote in a parliamentary by-election in West Bromwich in 1973 and comparable support in a handful of local government wards located in areas of high immigration in 1973 and again in 1977. But the fears which such performances aroused proved exaggerated. The Front never managed to elect a single councillor, averaged only 3 per cent per candidate in the fifty or so seats fought in the General Elections of 1974, and received a humiliating 1.3 per cent of the vote when it ambitiously contested over three hundred seats in 1979 (Taylor, 1982). Since then it has appeared a spent force.

The British National Party (BNP) has more recently had some success in profiting from racial tension in parts of the East End of London, Mosley's old stamping-ground, and received some media and public attention when a BNP candidate won a council by-election in the Isle of Dogs. Yet as with the National Front previously, fears of a surge in support for the neo-fascist right proved at least premature, as the BNP failed to make much impact in the subsequent 1995 council elections, and lost its Isle of Dogs seat.

The failure of British fascism to make a bigger impact may be variously explained. Benewick (1972) attributes Mosley's failure largely to the moderation, constitutionalism and parliamentarism of British political culture and tradition. Taylor (1982, pp. 179–80) similarly suggests the failure of the National Front could be attributed to 'resistance of the English to extremism' and an English 'commitment to moderation and democracy'. There is clearly something in this. Liberal democratic institutions and values were far earlier and more firmly established in Britain than in Italy, Germany, Spain, eastern Europe or even France, where fascist ideas had a more ready reception.

Yet perhaps one should not be too complacent about any inherent inconsistency between British political culture and fascism. Fascist movements achieved most support in countries which had suffered military defeat or national humiliation. In some cases fascist ideas flourished only in direct response to occupation and external pressure. A British defeat in 1940 would have produced the same pressures for collaboration, and the same encouragement for fascist and Nazi ideas as occurred in other occupied countries. The opposite happened in Britain. While earlier, fascism had considerable appeal for extreme nationalists, increasingly British patriotism seemed incompatible with fascism and Nazism. Hitler and Mussolini became figures of hatred and derision, and open espousal of Nazi symbols appeared treasonable. The National Front made some headway while it confined itself (in public at least) to exploiting racist and anti-immigrant feelings, but the firm identification of the National Front with nazism – 'The National Front is a Nazi Front' – perhaps helped erode support (Taylor, 1982, p. 138).

Indeed, while Britain has not been receptive to fascism, explicit or implicit racism has been widespread, and given some support by mainstream politicians and parties who have pandered to popular opposition to immigration in general, from the turn of the century onwards, and 'coloured immigration' in particular, after the Second World War. In the latter case, it was the speeches of Enoch Powell in 1968, then a Conservative shadow spokesman, and a former minister and challenger for the party leadership, which helped dramatise the immigration issue, and gave it political respectability (Taylor, 1982, p. 20). It was Mrs Thatcher who appeared to give some legitimacy to hostility to immigration, with her celebrated reference to fears of being 'swamped' (Taylor, 1982, p. 144). One explanation for the decline of the National Front and low levels of support for the BNP is simply that their natural constituency has been eroded by tough anti-immigration government policy and the appeasement of racism (Layton-Henry and Rich, 1986).

A neo-Nazi revival?

If there is now a bigger threat of a neo-Nazi revival it lies in the context of European and indeed global political developments. Explicitly racist and even openly fascist political parties and movements have attracted considerable popular support in France, Germany, Belgium, Italy, Russia and several other states of the former Soviet Union and eastern European Communist bloc. Indeed, the much heralded death of socialism in some countries has been followed not by the triumph of liberal capitalism but by a revival of nationalist conflicts and hatreds which have already plunged parts of Europe into chaos. The core liberal values of pluralism, toleration and individual freedom have been early casualties of a retreat into barbarism. Ideas which had apparently disappeared with the defeat of the Axis powers in 1945 have resurfaced.

Some of the worst manifestations of virulent nationalism can be blamed on specific circumstances in particular countries, such as the former Yugoslavia. Yet there may be a more general and more disturbing explanation of the revival of quasi-fascist or neo-Nazi ideas. Liberal democracy thrived in Europe in the post-war years on the back of relative economic prosperity. Recession, coupled with persistently high unemployment over much of Europe has revived the conditions in which fascism developed and thrived between the wars. Just as economic problems in the inter-war period led to the scape-goating of Jews, so immigrants and minorities became ready targets of blame for more recent economic distress. Moreover, the rapid transformation in the early 1990s of a post-war map of Europe which had remained virtually fixed for nearly half a century, created new minorities with bitter, new or newly revived grievances. In these circumstances the re-emergence in many countries of ideas which are either explicitly fascist or close kin to fascism is less surprising.

This may not mean a revival of the full Nazi ideology. Fascism took different forms in different countries between the wars, and the new political currents over much of Europe will develop in diverse ways according to local circumstances. Yet there are common elements across frontiers recognised by members of far-right movements themselves. Thus the British National Party acknowledge an affinity with the French National Front of Le Pen and with the far-right movements in Germany, the Low Countries, Italy and the United States.

In this context the future prospects for a British fascist or quasi-fascist movement are perhaps less remote than would appear from their past political record. In a political climate which is increasingly European and global, ideas are less constrained by national frontiers. Moreover, these ideas are no longer identified with countries perceived to be hostile to British national interests, which was a major problem for British fascism in the 1930s. Ethnic tensions in the cities, coupled with an English backlash against a possible disintegration of the United Kingdom, intensifying anti-European sentiments, and continuing economic problems could provide an explosive cocktail of ingredients for a far-right movement to exploit.

Guide to further reading

To appreciate some of the contending currents of thought on the British left it is necessary to put them into a broader context. George Lichtheim's *A Short History of Socialism* (1970) provides a helpful overall guide, and David McLellan (1979) is particularly useful on strands of Marxism. Bottomore's *Dictionary of Marxist Thought* (1991) furnishes lucid definitions and explorations of key concepts and thinkers. On the far left in Britain John Callaghan (1987) provides a general guide. On anarchism, George Woodcock (1963) and James Joll (1979) provide good accounts of mainstream left-wing anarchist thought. By contrast, Nozick's *Anarchy, State and Utopia* (1974) has become a cult book for some on the New Right.

On fascism in general M. Kitchen (1976) provides a useful introduction and F. L. Carsten (1967) the best short history. W. Laqueur (1979) has edited a thought-provoking collection of essays which look at some of the principal theoretical issues. On British fascism Richard Thurlow (1987) has written a useful general history of fascism in Britain which takes the story beyond Benewick's earlier study *The Fascist Movement in Britain* (1972). For Mosley, see his own self-justificatory autobiography (1970) and Robert Skidelsky's rather too sympathetic biography (1990, 3rd edn). Walker (1977) provides a good general account of the National Front, and Taylor (1982) is particularly useful on their ideology.

8

NATIONALISM

Introduction

Over the last two centuries, nationalism has been the political creed which has been most widespread and persistent, and inspired the most devotion or fanaticism. Men and women have been prepared to die for their nation, and to kill for it. Nationalism is thus, not surprisingly, a very controversial ideology. It has been condemned for promoting divisiveness and conflict, particularly in its more extreme variants, by those who have preached universalistic forms of liberalism or social-ism. The demise of nationalism has been regularly predicted, and indeed its survival seems incompatible with trends in the modern world towards a global economy and culture on the one hand, and the devolution of power to regions and localities on the other. Yet nationalism continues to confound predictions, and retains its appeal in a variety of circumstances, in the advanced industrial or post-industrial countries of the western world, in some of the most economically backward countries of the third world and, most con-spicuously of all, in the troubled fragments of the former Soviet empire, where nationalism is proving more potent than socialism or neo-liberalism.

Yet while at the level of popular consciousness nationalism is a potent creed with strong implications for political behaviour, it lacks theoretical substance. Nationalist thought is relatively thin. There are nationalist theorists, but they hardly approach the stature of the great liberal or socialist thinkers. Indeed, much nationalist writing is essentially particularist, promoting a specific nationalist case rather than nationalism in general. Thus academic accounts of nationalism tend to concentrate on why and how the ideology developed, rather than on a detailed exploration of nationalist thought. Moreover, while other ideologies, such as feminism or socialism, are often explored by broadly sympathetic academics, commentaries on nationalism generally range from distant critical detachment to downright hostility. Many would perhaps sympathise with the left-wing publisher, Victor Gollancz, who commented, 'Of all the evils I hate I think I hate nationalism most' (V. Gollancz, 1952, quoted in Alter, 1989, p. 27)

Others of course would take a much more positive view of the ideology. Yet whether nationalism is viewed as a beneficent or malevolent doctrine, its continued vitality and evident influence makes it important to analyse and explain. This chapter will seek to explain the essence of the doctrine and some of the surrounding controversy, particularly in terms of the application of the nationalist principle and its subsequent development. One aspect of nationalism which requires explanation is its chameleon character – it has been associated with very different ideas, with liberalism in the early nineteenth century, conservatism subsequently, and in the twentieth century with both racism and fascism on the one hand and anti-colonialism and socialism on the other.

The focus of this book is on British political ideologies. In one sense the analysis of nationalism in its domestic British context is unproblematic, because it is largely expressed in terms of specific national interests. Even so, there are problems in analysing nationalism from a British perspective, in part because of the ambivalence towards national identities of many people in the United Kingdom. These issues are explored in sections on English/British nationalism and on Scottish and Welsh nationalism.

A further section is included on nationalism and the European Union. For all European countries, but perhaps particularly for the United Kingdom, the progress towards closer European integration (and perhaps federalism) has clear implications for national sovereignty. The encouragement given by the European Union to regional devolution poses some threat to established nation-states, and assists peripheral nationalism. Yet although the European Union thus appears to undermine nationalism from above and below, the European ideal raises questions of identity, loyalty and exclusion which are not so far removed from familiar nationalist concerns.

A brief final section looks at the implications of trends such as globalisation, post-industrialisation and post-modernism for the future of sovereign states and for nationalism.

What is nationalism?

Ernest Gellner (1983) succinctly defines nationalism as 'a political principle which holds that the political and the national unit should be congruent'. In other words, nations should form states, and states should consist of nations. So successfully has this doctrine been promulgated over the last two hundred years that the terms 'state' and 'nation' are used almost interchangeably. Thus the United Nations is actually an organisation of states rather than nations, despite its name.

States of some kind are coterminous with recorded history. The notion of a state implies effective power and authority. A common formulation is that a state should have a monopoly of coercive powers within its own borders. In its relations with other states, a sovereign state is fully independent. No other state can interfere with decisions within its own boundaries.

This in turn relates the state to a particular territory. Thus the authority of a state is exercised within a geographical area, which may expand or contract over time, possibly through the fortunes of war or by dynastic alliances.

A nation is more difficult to define. It is essentially a community of people, bound together by some characteristic, real or imagined. Such a characteristic might be a common language. Thus the French or German or Polish nation would be defined substantially in terms of language. Yet it is well known that there are nations, like the Swiss, who are divided into several linguistic groups, while there are others, like the Americans or Australians, who share their language with different nations. Much more rarely, the nation may be defined in terms of some ethnic, racial or tribal group. A common history, culture, or economic life is more often cited as the bond which unites a people into a nation. Yet, in the last resort there are no satisfactory objective criteria – a nation exists where a people feel they constitute a nation. Nations exist in the minds of their members. They are 'imagined communities' (Anderson, 1983).

While states may be founded at a precise moment, nations emerge over time. Nationalist historians may argue that the nation is centuries old, its origins perhaps lying in pre-history, although people may only have become aware that they constituted a nation later. Yet in many cases national consciousness has only developed very recently, in some cases sponsored and assisted by ruling dynasties or states. There is considerable room for argument over when national consciousness developed in countries such as France, Germany or England. Shakespeare's history plays suggest that the educated classes at least had a developed national consciousness by the late sixteenth century.

A nation, like a state, may be associated with a territory. National consciousness may be closely bound up with a particular geographical area or homeland. Yet nations are not of course neatly arranged in self-contained parcels of land. Peoples migrate and intermingle, so that two or more nations may inhabit the same territory. A people who may consider themselves a nation may even be geographically scattered, like the Jews.

Political ideologies have implications for political behaviour. The nationalist ideology suggests that not only is the world naturally divided into nations, but the nation should be a focus of loyalty. For Breuilly (1993, p. 2) a basic assertion of nationalism is that the interests and values of the nation take priority over all other interests and values. The implication is that loyalty to the nation should override all other interests and loyalties: to self, family, tribe, class or religion. Perhaps not all nationalists would agree with such an extreme formulation, but they would generally assume that the nation deserves and requires loyalty and support. This clearly may have implications for obedience to the state, where the state does not consist of the nation. Thus Irish nationalists in Northern Ireland acknowledge no allegiance to the United Kingdom state, while Basque nationalists may similarly reject the Spanish state.

Not everyone would agree that nationalism necessarily has political implications. Some writers distinguish between political and cultural nationalism. The celebrated early German nationalist, Herder, was concerned exclusively with the German language and culture, and not with the state. Moreover, it may be possible to satisfy national sentiment by, for example, giving official status and support to a national language in administration, law, education and the media. Yet where the nation is regarded as the natural focus for pride and loyalty, this almost inevitably has wider political implications, involving at least demands for a measure of autonomy, and more

usually full independence as a sovereign state. Hence the principle of
national self-determination. The nation has a right to constitute itself
as a state. Nations should be states, and states should consist of
nations.

Thus stated the nationalist doctrine has an extensive application,
perhaps a universal application to all humankind. It was argued by
nationalists such as Mazzini that the world (or at least Europe) was
divided naturally into nations, which should each form states. When
this was done the resulting nation-states could coexist in peace and
harmony, freely trading with each other to mutual benefit. Yet many
nationalists have been less concerned, if at all, with nationalism as a
general principle, and have concentrated almost exclusively on particular national grievances and rights. Alleviating these particular
national grievances and asserting particular national rights may have
damaging implications for other nations. Quite simply, national
interests are often perceived to conflict. Such conflict may be regarded as inevitable, and it may even be welcomed. Success in
competition with other nations, in the military, economic, or even the
sporting arena may provide gratifying confirmation of the particular
merit or virtue of the nation, strengthening national loyalty and
pride.

Why nationalism developed

There is a widespread agreement among scholars that, although
nations and national sentiment may be much older, nationalism as an
ideology dates only from the French revolution. Kedourie (1991, p. 1)
baldly declares 'Nationalism is a doctrine invented in Europe at the
beginning of the nineteenth century' and this has been the general
consensus (Hobsbawm, 1990; Gellner, 1983; Breuilly, 1993),
although there is minority view that in certain parts of the world at
least it developed earlier (Kellas, 1991; Smith, 1991).

The French revolution is generally held to have given a particular
stimulus to nationalist ideas. The revolutionaries asserted that supreme power should reside, not in the monarch, but in the people of
France, the French nation. This denied the conventional assumption
that states were the property of their ruling dynasty, and had implications for rulers everywhere. While principally concerned with the
rights and interests of the French people, the revolutionaries did give

some encouragement to the national sentiments of others, such as the Italians and the Poles. Moreover, both in imitation of, and in reaction against, French nationalism, the revolution helped stimulate German, Spanish and Russian nationalism.

Nationalists would argue that nationalist demands developed as the natural and inevitable consequence of peoples becoming conscious of their national identities and loyalties, asserting their right to self-determination, and ultimately securing their aim – a fully independent national state. Others would point out that this implied sequence was not commonly followed. Nation-states might be created, perhaps as a consequence of the successful agitation of a relatively small intellectual elite, and a mass national consciousness created subsequently. Thus the Italian nationalist d'Azeglio (1792–1886) declared after the creation of the Italian state in 1860, 'We have made Italy; now we must make Italians' (quoted in Hobsbawm, 1988, p. 111). Gellner (1983, p. 55) roundly declares, 'It is nationalism which engenders nations, and not the other way around'.

Some critics of nationalism would argue that the spread of nationalism was not the result of national communities becoming conscious of their own common identity but the consequence of a minority of nationalists deliberately disseminating their 'invented' doctrine (Kedourie, 1991). For some socialists it was a creed fostered by dominant classes in society to divert the workers from their common economic interests and class loyalty. Thus nationalism was a kind of false consciousness from which the masses (who 'had no country') needed to be freed before they could perceive their own real interests. Yet neither Kedourie's right-wing perspective nor the mainstream Marxist position can readily explain the extraordinarily tenacious hold nationalist ideas have had among the working classes and indeed all classes.

Perhaps such accounts attribute too much to the persuasive power of nationalist propagandists. Gellner (1983, p. 125) explicitly criticises Kedourie for treating nationalism 'as a contingent, avoidable aberration, accidentally spawned by European thinkers'. Eric Hobsbawm, working within a broadly Marxist theoretical framework, makes a similar point. It is not ideas, like nationalism, which change history. Instead, new ideas are articulated in response to historical change. This is perhaps particularly plausible in the case of nationalism. Indeed, it might be said that if the spread of nationalism was dependent on the quality of nationalist thinking, it would not perhaps have spread very far. Virtually all academic writers on nationalism, whether sympathetic, relatively neutral, or hostile, agree that nationalist theory is thin and nationalist thinkers predominantly second-rate.

Yet it is still necessary to explain why it developed when it did, and spread so fast. In the eighteenth century there were only a few states which might in retrospect be described as nation-states: France, Spain and (with qualifications) Britain. In the course of the nineteenth and twentieth centuries the number of nation-states multiplied rapidly, to the extent that the term 'nation' and 'state' were conflated. Why?

One widely accepted explanation is that nationalism was the consequence of industrial modernisation. Industrialisation required the breakdown of traditional and local restraints on trade, and a mass, fluid and mobile society, and thus provided an impetus for the development of a national economy. It also required, as previous agrarian societies had not, mass education and mass literacy. This and its associated print culture required a standardisation of language, officially recognised and taught, which became the accepted language of administration and commerce to the extent that personal advancement depended on its mastery. Thus the need for industrial modernisation created a national culture in place of the essentially local or regional cultures which predominated earlier. One version of the development of nationalism was that it was essentially the consequence of a revolution in the technology of communication. 'It is the media themselves, the importance of abstract, centralized, standardized, one-to-many communication, which itself automatically engenders the core idea of nationalism' argues Gellner (1983, p. 127).

Compatible with the linking of nationalism with industrial modernisation is a quasi-sociological/psychological explanation which points to the needs of individuals in a modern atomised mass society to find some identity or allegiance to which they can attach themselves, following the breakdown of traditional ties and communities brought about by the development of modern industrial capitalism. Thus nationalism is the consequence, not the cause (as Kedourie implies) of the breakdown of other allegiances.

One implication of identifying the rise of nationalism with a particular phase of historical development is that another phase might see its decline or extinction. Indeed, just as nationalism has been identified with modern industrial society, so it has been suggested that it is incompatible with post-modern, post-industrial global economy and society. This may eventually prove to be the case, but nationalist ideas currently survive and thrive. Perhaps this indicates that ideas, however they originate, can take on a life of their own. Part of the appeal of nationalism possibly lies in its very simplicity. It does not need elaborate formulation or the advocacy of great thinkers. It is easily grasped, and, in terms of personal commitment at least, easily applied. Moreover, its ready acceptance so widely by peoples in very different circumstances suggests that it continues to answer some psychological need in modern humanity.

How nationalism has developed – revolutionary and liberal nationalism

Some political ideologies, notably socialism and liberalism, involve considerable internal tensions and have been subject to extensive evolution or revision. In comparison, nationalism has changed very little. For two centuries the simple core principle of nationalism has been that nations should form states. Even so, the ideas with which nationalism has been associated have changed quite considerably. Indeed, nationalism has a chameleon quality, taking colour from its ideological surroundings. Thus while other political ideologies discussed so far in this book can be readily placed on the conventional left–right political spectrum, nationalism has been promiscuously associated with ideas across the spectrum.

It began as a revolutionary doctrine, posing a profound threat to the prevailing social and political order in Europe in the early nineteenth century. The idea that political authority should derive from the nation was particularly damaging to foreign dynasties or those who ruled over multinational states. Thus nationalism threatened the security and independence of the petty Italian and German princelings. It threatened Russian rule in Poland and Austrian rule in north Italy, Hungary, Czech Bohemia and elsewhere.

Much of this rule was associated with absolutism and reaction and thus opposed by liberals who sought individual political freedoms and constitutional reform. Liberalism and nationalism in the early nineteenth century were closely associated. Individual self-determination appeared to go hand in hand with national self-determination. Freedom from tyrannical rule often seemed to involve freedom from foreign rule, and vice versa. The demand for popular sovereignty entailed both the extension of political rights and the creation of states by national communities.

The application of the principle of self-determination depended on circumstance. A distinction is sometimes drawn between unification nationalism and separation nationalism. Where a nation was divided into several separate states, as in early nineteenth-century Italy and Germany, nationalists sought to unite them to form a single nation-state. Where a nation was part of a state made up of several national groups, as was the case with Greeks, Poles and Hungarians, nationalists sought to secure its separate political existence as a sovereign independent state.

Yet early liberal nationalists tended to assume limits to this process of self-determination and separation. States had to be economically, politically and militarily viable, which implied a certain minimum size and secure frontiers, as well as a developed national consciousness. Very small states were held to be inconsistent with economic modernisation and cultural progress. Mazzini (1805–72) envisaged a Europe divided into no more than twelve nation-states, of which Ireland was not one. John Stuart Mill's support for the nationalist principle in general did not extend to Bretons and Basques. Indeed, he argued that such peoples benefited by being brought within 'the current of ideas and feelings of a highly civilised and cultivated people – to be a member of the French nationality' rather than 'to sulk on his own rocks, the half savage relic of past times'. Progress involved the extinction of the Breton nation. Almost parenthetically, Mill suggested that the same was true of Scottish Highlanders or the Welsh, with reference to Britain (Mill, 1861, ed. Fawcett, 1971 edition, p. 385).

This 'threshold principle', as it has been termed, was subsequently largely abandoned (Hobsbawm, 1990, 1994a). Thus the principle of self-determination was applied to some relatively small and poor nations, most notably in the Balkans, leading to the derogatory expression 'Balkanisation' to describe the proliferation of small states, considered potentially unstable and a threat to international political order. Yet the problem with the liberal nationalist principle of self-determination was that there was never any clear criteria to determine limits to the process. Thus the American President Woodrow Wilson in his attempts to apply the principle to Europe at the end of the First World War was confronted with demands for self-determination from peoples of which he had never previously heard.

A more intractable problem was the inter-settlement of peoples and the continued existence of national minorities within new nation-states. Unfortunately, whole peoples have rarely settled, over time, in neat parcels of land with clearly defined and defensible frontiers. Often they live in close proximity with members of other national groups. Here, the application of self-determination is necessarily an untidy affair at best, with undesired consequences for the resulting minorities. The national principle often proved inimical to the individual rights which liberals championed. National minorities were sometimes subjected to discrimination or even persecution, while the protection of majority nationalist susceptibilities could involve limitations on freedom of speech and toleration. At worst, the application of national rights to self-determination meant expulsions, forced transfers of population, and even extermination. 'Ethnic cleansing' is the modern sanitised term to describe the process.

Liberalism is an ideology with universal implications, and for some of its early liberal exponents nationalism too was a doctrine which was generally applicable. Self-determination for one nation was quite compatible with self-determination for others. Indeed Mazzini, the most celebrated liberal nationalist, envisaged that his planned future Europe of free and independent nation-states would exist in peaceful harmony. The reality proved otherwise. Most nationalists it seemed were more interested in the advance of specific nationalist causes rather than nationalism in general. To the disillusionment of some early liberal nationalists, these rival particular nationalisms subsequently appeared a spur to conflict and war.

Conservative nationalism and imperialism

But if some liberals became disenchanted with nationalism during the course of the nineteenth century, some conservatives increasingly found it useful as a political creed which could be harnessed in the interests of the existing social order. While in the early nineteenth century the concept of the nation was invoked against the state, once nation and state were conflated, an official state-sponsored nationalism could be handily utilised to promote unity and harmony, particularly against radicals and socialists preaching class conflict and revolution. Moreover, with an expanding electorate in many western states, it was essential for parties of the right to find some means of winning working-class votes if they were to have any prospect of survival in the new era of parliamentary democracy. Outbidding the parties of the left by promises of social reform was one possibility, but this risked conflict with the propertied interests of their own core supporters. Nationalism proved to be a cheaper and more effective alternative. The appeal to patriotism as involving a higher duty than sectional class loyalties, sometimes through the combined efforts of the state education system, the Established Church and the mass media, proved remarkably successful among all classes including the industrial working class. To the dismay of those liberals and socialists who continued to proclaim international or cross-national values, the mass of workers in all western European countries demonstrated the overriding strength of their national allegiances in 1914.

Yet although nationalism was an ideology to unite the nation, including all classes, and both men and women, it inevitably involved also some exclusions. However the nation was defined, it did not normally extend to everyone who happened to live within existing state borders. Thus the national identity of those who did not share the self-defined characteristics of nation communities was at best doubtful. At worst they might be perceived as actual or potential traitors, threats to the security and prosperity of the nation. Thus many patriotic French at the turn of the century could not acknowledge an Alsatian Jew like Dreyfus as a fellow citizen. His background made him automatically suspect, which is why he remained in prison for selling military secrets to the Germans even after it became clear that he could not be the traitor involved. German nationalists similarly could not accept that Jews could be Germans.

Much of the nationalism of the late nineteenth and early twentieth centuries was also more assertive and aggressive than the earlier essentially liberal nationalism of Mazzini and others. Instead of proclaiming the universal rights to self-determination of all national communities, it involved advancing the claims of particular nations, often at the expense of other national interests. Behind it there were more competitive assumptions, bound up with Darwinian notions of the survival of the fittest in international relations. Strong nations could and indeed should flourish at the expense of their weaker adversaries. Economic, diplomatic and military success could be attributed to the superior virtues of the nation.

The nationalism of western European countries such as France, Britain, Germany and Italy was closely bound up with colonialism and imperialism. It rarely seems to have occurred even to the most progressive-minded nineteenth-century liberal that the rights to self-determination they proclaimed for peoples in Europe might also be applied to peoples in Africa and Asia. They were 'lesser breeds without the law', incapable of self-government. Indeed, such comforting assumptions of cultural and racial superiority enabled Europeans to see imperialism as an idealistic crusade – a 'white man's burden' to bring good government, religion and civilisation to savages. The easy acquisition of colonial empires was further confirmatory evidence of the superior qualities of Europeans in general, and of specific European countries in particular (although it was largely a consequence of a temporary advantage in military hardware, particularly the possession of rifles and, later, machine guns). Thus the 'scramble for Africa' was a Darwinian competition between European nations in which the strongest secured the most desirable prizes.

Both assertive nationalism and imperialism were closely (although not exclusively) associated with the right and conservatism. The concept of national community fits comfortably with an organic theory of state and society, advanced by some conservative thinkers in opposition to the atomised individualism of liberalism. Yet if nationalism is associated with modernity, it seems a strange element to become a core component of conservatism, which is generally identified with stability and tradition. However, nationalism, although in once sense a product of the modern world, derives much of its appeal from the past and from an interpretation of history. Thus the history of the emerging nation is portrayed in terms of key defining moments, of brave struggles by national heroes, of potent historical myths and symbols. Even ruling dynasties of foreign descent could, through the rediscovery or invention of appropriate traditions or ceremonies, hope to identify themselves with the national spirit. In Britain, coronations, jubilees and other more routine ceremonial occasions, such as trooping the colour or the state opening of parliament, helped to promote a nationalist sentiment steeped in tradition, even if some of that tradition was of relatively recent origin (Cannadine, in Donald and Hall, 1986).

However, if nationalism could become associated with such (real or imagined) traditional values, in some countries, such as Japan and

Turkey, it was aggressively employed as an instrument of modernisation by a ruling order determined to overcome traditional practices and loyalties which were seen as an obstacle to progress. Here a state-sponsored nationalism deliberately rejected traditional culture and dress, encouraging alien western ways as part of a process of national regeneration. This confirms further the chameleon character of the ideology.

Both the traditional and modernising implications of nationalism were present in fascism, which was perhaps the most extreme manifestation of the ideology, employing racist ideas to establish the superiority of specific national communities over others. German nationalism from the late eighteenth century was based particularly on German language and culture, but some German nationalists went on to claim that the German *volk* were a distinctive race which could be marked off from Slavs or Latins or Jews. This was generally combined with some assumptions of racial superiority. Such ideas provided a key component of the Nazi ideology. Nazi textbooks outlined the characteristics of the true 'Aryan' and compared these with the physical characteristics of other races. They also assumed the superiority of the Aryans particularly over other backward or degenerate races. Such ideas could be used to justify the subordination of Slavs to Germans, or even the extermination of entire peoples, such as the Jews.

The extreme example of Nazism demonstrates that racism is not necessarily based on skin colour. Indeed, there was an element of such racism in some other European nationalist movements. However, racism has lately been more commonly linked with colour, particularly in countries where some ethnic minorities are marked off from the majority by skin colour. This has been often associated with assumptions of white superiority, deeply rooted in language and culture. The colour white is linked with goodness and virtue, black with evil.

Where nationalism is combined with racism it involves an aggressive, assertive and highly exclusive form of nationalism. Yet of course nationalism does not necessarily involve racism, and racism often transcends nationalism. Thus overt racists, while they may employ national symbols and imagery, recognise an affinity with racists in other countries. While British racists freely display the Union Jack, they may at the same time adopt German Nazi insignia, or express solidarity with the French racist politician Le Pen.

Nationalism, anti-colonialism and socialism

While nationalism became closely associated with the right and particularly the far right in Europe in the late nineteenth and first half of twentieth century, there were also nationalist movements which were supported by socialists, particularly those which involved resistance against colonialism and imperialism.

At first sight, socialism and nationalism would seem incompatible doctrines. Socialism essentially involved a reaction against, and an alternative to, capitalism. For a socialist the fundamental divisions in human society were economic class divisions. Other divisions were either essentially derived from class divisions. or were artificially fostered. The common interests of the working class, those who owned little beyond their own labour, transcended national boundaries. The orthodox socialist position was that the working man had no country. Nationalism was a doctrine fostered by the ruling classes to obscure the common interests of the working class. Socialist parties proclaimed instead the universal brotherhood of man. Indeed, it was widely anticipated by socialists before the First World War that workers would refuse to fight their brothers in other countries. Socialism, as a universalist doctrine, was naturally hostile to the particularist claims of nationalists.

Yet socialists had to provide some explanation of nationalism and imperialism. Lenin neatly linked the phenomenon of imperialism with another problem for Marxists – improved living standards for the working classes in advanced capitalist countries. Marx had predicted increased pressures on working-class living standards as competition between capitalists forced down profits. It was this increased misery of the proletariat which would eventually provoke revolution. Yet instead, in countries like Germany, Britain and France, living standards were apparently rising, and large parts of the working class weaned away from revolutionary politics. For Lenin, imperialism was the way in which advanced capitalist countries could temporarily postpone the collapse predicted by Marx. Exploitation of peoples and resources in other continents would enable western capitalist states to avoid intensifying the exploitation of their own working class, who instead would reap some of the rewards of imperialism. That in turn might explain something of the apparent popularity of nationalism and imperialism among sections of the working class.

For Marxists and indeed for most socialists imperialism involved exploitation which should be opposed and resisted. Thus they supported anti-colonial movements in territories which had been absorbed into the empires of Britain, France, Germany and other countries which had acquired colonies. Yet in demanding freedom and independence from the colonial power, these movements inevitably borrowed the terminology and ideas of European nationalism. Thus socialists supported nationalists, notably in India between the wars, and in the African continent after the Second World War.

Many of the nationalists themselves proclaimed their own socialism. This may have been in part because of the support received from the Soviet Union and other communist and socialist countries, and from largely socialist pressure groups in western countries, such as the Movement for Colonial Freedom. But it was also because the westernisation which accompanied imperialism had introduced western ideas. The unwilling subjects of imperial powers could use against them their own slogans of freedom, equality and self-determination. The language of socialism could be readily applied to their own situation. Their position, compared with that of their colonial masters, was profoundly unequal, and they were exploited, indeed more manifestly exploited than the working classes of the colonial powers. Their leaders, largely western educated, imbibed western socialist teaching, particularly Marxism, although some of them also discerned a distinctive form of socialism in their own native cultures. Thus some African nationalists argued that African society involved co-operation and collectivism rather than western competition and individualism.

The extent to which socialism and nationalism are ultimately compatible remains contentious. If nationalism requires an over-riding loyalty to the nation (Breuilly, 1993, p. 2) this presents problems for socialists. As Hobsbawm (1989, p. 125) tartly observes, 'any Marxists who are not, at least in theory, prepared to see the "interests" of their own country or people subordinated to wider interests, had best reconsider their ideological loyalties'. Yet other socialists and Marxists have seen no incompatibility between their nationalist and socialist convictions. In part, the debate clearly depends on the definition of nationalism, and the extent to which nationalism is, or is not, exclusive. This in turn relates back to different interpretations of nationalism from the nineteenth century:

from the universalist nationalism of Mazzini to the more assertive and exclusive nationalism of Bismarck or Joseph Chamberlain.

The relationship between nationalism and socialism has sometimes appeared less problematic in the third world than in Europe, although conflicts of interest can arise. Thus in South Africa a Communist within the African National Congress such as Joe Slovo had to subordinate his socialist aspirations to the need to promote national unity and reassure the business community, within the short term at least. Elsewhere, the socialist rhetoric of some regimes has not prevented wars with neighbouring states, or the ruthless internal suppression of minorities.

There have been some particular problems with anti-colonial nationalism. One is that the nations themselves are often the products of colonialism, with boundaries the arbitrary products of compromises between the colonising powers. National unity was often promoted in the face of cross-cutting tribal and religious loyalties, which sometimes resurfaced following the achievement of political independence, once the common enemy was removed. Another response to the same problem is to suggest that there is a coincidence of interest among the former subject peoples which should transcend colonial state boundaries. Thus in Africa there are pan-African movements which strive towards African unity, which have some affinity with the earlier pan-Slav and pan-German movements in Europe.

English and British nationalism

If nationalism requires that nations should form independent states and states should consist of nations, there is an immediate difficulty in applying the ideology to Britain, where the very identity of state and nation is clouded in ambiguity. The state is officially the United Kingdom of Great Britain and Northern Ireland, but is often referred to as the UK, Great Britain or simply Britain, while part of the state, England, is occasionally mistaken for the whole. It is sometimes suggested that this political unit constitutes a nation-state, which implies a single 'British' nationality. More commonly, the United Kingdom is reckoned to include four nations, English, Scots, Welsh and Irish (although there is some difficulty with the national allegiances of the inhabitants of Northern Ireland). Some of those living

Type of nationalism	Associated ideas	Countries	Politicians/thinkers
Revolutionary nationalism	Popular sovereignty	Revolutionary France and client states	Rosseau, Abbé Sieyes
Cultural nationalism	Language and culture	Germany early 19th century, Wales 19th century	Herder
Liberal nationalism	National self-determination Constitutionalism Protection of minority rights Threshold principle Europe of nations Free trade	Unification nationalism: Germany, Italy Separation nationalism: Greece, Belgium, Hungary, Poland	Mazzini John Stuart Mill
Conservative nationalism	Patriotism, social integration, national unity, fatherland, imperialism, social Darwinism, 'manifest destiny' economy protection, autarky	Bismark's Germany Czarist Russia Late 19th-century Britain and France	Bismarck List Disraeli Joseph Chamberlain Renan
Modernisation nationalism	Modernity, industrialisation, westernisation, breach with tradition	Japan from 19th century Turkey in 20th century	Kemal Attaturk
Fascist and Nazi nationalism	'Blood and soil' Identification of people, state and nation (Master) race, racial purity, persecution, extermination of minorities	Nazi Germany Fascist Italy Japan to 1945?	Houston Chamberlain Mussolini Hitler Mosley
Anti-colonial nationalism	Colonial freedom, socialist nationalism? Imperialism as the higher stage of capitalism	India South East Asia African continent	Lenin Gandhi Nyerere
Modern separation nationalism	Language, culture, national identity, federalism, internationalism	Scotland Wales, Baltic states, Basques Former Yugoslavia	Hugh MacDiarmid Tom Nairn

Figure 8.1   Varieties of nationalism

within the United Kingdom would claim a dual national allegiance – British and Irish, or British and Scots, while others would arbitrarily describe themselves as English or British depending on mood or circumstances. There are also some members of ethnic minorities who are full citizens of the United Kingdom, but whose allegiance is doubtful in the eyes of others, and sometimes perhaps to themselves.

Most of these difficulties surrounding national identity are derived from the history of the British Isles and its changing political units. England was politically united from the tenth century, with strong links with Scandinavia until the Norman conquest, and then with France until the fifteenth century. It was then, and particularly under the Tudors, that a strong English national consciousness seems to have developed, eloquently articulated in Shakespeare's history plays. Yet Kings of England also ruled Wales from the thirteenth century, and Henry Tudor was conscious of the propaganda value of his own Welsh ancestry in cementing the allegiance of the principality. Partly to this end also, the Tudors exploited the Arthurian legend – Henry VII's eldest son was named Arthur – establishing their Celtic British credentials. The union with Scotland gave a further impetus to a British rather than English identity, symbolised by the figure of Britannia on coins, and celebrated in Thomas Arne's bombastic patriotic number, 'Rule Britannia'. Many educated Scots willingly acquiesced in their new designation as North Britons in the eighteenth century, and the incorporation of the Cross of St Andrew into the Union Jack. Moreover, they and the Welsh could share in the reflected glories of the growing overseas 'British' empire.

All this implied a deliberate attempt by the rulers of the British state to secure the full political integration of its once separate elements. Yet the new officially sponsored British identity never succeeded in obliterating older national loyalties. Ireland in particular, erratically controlled by the English crown from the twelfth century, obstinately maintained a distinctive Irish national identity, which was intensified rather than destroyed by the Act of Union of 1801. A sense of Scottish nationhood also persisted – to the extent that Britain's ruling class came to appreciate that a 'state-fostered cult of a depoliticized Scottish identity' was a more reliable tactic for securing Scotland's allegiance than cultural integration (Crick, 1991, p. 91). Significantly also the most numerous participants in the British state maintained an attachment to 'England'. which was proudly or sentimentally celebrated by poets from Blake to Tennyson.

Nationalism in its early nineteenth century liberal form as a political doctrine asserting the right to self-determination did not appear at first to have much relevance to Britain, although British politicians and intellectuals gave enthusiastic support to a whole range of nationalist causes abroad – notably Greek, Belgian, Hungarian, Polish and Italian nationalism. Nationalism was thus a principle to be applied to other people. Britons, by contrast, did not need to be freed from foreign rule or united. It was assumed that Britain was already a nation-state. Moreover, there was in the nineteenth century no significant movement for Scottish or Welsh independence. Ireland of course was a very different matter. Yet even Mazzini, the champion of a new Europe of nation-states, did not envisage an Irish nation-state. Britain's rulers continued to regard Ireland as an integral part of the Union, until Gladstone became converted to Irish Home Rule.

However, nationalism in its later nineteenth century version as a political doctrine asserting the primacy of national loyalties over other loyalties, and glorying in the superiority of one's own nation over other nations was deliberated stimulated in Britain – by the revival or invention of ritual, through the arts and popular culture (particularly the music hall) and through education. Nationalism and imperialism became key ingredients of conservatism from the late nineteenth century, but were also enthusiastically endorsed by large sections of the Liberal and Labour parties. British colonial acquisitions, and British victories in wars, provided convincing confirmation of national superiority.

Loss of empire and great power status after the Second World War, coupled with economic decline, rendered the United Kingdom a less obviously successful political enterprise. British decline was doubtless one factor in stirring nationalist currents in Scotland and Wales, but it also intensified doubts over national identity in England. For some, the loss of a world role required a reorientation towards a European identity. For others, it involved a re-emphasis of links with other English-speaking countries, and particularly the 'special relationship' with the United States of America. For still others it perhaps helped to stimulate a narrow chauvinist British racism, in which national pride was bound up with skin colour. Even here there was a continuing ambiguity over national identity, with English and British symbols used almost interchangeably, although the largest surviving neo-fascist group significantly calls itself the British National Party. Yet ironically it was perhaps easier for ethnic minorities to adopt a British rather than an English identity.

By the late 1970s there were, for the first time almost since its establishment, serious doubts about the long-term survival of the British state, with Northern Ireland in turmoil, and nationalism on a steep upward curve in Scotland and Wales (Birch, 1977). After 1979, however, the nationalist tide receded for a period, and British nationalist sentiment was stimulated by the 1982 Falklands War, a generally more assertive foreign policy, and a reaffirmation of commitment to the Union under the premiership of Margaret Thatcher, which the Major government endeavoured to maintain. Yet the fundamental problems of the British state remain, involving uncertain and changing internal loyalties, and questions over the United Kingdom's external relationships, particularly with Europe.

Scottish and Welsh nationalism

Scottish and Welsh nationalism are both relatively new, at least as political doctrines rather than sentiment. While Irish nationalism was clearly a significant political factor throughout the nineteenth century, most Scots and Welsh then seemed content with their participation within the United Kingdom, from which, it could be argued, they profited economically and politically.

Substantial support for nationalism in the sense of full independence for Scotland and Wales is very recent. Plaid Cymru was only founded in 1925 and the Scottish National Party in 1928 (Marr, 1992, pp. 63–7) and neither achieved much electoral success before the late 1960s (Butler and Butler, 1994, pp. 163–4), so that they are essentially modern political movements. However, although nationalism is a modern creed, it derives much of its sustenance through an interpretation of the past, and evocation of national myths, symbols and heroes. This is true of both Welsh and Scottish nationalism.

Wales has never really been an independent sovereign state. It was part of the province of Britannia during the period of the Roman Empire, but after the departure of the Romans it was not colonised by waves of invading Angles, Saxons and later Danes like much of Britain and remained a collection of Celtic tribes and principalities.

From the twelfth century Wales was increasingly subject to encroach-
ments by Norman barons from England. In the thirteenth century
Edward I of England defeated the most powerful of the Welsh
princes, Llewelyn of Gwynedd, and gave his own infant son the title
'Prince of Wales'. In the early fifteenth century English rule was
briefly threatened by Owen Glendower, but Wales was more firmly
united with England under the Tudors (Act of Union, 1536). The
Welsh themselves had little say in the process of absorption under
English rule. They retained their own language and culture, but this
seemed under threat by the nineteenth century.

It was rather different with Scotland which existed for several
centuries as an independent state with its own crown, parliament, and
legal system, although it had a troubled relationship with its more
powerful neighbour to the south, and might like Wales have been
brought under English rule from the reign of Edward I, had it not
been for the exploits of William Wallace and then Robert the Bruce,
which effectively preserved for three more centuries Scottish independence, eloquently asserted in the Declaration of Arbroath of
1320.

Scottish nationalists have derived powerful inspiration from these
early indications of a separate national consciousness, although it is
not clear how far it extended beyond a tiny elite. Moreover, Scotland
was internally divided almost throughout its history, with clan rivalry
in the Highlands and conflicts between rival noble families in the
Lowlands on top of old ethnic and linguistic divisions. To these
divisions was added religious conflict when John Knox converted
most of Scotland to Protestantism. This was significant in terms of
Scotland's external relations. Previously Scotland had been a natural
ally of France against England. After the Reformation the dominant
Protestant elites in both England and Scotland had a common interest
in resisting Catholic France and Spain. Thus it was not just the chance
succession of James VI of Scotland to the English throne in 1603
which brought the two states together, and Scottish and English
interests remained closely entangled throughout the seventeenth century. It was the combination of Scottish Presbyterianism and English
Puritanism which effectively destroyed the government of Charles I,
while Scottish and English interests were involved in both the
restoration of the Stuarts and the Glorious Revolution of 1688.

Scottish nationalists have generally regarded the Act of Union of
1707, in which the majority of the separate Scottish Parliament

accepted its own demise in return for Scottish representation at Westminster, as a craven betrayal of Scottish interests. Equally, it can be seen as a natural development in the interests of the ruling elites of both countries. Advocates of the union in Scotland saw positive benefits in terms of peace, security for the Scottish religion, a degree of political freedom and, most of all, trade. Subsequently, although not necessarily as a consequence of union, Scotland enjoyed a flowering of economic, intellectual and cultural life in the eighteenth century, and the Scottish establishment became enthusiastic proponents of a British identity. After the threat from the Highlands was safely destroyed with the defeat of Bonnie Prince Charlie at Culloden in 1746, the writer Sir Walter Scott helped to invent a powerful romantic Tartan myth, which was enthusiastically adopted by the British royal family. This rather phoney Scottish tartan culture, while it did much for the tourist trade, had little to do with any incipient Scottish nationalism.

While Irish nationalism was a potent political force in British politics throughout the nineteenth century, there was nothing remotely comparable in Scotland and Wales. A possible explanation is that Scotland and Wales substantially shared in the benefits (as well as the costs) of the industrial growth and imperial expansion of the British state. Yet there was a consciousness of a separate national identity which had some basis in real differences. Scotland had its own religious and legal system, and an educational system developing on distinctive lines. Wales had its own language and culture, and a developing Nonconformist chapel tradition which was at odds with the Established Church. Yet national consciousness in Scotland and Wales did not develop then into demands for national independence as it had done in Ireland and over much of the continent of Europe.

Nationalism as an ideology is generally taken to involve demands for full political sovereignty for the nation, although some writers distinguish between political and cultural nationalism, with the added implication that the latter does not require political independence. Thus national feelings may be assuaged by full recognition of a people's language and culture. Moreover, demands for a degree of autonomy may be met by an element of administrative or political devolution, or possibly by a fully federal system of government. It is debatable how far a recognition of the interests of minorities within a state assuages or stimulates separatist feeling. Those wishing to preserve the union of a state may be divided over how this is to be best achieved – concessions to national sentiment may shore up the union, or may be a slippery slope to independence. Similarly, nationalists have awkward tactical decisions to make over their attitude to proposals which stop short of independence.

In the case of Scotland and Wales the British state has made a number of concessions to national sentiment. Thus Scotland, which already had its own system of courts, local government and education, acquired a Secretary for Scotland from 1885, while Scottish administration was progressively reorganised and rationalised under a largely autonomous Scottish Office in the course of the twentieth century. Wales, which had (and still has) similar administrative legal and educational systems to those in England, did not acquire a minister until 1951, and a full Secretary of State with a separate Welsh Office only in 1964. Yet from the late nineteenth century onwards there were also concessions to Welsh national feeling on religion, temperance, education and the use of the Welsh language in administrative and judicial proceedings, and on television.

Some British politicians and parties have, from time to time, proposed some transfer of political power to Scotland and Wales. The notion of Home Rule for Scotland and (to a more limited extent) Wales, began to appear on the political agenda in the late nineteenth century largely as a consequence of the bitter controversy over Irish Home Rule. Home Rule all round was one attempt by Liberals to popularise a cause which did not greatly appeal to the British electorate, and they and their Liberal Democrat successors have fairly consistently supported it. Labour's record has been more erratic. They favoured Home Rule up to 1945, then opposed it, becoming reconverted in 1974 when they promised Scottish and Welsh Assemblies. Failure to secure sufficient support for their 'devolution' proposals in referendums in Scotland and Wales in 1979 precipitated the fall of the Labour Government in 1979. Since then they have remained committed to a Scottish Assembly, co-operating with the Scottish Liberal Democrats in a Scottish National Convention. The Conservatives have been in name and spirit a Unionist party, but even they have from time to time flirted with a measure of devolution, notably under Heath, and there have been more recent suggestions of concessions to Scottish national feeling, although Major has made much of his continued commitment to the Union, arguing that Labour proposals threaten the breakup of the United

Kingdom, a point also made by some Labour dissidents like Tam Dalyell (Marr, 1992).

None of these concessions or proposals remotely satisfy the aspirations of the modern Scottish National Party (SNP) or Plaid Cymru, who seek full independence, in accordance with the general interpretation of the ideology of nationalism. Both nationalist movements were slow to get under way, at least in comparison with similar parties on the European continent, and both at first made little progress in terms of electoral support or parliamentary representation. However, the SNP and to a lesser extent Plaid Cymru made a political breakthrough in the late 1960s and early 1970s. The SNP won 21.9 per cent of the Scottish vote and seven seats in February 1974, and 30.4 per cent of the vote and eleven seats in October, when the Welsh nationalists won over 10 per cent of the Welsh vote and three seats. Since then support has fluctuated, but the SNP has recovered from a slump to secure over a fifth of the Scottish vote in 1992, while Plaid Cymru saw the election of four MPs. Thus if the nationalists have failed to sustain their momentum of the early 1970s, they have established their political presence.

Describing the growth of Scottish and Welsh nationalism is simple. Explaining it is more difficult. It may be seen in part as a consequence of the end of empire and relative economic decline. Scotland, and perhaps to a lesser extent Wales, benefited from the opportunities for trade and settlement opened up by the British empire, and Scots and Welsh as well as English were encouraged to take pride in their partnership in a successful political enterprise. The rapid loss of empire relegated Scotland and Wales to the declining periphery of a shrunken state. Moreover, partly because of their peripheral location, both suffered disproportionately from the economic decline of the United Kingdom as a whole in the twentieth century, particularly more recently. The decline of the textile industry, shipbuilding, and latterly coal mining hit the Scottish economy, while South Wales was similarly damaged by the run-down of iron and steel and mining.

Welsh nationalism, however, was not essentially a question of economics. Indeed it has never caught on in the valleys of South Wales which were hard hit by industrial decline, but has been associated with the core Welsh-speaking areas of the north west, where preservation of the Welsh language and culture has been the key concern. Education in Welsh, Welsh television and Welsh as the language for legal and administrative business have been important issues, although supplemented to a degree by concerns over English immigration, which is partly related to the protection of Welsh culture, but also has an economic dimension (particularly in terms of housing). Yet Wales is essentially divided rather than united by the language issue, which provides a powerful motivation for nationalist sentiment in North Wales but is an explanation for lack of enthusiasm in the south where Welsh is not generally the first language in the home. The language question helps to explain the consistency of support for Welsh nationalism, but also its failure to grow.

Support for nationalism in Scotland is much more volatile. There, language is a negligible issue, enabling the SNP to make a wider appeal based on national sentiment and Scottish economic and political interests. The negative part of this appeal is a perceived neglect of Scottish issues by a remote United Kingdom government, alien both because it is essentially English and Conservative. Thus from 1979 the Scottish Office was headed by ministers from a party for whom only a diminishing minority of Scots voted. One consequence was the imposition of policies such as the Poll Tax and privatisation measures which were strongly opposed in Scotland. Yet with the discovery of North Sea Oil, largely off the coast of Scotland, the SNP could claim that Scotland would be economically better off with independence. 'It's Scotland's Oil' became a potent election slogan, although the force of it diminished with the depletion of oil reserves and the fall in world oil prices.

Such naked appeals to Scottish self-interest provided some ammunition for critics who denounced the nationalists as narrow and materialist. Since then the SNP have sought to counter charges of narrow chauvinism by campaigning on the platform, 'Scotland in Europe', aligning themselves with progressive tendencies favouring closer European integration. This involved a marked policy reversal from earlier opposition to membership, yet it is logical that Euro-federalists and aspiring regional and national interests should make common cause against the entrenched power of existing European states.

There were at one time some significant differences in the location of Scottish and Welsh nationalism on the political spectrum. Whereas Plaid Cymru was firmly associated with the left and socialism, a common gibe by Labour opponents of the SNP was that they were 'Tartan Tories'. The rapid growth of the SNP in the 1970s and the defection to it of erstwhile Labour supporters has weakened that charge, although it is still true that the SNP covers a wider range of views on domestic and economic policy than Plaid. Yet it is now easier for some socialists and Marxists like Nairn (1981) to identify Scottish and Welsh nationalism with progressive neo-nationalism rather than the older reactionary nationalism of the nineteenth and early twentieth centuries.

Changes in the European political map since 1989 make it easier to contemplate a Scottish or Welsh state. If Slovakia or Slovenia, or Latvia, why not Wales? What actually constitutes a nation, and how far in practice might the process of national separation go? Hobsbawm (1989, pp. 120ff.) suggests that requirements of political and economic viability for states in the nineteenth century provided some restraint then on political fragmentation or 'Balkanisation'. The development of an international economy on the one hand, and an (albeit imperfect) European and global political order on the other, has rendered outmoded old assumptions about economic self-sufficiency and defence capability, enabling tiny states to emerge and survive in the modern world. Thus there is no practical brake on nationalist aspirations. The Basques or the Bretons, like the Scots and Welsh, can reasonably aspire to full sovereign independence. But if an independent Scotland, why not an independent Shetlands? One problem, as President Woodrow Wilson discovered in 1919, is that there is no clear criteria for nationhood, and no minimum size as a qualification for membership of the club of independent sovereign states.

Nairn (1981) argues that the breakup of Britain could have a progressive, beneficial effect, enabling all its former constituent parts, including England, to rediscover or invent separate national identities which could co-exist and co-operate fruitfully in a European or global environment. Hobsbawm (1989, pp. 134–5) considers reactionary consequences more likely. One possibility is a narrow exclusive chauvinism, which would discriminate against non-Welsh speakers in Wales, English settlers in Scotland, and all kinds of ethnic minorities in England, with bitter inter-state disputes over assets, debts, off-shore fishing and mineral rights. Interpretations and expectations rest heavily on different perspectives of the nature of nationalism.

Europe, regionalism and nationalism

Perhaps one of the most interesting challenges to traditional nationalist assumptions has been provided by the development of the movement for European union. A large part of the attraction of the idea of
European unity for some of its original advocates was precisely that
it would transcend and render redundant the old national rivalries
within Europe which had culminated in two world wars. It involved
a different vision and a distinctive political programme. From the
beginning the founders of the European Community envisaged a
political as well as an economic union. It has also involved the
development of a European as opposed to a national consciousness –
in the early days some Germans in particular were fond of sporting
'EU' plates on their cars rather than a 'D' for Deutschland, but a
European consciousness appeared well developed in most of the
original six members. The concept of European citizenship was
advanced.

The developing institutions of what is now the European Union
involve in embryo all the apparatus of a sovereign state – an
executive in the shape of the European Commission, a legislature
(potentially, if hardly yet in reality) in the European Parliament, and
a judiciary in the Court of Justice in Luxembourg. It is true that
alongside these institutions there are others which reflect the national
interests of the member states, and that these often appear more
influential on key decisions, yet the elements of federal super-state
are already in place.

In the long debate over British membership of the European
Community from the early 1960s onwards, there has been some
discussion on the implications for sovereignty, an issue particularly
raised by opponents such as Enoch Powell. Supporters of British
membership then and since largely played down the political implications, and emphasised instead the economic advantages. In so far as
they addressed the issue of sovereignty, it was to deny that it was
affected.

The term sovereignty is used to describe two linked concepts:
sovereignty, or independence, in relation to other states, and supreme
power within the state, involving 'parliamentary sovereignty' in the
case of the United Kingdom. Both have been affected by British
membership of the European Union. As with membership of other
international associations, such as the United Nations or NATO,

membership of the European Union has some practical implications for British freedom of action in relation to other states. More significantly perhaps it also has implications for the traditional constitutional doctrine of the sovereignty of Parliament. European law overrides state law and is automatically applied within member countries. It is still possible to argue that a vote of the Westminster Parliament took Britain into Europe and a similar vote could take Britain out again; thus parliamentary sovereignty is unaffected. Yet as the real possibility of withdrawal recedes as a political option, the argument weakens.

The European Union thus has considerable consequences for existing European states, and for the ideology of nationalism. A belief in some forms of European Union, particularly a federalist vision of Europe, seems incompatible with most variants of nationalism. The idea that nations should constitute independent sovereign states does not sit easily with the concept of European unity in which such sovereignty may be 'pooled' or effectively abandoned.

One way in which European unity may be reconciled with nationalism is through the adoption of a relatively loose and weak form of political association: a 'Europe des Patries' in de Gaulle's formulation, or what has been called confederalism rather than federalism. This seems to be what British governments have implicitly or explicitly favoured. Thus strong, virtually independent sovereign states co-operate with other members, but in the last resort retain the right to protect their own separate state interests.

Equally, a rather stronger form of European unity involving a federal structure is quite compatible with a form of nationalism which does not necessarily demand full sovereign independence. Indeed, the European Union may give some tacit encouragement to nationalist movements within existing member states. The European ideal may combine relatively easily with what is sometimes described as 'peripheral nationalism' such as Welsh, or Basque nationalism. The existence of the Union weakens old objections to such nationalism on the grounds of lack of viability or economic dependence. Moreover, it enables nationalists to avoid accusations of narrow chauvinism. They can proclaim their national and European loyalties together, as in the slogan 'Scotland in Europe'.

Even if the European Union does not give overt encouragement to 'peripheral nationalism' there are certainly some institutional pressures towards regional devolution which also have implications for existing states and nationalist assumptions. Local and regional governments have long sought direct links with Brussels, and regional subsidies have become a growing element of the European budget. The Committee of Regions further institutionalises this strong regional element in European policy-making. In so far as it involves links which bypass the national state level, it could be argued that the nation-state is being eroded from above and below. The notion of subsidiarity, that decisions should be taken at the lowest level compatible with efficiency, has been used by the British government to justify taking decisions at the national rather than European level, but it can equally be used to devolve decision-making further to regional or local bodies. Thus there is some commonality of interest between those advocating closer European union and more devolution of decision-making within states. Strong regions threaten strong nation-states. Indeed, some of these regions, sometimes called 'super regions', transcend national state boundaries. Kent, for example, has developed strong links with its cross-channel neighbours in northern France and Belgium.

So far it has been assumed that the European ideal is scarcely compatible with older more aggressive and exclusive forms of nationalism within Europe, but the debates over enlargement have raised or revived some awkward questions about European identity. Some who opposed the European Community did so because they perceived it as a rich man's club, a narrow group of rich capitalist European nations banding together in a protectionist association against perceived threats and competition from the second and third worlds. European federalists have tended to counter such arguments with reference to the aid given by the European Union to the developing world, and special trade arrangements, yet there was always something in the critics' case, and new applications to join the Union have given an urgent practical consideration to previously largely theoretical debates over the nature of Europe. Formerly, despite its name, the European Community was an association of western European states. Enlargement to include Scandinavian or other western states pose some practical problems but few issues of principle. Applications from former Communist states of eastern Europe raise other concerns. Beyond that there is the question of whether Russia is part of Europe, and could be reasonably refused membership. Moreover, there is a longer-standing issue, the question of Turkey, which applied to join before any of the other aspiring new members.

The issues raised by enlargement of the European Union are not dissimilar in nature from the issues raised by German or French nationalism. Just as those nationalisms posed questions about German and French national identity and national boundaries, so the debate over the future of Europe involves, implicitly or explicitly, arguments over who is, or is not, a European, and what are the boundaries of Europe. As with France, the 'natural frontiers' suggested by geography may not be the same as those indicated by language and culture. The European Union has always been multilingual, but awkward questions include the very nature of European culture and civilisation. Is it essentially Christian? That would apparently rule out Moslem states or communities. Some other parts of what might be regarded as the continent of Europe, such as Albania or Bulgaria, have been outside the orbit of western European civilisation for longer than they have been within it. Even more delicate is what some might call implicitly racist assumptions behind the European ideal. Is Europe essentially white? Of course some of the existing member states have substantial black minorities, but to what extent do these share in the European dream? Ethnic minorities in Britain may not always feel a British identity. Is it easier or more difficult for them to feel a European identity? In theory, citizens of member states are automatically European citizens, but the rules governing citizenship in some member states might be regarded as implicitly racist. It is much easier for former Russian residents of German descent to claim German citizenship than for those of Turkish descent who have lived in Germany all their lives (Schlesinger in Hutchinson and Smith, 1994).

Thus at one level the European ideal appears to transcend narrow national rivalries and to promote a spirit of international co-operation, yet equally at another level it raises issues not dissimilar from those associated with old-fashioned nationalism. European unity, just like national unity, poses questions about identity and territory, and can be interpreted in an exclusive way, although many would argue that it does not have to be so interpreted.

Globalisation and the future of nationalism

The movement towards European unity is just one among many trends in the modern world which appear incompatible with nationalist doctrines. Just as it can be argued that the rise of nationalism was connected with industrial modernisation and associated economic developments, so it can now be argued that in the modern industrial or post-industrial world, nationalism is outdated. Globalisation on the one hand, and pressures towards decentralisation on the other, have combined to render nationalism redundant.

It is increasingly clear that nation-states can no longer immunise themselves from the international economy. Movements in money or security markets in New York or Tokyo almost immediately have repercussions for London. The operations of multinational corporations have massive implications for domestic economies. Interest rate policy and increasingly fiscal policy are heavily constrained by international pressures. There are tight rules governing trade restrictions and direct and indirect subsidies for domestic industries.

Similarly, developments in communication technology are rapidly creating a global culture. Much popular music now finds an international audience. Television programmes may have a global market, particularly with the development of satellite and cable television. It is much more difficult for regimes to exclude material from the outside world than it used to be. Neither the Communist regimes nor the former apartheid regime in South Africa could immunise their people from the alternative perspectives and implicit promises held out by the western media.

Just as industrialisation in the nineteenth century helped create a national culture instead of diverse regional and local cultures in many European states, so post-industrial society has created cultures which transcend national boundaries. This has created tensions, particularly in countries determined to preserve a distinctive national culture. Thus France tries to resist Anglo-American imports into its language, and restrict English language film and television.

But if nationalism is apparently being undermined by globalisation, it is also threatened by other pressures towards decentralisation. Industrialisation involved Fordist assumptions about economies of scale, mass production and standardisation. It is now suggested that we live in a post-Fordist economy and society, where small is once again beautiful, and where the emphasis is on flexibility, and meeting customers' requirements. This has affected government and public services as well as the private sector. In most European countries (the United Kingdom at present is an exception) there has been a significant devolution of power from central government to regional and local authorities. In Britain and also in many other countries the introduction of increased competition and quasi-markets into the public sector has transformed patterns of service delivery. In theory, power is devolved to consumers, which is questionable in practice, but certainly there has been a significant decentralisation of decision-making to institutions, managers and professionals away from centralised bureaucracies.

Many of these changes remain problematic and acutely controversial. Yet although the privatisation and commercialisation involved in New Right reforms have been strongly criticised from the left, few seem to want to return to bureaucratic central control, or older models of centralised state socialism. More emphasis instead is placed on the values of community and locality.

The implications of all this for mainstream nationalist ideology should be manifest. Nationalism suggests that national communities should have their own political and governmental framework in the form of sovereign independent nation-states. That implicitly is the only level of government which ultimately counts. Yet in the modern world national state government is increasingly being undermined from above and below: by globalisation and decentralisation. These in turn are not just fashionable ideas but reflect changes in the economy, society and technology which are probably irreversible. On this analysis, nationalism, perhaps the most potent political ideology of the nineteenth century and most of the twentieth century, should be doomed to extinction.

Yet the decline of nationalism has been long prophesied, while there are few indications that such prophecies are being fulfilled. On the contrary, nationalism seems as vigorous as ever in most parts of the world, and has flourished in extreme forms particularly in former Communist countries where a counter ideology stressing universalism and international working-class solidarity has been inculcated for half a century or more. Thus in Russia and other former constituent elements of the Soviet Union, in the Baltic States, in former East Germany, in Slovakia, and most of all in former Yugoslavia, the strength of nationalism is evident. It is also a growing phenomenon in parts of the western world – in the United Kingdom, Spain and France, for example, where 'peripheral nationalism' thrives. It remains manifest over much of the third world also. Nationalism may logically appear redundant in the modern world, but it continues to defy all predictions.

Guide to further reading

The literature on nationalism is extensive. A good brief introduction to some of the main issues surrounding nationalism is provided by Richard Jay in Eccleshall *et al.* (1994). Among the best recent single volume accounts is P. Alter (1989) *Nationalism*. Contrasting explanations of nationalism are offered by E. Kedourie (1960, 4th edn, 1991), E. Gellner (1983), B. Anderson (1983), J. Breuilly (2nd edn, 1993), Hobsbawm (1990) and A. D. Smith (1991). Extracts from all these and much else besides can be found in a reader on nationalism by J. Hutchinson and A. D. Smith (1994). In addition to his slim volume *Nations and Nationalism since 1780* quoted above, Hobsbawm's four volumes on modern history *Age of Revolution*, *Age of Capital*, *Age of Empire* and *Age of Extremes* all contain valuable material on nationalism. For the troubled relationship between nationalism and socialism J. Schwarzmantel (1991) is useful. J. Hutchinson (1994) is good on nationalism in the modern world.

It is more difficult to find books which can be confidently recommended on nationalism in Britain. At the height of the devolution debate in 1977, A. H. Birch produced a slim volume, *Political Integration and Disintegration in the British Isles* which is still useful but inevitably dated. T. Nairn (1981) *The Break-up of Britain* is more wide-ranging, theoretical as well as provocative, but also reflects the political climate in which it was originally written. B. Crick has edited a more recent (1991) collection of essays on *National Identities*. On Scottish nationalism D. McCrone (1992) is useful and A. Marr (1992) journalistic, but fair and penetrating.

9

FEMINISM

Introduction

Like other ideologies, feminism involves a critique, an ideal and a programme. The critique contains an analysis of the discrimination and injustices suffered by women in existing society. The ideal is justice for women, generally but not exclusively interpreted to mean sexual equality. The practical programme has included action to achieve political and legal rights, equality in the economic sphere, the elimination of sexual discrimination in education, the workplace and the home and protection against physical and sexual violence. All political ideologies contain implications for political action, but feminism is markedly action-oriented.

Feminism clearly differs from most of the other political ideologies discussed in this book. It is not a party ideology, as it is not closely linked with a particular political party in Britain or most other western countries. Moreover, many of its practical implications have more to do with the private sphere of family and interpersonal relations than the public sphere of government and conventional politics. Yet the definition of what is and what is not political is itself an essentially ideological question. While many Conservatives or Liberals would distinguish between state and civil society, and between a political and personal sphere, feminists have argued that 'the personal is political'. Thus issues of identity and interpersonal relations, the exploitation of women within the family, or the sexual abuse of women are political questions, just as more conventionally

231

political issues such as civil and political rights, and equal opportunities. Feminism involves a distinctive and radically different perspective which has important implications for politics in its broadest
sense.

Analysis of feminism, as with other ideologies, has tended to
involve distinctions and classifications into periods and sub-
categories. Thus the literature commonly refers to two main periods
or waves of feminism: the first from the nineteenth century until
around 1920, and the second from the 1960s to the present. Largely
cutting across this time dimension there is also a conventional
distinction between three varieties of feminism: liberal feminism,
socialist/Marxist feminism and radical feminism. Such classifications
are helpful, particularly to the student struggling to make sense of a
complex range of feminist thinkers, ideas and issues, and some use of
them is made in this chapter. However, categorisation always involves oversimplification and often distortion. There are feminists
who are difficult to pigeon-hole and newer strands of feminist
thinking which cut across or lie outside the conventional categories.
Moreover, some feminists would object that categorisation exagger-
ates the differences within the women's movement, and downplays
the essential central issues on which feminists are broadly united.

An implicit and often explicit assumption in this book is that
British ideologies are sufficiently distinctive at least in some aspects
to warrant separate treatment. This is problematic for some ideologies, and particularly for feminism. Mainstream feminist literature
studied in Britain might be described as Anglo-American, but influences from France and other countries are also evident, while perhaps
the most well-known modern 'British' feminist was born and brought
up in Australia (Greer, 1970). Many feminists moreover would argue
that their theory and analysis has a universal application. Women are
exploited everywhere, regardless of economic, political and cultural
differences between societies.

However, many feminists would acknowledge that the problems of
women in advanced capitalist western societies and cultures like
Britain have distinctive aspects. Some British feminists question
whether even American analysis and prescription has anything to do
with 'the state of feminism in Britain' (Linda Grant, *Guardian*,
11/5/95). Action to remedy discrimination and exploitation in particular countries like Britain inevitably relates to the specific economic,
social, political and legal context (Carter, 1988; Lovenduski and

Randall, 1993). Theory is also affected by context, and socialist and Marxist feminism has featured relatively strongly in theoretical debates within the British women's movement. Thus while this chapter will draw on feminist thought from other countries, it will focus principally on British feminists, and most of the policy implications will be related to British experience.

The origins and development of feminist thought – liberal feminism

Women, and women's rights and issues, have not been a major focus for most of the 'great writers' who figure prominently in histories of political theory, although some of them, such as Plato, have interesting things to say about women (Coole, 1988, ch. 2). Modern feminists have rediscovered a number of (largely women) writers who have drawn attention to the exploitation of women from the late Middle Ages onwards, but who have been ignored in conventional male-oriented histories of political thought. However, the first significant modern feminist text is still generally reckoned to be Mary Wollstonecraft's *A Vindication of the Rights of Women*, first published in 1792.

Mary Wollstonecraft (1759–97) had a turbulent, unconventional and brief life, famously (or notoriously) described after her death by her husband, the anarchist thinker William Godwin (Tomalin, 1974). Her fundamental assumptions were those of liberalism – the rights, freedom and equality of the individual – applied specifically to the position of women. Wollstonecraft argued that women were as capable of reason as men, and should be educated in the same way as men. They should be free to exercise their reason and choose their role in life. An equality of worth between men and women implied an equality of rights, including political rights.

Liberalism is a universalist ideology. Theoretically, its analysis and programme is applicable to all mankind, which might be taken to comprehend also womankind, although in practice many liberals were reluctant to extend the rights of man to woman, as Arblaster (1984) among others has noted. Even so, there were some honourable exceptions to this generalisation among prominent male liberals who did seek to apply their liberal principles to the position of women and there were many women brought up within the liberal tradition who perhaps made the connection more readily. Thus Mary Wollstonecraft and subsequent nineteenth-century writers such as Harriet Taylor and John Stuart Mill (1806–73) in Britain, and Elizabeth Cady Stanton (1815–1902) in the United States, articulated what has come to be called liberal feminism. The essential project was to assert full legal and political equality between the sexes.

The liberal feminists, it might be said, did not develop any essentially new theories. What was novel in their work was the application of liberal assumptions, theories and claims to the position of women. In some respects it could be said that they placed the burden of proof on those who opposed women's rights to justify their exclusion of the grounds of some innate difference or inferiority (Mill, 1869, ed. Fawcett, 1971). Liberal feminists shared the general liberal presumption that human nature was pretty much the same everywhere, regardless of differences in culture, social class or indeed gender. Thus they were critical of assumptions about feminine nature, suggesting that many perceived differences between the sexes were the product of nurture. Mill in particular was scathing over the way in which even the proclaimed superior virtues of women were used in debate to deny women rights. However, in countering the arguments of the opponents of feminine emancipation, the liberal feminists tended to deny or downplay any psychological differences between the sexes, and even the implications of the biological differences were minimised. This was in marked contrast to the line adopted by some radical feminists subsequently.

The main focus of the campaign for women's rights in the first wave of feminism was the franchise. This was the most obvious and blatant symbol of their inequality and exclusion from full participation in modern politics and society. Women who joined in the successful campaign for the abolition of slavery in the United States soon came to appreciate the irony of their own exclusion from political rights and privileges. In Britain a long and high profile campaign for 'Votes for Women' ultimately led to their enfranchisement in Acts passed in 1918 and 1928.

However, it should not be supposed that liberal feminists were exclusively concerned with either the relatively narrow issue of the right to vote, or more general political rights. There was a concern to remedy legal restrictions on the right to inherit and own property, to develop education, including higher education, for girls and young women, and to open up some of the most esteemed careers and professions to women, to provide apparently a degree of equality of opportunity. Nor should the significance of some of the victories secured by liberal feminists in the nineteenth and early twentieth centuries be downplayed. They involved a real and not just a symbolic improvement in the position and status of women.

Moreover, this essentially liberal strand was significant also in the 'second wave' of feminism from the 1960s, drawing attention to inadequacies in the legal protection of women's rights and to the cultural and educational factors which contributed to the continued subordination of women, and their exclusion or marginalisation from leading positions in management and the professions. In Britain such pressures led to further legal reforms outlawing discrimination on grounds of sex. An Equal Pay Act was passed in 1970, and a Sex Discrimination Act in 1975. A new body, the Equal Opportunities Commission, was established to monitor implementation of both Acts and to investigate allegations of discrimination. Pressure to improve the position of women also produced significant changes in the education of both sexes and in the recruitment and promotion of women in a range of occupations.

This second wave of liberal feminism produced some notable additions to feminist literature, from Betty Friedan's popular *The Feminine Mystique* (1965) and subsequent works (1977, 1982), to Janet Radcliffe Richards' more philosophical *The Sceptical Feminist* (1982). Friedan's book appealed to a generation of American women who wanted careers and fulfilment outside the home, without necessarily wishing to reject the traditional values of motherhood and family, and led to the formation of the liberal pressure group, the National Organisation for Women. Richards' book, by contrast, involved a reaffirmation of the traditional liberal feminist appeal to reason, equality and social justice in the face of a radical feminist assault which downplayed or rejected their relevance.

Yet many feminists would argue that the analysis and achievements of both nineteenth-century and more recent liberal feminism are strictly limited. From a theoretical standpoint, if the case for women's emancipation was as clear as Mill and others suggested, how could their subjection for so long and in so many parts of the globe be explained? Liberal feminists failed to provide an adequate explanation for the injustices so universally inflicted on women. Liberals tended to assume that the liberty, formal equality and individual rights which they proclaimed actually existed in reality, or were capable of introduction through rational persuasion and appropriate action. They were less concerned to account for the power relations which prevailed in practice (Coole, 1988, ch. 6; Bryson, 1992, pp. 58–64).

To critics, this central failure to explain women's inequality meant that the liberal strategy for tackling it was inadequate. Indeed, it could be argued that the political and legal gains of the liberal feminists failed to secure a really significant amelioration in the position of all women, despite the acknowledged improvement in opportunities for some women. The evidence of continued discrimination after the achievement of formal equality in so many spheres was extensive and damning. Thus levels of participation by women in the Cabinet, Parliament, the Council Chamber and other spheres remains low or derisory half a century or more after the achievement of full political rights for women in the United Kingdom (Randall, 1987).

Thus even after the passing of an Equal Pay Act in 1970, average earnings for men and women appeared as far apart as ever (Barrett, 1980, pp. 153–4). Thus despite the outlawing of discrimination on grounds of sex, and the establishment of the Equal Opportunities Commission, only a handful of women have reached the highest levels in the civil service, the judiciary, the professions and company boardrooms. The failure of legal remedies to secure the desired changes tended to cast a doubt not only on specific remedies but also on the underlying liberal feminist analysis. Neither rational persuasion nor legal compulsion seemed adequate to secure justice for women.

Particularly glaring were the continuing and perhaps increasing differences among women themselves. A minority signally gained from the changes in the legal and cultural climate, but the majority hardly profited. Those women who did succeed in what was still so evidently a man's world, such as, most conspicuously, Mrs Thatcher, Britain's first female Prime Minister, were very much the exception, and apparently had done little to assist their sisters. Indeed, the opportunities opened up for a minority of professional career women were often dependent on the provision of child-care, catering and cleaning services, which were in practice performed by other women, commonly among the most exploited in terms of pay and conditions of employment. Sometimes the apparent corollary of the emancipation of a successful professional woman was the virtual enslavement of a foreign au pair. Moreover, the 'glittering prizes' available to a few were quite out of reach of the majority of the female population, still largely confined to low status and low pay jobs in manufacturing, retailing, catering, cleaning, and that ubiquitous category, caring. While some women preferred or were pressurised to concentrate on child-rearing and household chores without pay, increasingly economic necessity forced more to combine the dual role of low-paid wage earner and unpaid carer.

This is still largely true in Britain today. The marked expansion in the employment of women compared with high unemployment of men in the 1980s and 1990s is not largely the consequence of egalitarian pressures or legal constraints, but of reduced employment opportunities in traditionally male-dominated mining and heavy manufacturing industries, and rising demand for casual and part-time labour in retailing and services. The demand for female labour reflects the willingness (or necessity) of many women to accept low pay, 'flexible' working arrangements and lack of job security. It is debatable whether their increased participation in the labour force means most women are really better off. Moreover, if there are real gains for some women at least, these would seem to owe more to the way market forces are currently operating than the result of liberal legislation.

Finally, some modern critics from within the women's movement would argue that while the liberal feminists at least tried to address discrimination and injustice in the public sphere of the law, politics, school and work, they generally had less to say on the position of women in the private world of home and family, which to many feminists is the very seat and centre of women's exploitation and subordination. Although some first wave liberal feminists like Mill and Taylor, and second wave feminists like Friedan have quite a lot to say about the domestic sphere, the criticism is basically fair, for liberals generally assume a strict separation between the public and private spheres, and a distinction between the legitimate role of the state on the one hand and civil society on the other. As a consequence of this assumption, while liberals lay emphasis on political and legal remedies for abuses, they tend also to narrow the scope of those remedies. Behaviour within the private world of the home and family was not regarded by most liberals as a legitimate field for state intervention, although Mill, surprisingly perhaps, did advocate considerable state interference (Coole, 1988, p. 137).

Yet while both their analysis and prescription has been subjected to extensive criticism, the achievements of liberal feminists should be acknowledged. While formal legal and political rights have not produced equality between the sexes they have involved real concrete gains for women. Moreover, there has also been a significant change in the climate of opinion, which has involved a marked change in the portrayal of women in the media – notably in films, in television soap opera and comedy, and in advertisements. Changes in stereotypes and role models suggest that changes in the law and formal codes can influence culture, and ultimately thought and behaviour. Politicians and public figures are now far more careful to avoid language which is deemed sexist. To that extent it may be claimed that most of the liberal feminist agenda has been incorporated into mainstream political ideology. Thus while it is easy to decry the limitations of liberal feminism, it has perhaps done more to date to improve the position of women than the more ambitious but largely unachieved programmes of socialist and radical feminists.

Socialist and Marxist feminism

Socialists and liberals start from different assumptions over the relationship of individual men and women to society. For the liberal, society is the sum of its individual parts, and social change is the cumulative consequence of free choices made by individuals. For the socialist, individual men and women are severely constrained, if not moulded, by social pressures outside their control. While the liberal relates the position of women to fundamental underlying assumptions about individual liberty and formal equality, the socialist naturally attempts to explain women's exploitation in terms of broader trends and pressures within society.

For Marxists this entails an analysis involving inevitable conflict between economic classes, as created and conditioned by the dominant mode of production – capitalism in the modern western world. Thus the position of women can only be understood in terms of capitalism and class. The exploitation of women in modern society is a consequence of the exploitation of the industrial working class under capitalism. The unpaid domestic labour largely performed by women in modern western societies is related to the requirements of capitalism. Women may also be exploited in the labour force – used as part of the industrial reserve army of labour to swell the ranks of workers in times of boom and to undercut the wages of male workers more generally. It follows that liberal remedies are at best mere palliatives and that the emancipation of women can only be truly achieved by a revolution which will end capitalism and those bourgeois social relations associated with capitalism.

Marx himself paid relatively little attention to gender issues, although he and Engels agreed in the Communist Manifesto that their proposals entailed the abolition of the bourgeois family, which they claimed would 'do away with the status of women as mere instruments of production'. Engels later provided a more sustained analysis of the modern family and the exploitation of women in *The Origin of the Family, Private Property and the State.* Subsequently Lenin, Trotsky and Bebel all made significant theoretical contributions to the Marxist analysis of the position of women, while Alexandra Kollontai (1872–1952) attempted to implement what she conceived as a socialist programme to advance the position of women in the Soviet Union (Coole, 1988, pp. 220–31; Bryson, 1992 pp. 134–44), without much assistance, it might be said, from her male Bolshevik colleagues, particularly Stalin, who ultimately reversed any modest gains which had been made (Millett, 1977). All the same, modern Marxist feminists thus have a strong theoretical and practical tradition to draw upon.

By no means all socialist feminists are Marxists. There were pre-Marxist socialist thinkers who addressed the position of women, such as, notably, William Thompson (1775–1844) in Britain (Coole, 1988, pp. 158–65). Subsequently, there were many other writers and active politicians who claimed to be socialists but who did not wholly subscribe to a Marxist analysis or totally rejected it, and who promoted arguments and practical proposals to advance the position of women. These included both Keir Hardie and Ramsay MacDonald in the British Labour Party, the indefatigable campaigner for family allowances, Eleanor Rathbone, and modern mainstream Labour socialists, such as Barbara Castle. Yet while some writers make a distinction between Marxist feminism and other socialist feminism, the line between them is in practice blurred, and it is difficult to construct a coherent socialist or social democratic feminism which comprehends all the various feminists who were socialists but not Marxists.

However, socialist feminists of all kinds tend to differ from liberal feminists in the importance they attach to class. Most women, it is argued, suffer from a double exploitation, belonging both to a subordinate class and disadvantaged by their sex. The link between class and sex is more problematic. Marxist analysis suggests that the exploitation of women both in the workplace and the home is the consequence of the class conflict associated with capitalism. There is thus an assumption that it is the differences and conflict between economic classes which is ultimately fundamental, rather than the differences and conflict based on gender (Coole, 1988, p. 193).

The social class of women is itself a contentious issue. It might be noted that social class categories to which married women are conventionally assigned tend to be based on their husband's occupation, particularly if they are not in paid employment themselves. Thus an alteration in family circumstances may imply a change in social status, which in turn suggests some fluidity in their class allegiance. However, it is often suggested that, regardless of their own formal status, or that of their husband, many women have what might be described as a working-class lifestyle. Thus while their husbands may be driving a prestigious company car or enjoying expense account meals, wives are more likely to be using public transport or a small family car, and eating fishfingers and baked beans with their children. The life which they experience has more in common with the working class than the middle class to which they are formally assigned. Some feminists have tried to solve the knotty relationship between class and gender by simply declaring that women constitute a distinctive class.

Laying aside problems of analysis and classification, all kinds of socialist feminists would proclaim a practical concern for the condition of ordinary women, or more specifically, working-class women. There is specifically a concern for women in paid employment, particularly those in low-paid casual and part-time employment who lack even the more basic legal protection afforded to most full-time workers. One remedy might be shared with liberal feminists – specific legal reforms to extend existing rights to part-time and casual workers – but socialist feminists would also seek to empower female workers themselves through organisation, unionisation and consciousness-raising.

Another characteristic practical concern of socialist feminists has been the provision of adequate child-care for ordinary women workers for whom the facilities commonly utilised by professional women are unavailable, unsuitable, or simply far too expensive. Thus socialist feminists commonly demand the availability, as of right, of both state day nurseries and nursery schools, and workplace crèches.

Some socialist feminists would argue that the provision of child-care for women in paid employment does not assist those women who, either through circumstances or choice, are obliged to perform housework and child-care services unpaid in the home. This practical concern was linked with a long-running theoretical debate among Marxist feminists over domestic labour, which was seen as providing a crucial underpinning for the whole capitalist system. It was argued that the low dependent status of domestic labour could only be significantly improved by an acknowledgement of the value of the services performed through regular payment – hence the demand for wages for housework, a campaign not supported by all feminists, in part because it appears to condone and legitimise existing specialised gender roles within the family. While domestic labour can be performed by either sex, of course it has been traditionally associated with women.

The demands of socialist feminists have been more ambitious than those of liberal feminists, and it is probably fair to say that the achievements have been correspondingly less. Some progress has been made towards the increased unionisation and politicisation of women workers. Moreover, the former male-dominated British labour and trade union movement has become rather more sensitive to women's issues and women's demands. These are real gains, even if they have been somewhat offset by the effective marginalisation of the whole labour movement in Britain in the Thatcher and post-Thatcher years. There have also been some piecemeal improvements in the provision of child-care facilities. However, both the recession in the private sector and cuts in resources in the public sector have contributed to undermining any real progress in this direction. 'Fringe' benefits or non-statutory services are commonly the first to suffer in any cutbacks. Needless to say, the more radical and ambitious proposals, such as wages for housework, have proved non-starters in the recent economic and political climate. Even universal child benefits (one positive achievement of previous generations of feminists) have been under threat.

Feminists who are also socialists are frequently faced with a conflict of loyalties or priorities. Socialism and feminism do not invariably go together, even if in theory they should. Some feminists have learned from bitter experience that male socialists and trade unionists can display as much male chauvinism as their reactionary counterparts on the right of the political spectrum. Indeed, it was the disillusionment of female radical activists with the conduct of their male colleagues in the civil rights movement which sparked the feminist upsurge on the American campus from the late 1960s onwards. Yet socialist feminists are generally only too aware that the treatment of women is only one, and not always the most important, of the manifestations of 'man's inhumanity to man'. Thus they are sometimes accused by other feminists of not giving sufficient priority to women's issues.

There has also been a more fundamental questioning of the theoretical assumptions underpinning Marxist feminism. In so far as the injustices suffered by women are linked with capitalism, there is a tacit assumption that the end of capitalism would entail the end of women's subjection. Ultimately, it is implied, inequality of the sexes derives from the inequalities between different economic classes. Thus issues of class are primary, and issues of gender secondary. This hardly provides an adequate explanation for the extensive evidence of women's oppression across time and cultures. As Coole (1988, p. 193) points out, although Marxism is relevant to women 'because of its general analysis of the dynamics of oppression' it is also 'problematic . . . because it cannot account for a specifically sexual form of oppression except in so far as it is functional to private property and production'.

There has been some anguished reassessment of *The Unhappy Marriage of Marxism and Feminism* (Sargent, 1981). Many Marxist feminists themselves today would acknowledge that male domination and the exploitation of women is a feature of most if not all known societies, which implies at least a need to extend Marxist analysis by borrowing from other approaches. Thus Juliet Mitchell (1974) has combined a Marxist class analysis with insights drawn from psychology and psychoanalysis to explain the subordination of women within the family and domestic sphere. Through childhood social-isation gender roles are learned which have an enduring significance. Other Marxist feminists have acknowledged a need to incorporate the radical feminists' theory of patriarchy into their analysis. Thus women are exploited because of their class position within a capitalist society, but also because they are women, and generally subject to male domination. This does raise the question of the connection, if any, between capitalism and patriarchy, and of the fundamental source of women's oppression. MacKinnon (1989) has argued that while Marxism focuses on work, feminism focuses on sexuality, and it is the latter which is the real basis of women's subordination. While this assumption would not be shared by all feminists, it is a position taken by those who have been described as radical feminists.

Radical feminism

Marxist feminism involved a widening of the focus of the women's movement away from specific legal and political concerns of the liberals towards an analysis of the underlying economic and social causes of women's oppression. At first sight, the work of the radical feminists implied, by contrast, a drastic narrowing of horizons to sexual and personal relations between men and women. However, if the focus appeared to be narrow, the radicals argued it had a universal relevance. Moreover, they could argue that the central concept of patriarchy provided feminism with a theory which was not essentially derivative, not just an application of theories like liberalism and Marxism which were not primarily concerned with women's oppression.

Simplifying drastically, the nature of the problem for radical feminists is neither an inadequate political and legal framework, as liberal feminists imply, nor capitalism, as Marxist feminists suggest, but just men. Everywhere men exploit women. It is the sex war, not the class war, which is fundamental. The central concept of radical feminists is patriarchy, rule by the father, or the male head of the household.

It should, however, be immediately acknowledged that the clear distinctions implied in such typologies are considerably blurred in practice. Even someone regarded as an extreme radical, such as Shulamith Firestone (1979) both incorporates Marxist ideas and pays tribute to 'liberal' predecessors. Many Marxist feminists would endorse much of the analysis of the radicals, and indeed regard themselves as radicals. Each arbitrary category involves a wide range of ideas and internal tensions, and there is considerable overlap between them.

Who are the radical feminists? Three key texts first appeared around 1970. Kate Millett's *Sexual Politics* came out in the United States in 1969, and the United Kingdom in 1971. Germaine Greer's book *The Female Eunuch* first appeared in 1970. Shulamith Firestone's *The Dialectic of Sex* came out in the States in the same year and was published in Britain a year later. What these books had in common was a preoccupation with the biology and sexuality of women. Indeed, the term 'woman's liberation' was closely linked with what was seen as a sexual revolution in the 1960s. These writers were all less concerned with the discrimination against women in the political and public sphere, and more concerned with the everyday relations between men and women in the home, family and bedroom. All three illustrated their themes of feminine exploitation with examples from literature, journals and popular culture.

In one sense the focus on male–female relations in the home seemed to involve a retreat from politics. Yet essentially it involved a rejection of conventional politics coupled with a deliberate widening of the political sphere. The title of Kate Millett's book *Sexual Politics* was not accidental. The implication was that sexual relations involved power and were inherently political. Hence the slogan of the radical feminists, 'The personal is political'.

Another characteristic of much radical feminism is its style. They freely use the language of revolution rather than reform. They challenge and set out to shock. The prevailing tone is anger and outrage. It would not be fair to suggest that radical feminism is more inspired by anger than reason, for the two are not necessarily in contradiction, yet there is a clear difference in approach in the writings of Millet, Greer and Firestone, from that of Mill and Betty Friedan.

The enemy was male power, embodied in the universal institution of patriarchy. Patriarchy may be variously defined, but is a term most usually employed by radical feminists to signify, simply, male dominance. The power of the husband over his wife, the power of the father over his children, and the power of the male head of the household over everyone within it was seen as the ultimate symbol and source of male power in politics and society. Equality between the sexes and justice for women could thus never be achieved unless the institution of patriarchy was destroyed. In this context the absence of legal rights and privileges were beside the point. These were not the cause of female inequality, only its visible manifestation. Likewise a socialist revolution which ended the oppression of one class by another would not by itself end the oppression of women by men.

For radical feminists it was in the sexual relations between men and women that male domination and female subjugation were most evident. A prime practical concern of radical feminists was violence against women, and most particularly rape, which was not perceived as an occasional and highly aberrational act of violence, but as a widespread and typical aspect of male sexuality. Thus radical feminists drew attention to the extent of unreported rape, and, more controversially, the phenomena of 'date rape' and rape within marriage (Brownmiller, 1977). Another target was pornography which involved degrading images of women, reinforced their role as sex-objects, and arguably incited sexual violence against women (Dworkin, 1981).

In view of the significance attached to sexual relations between men and women by the radical feminists it was not surprising that a prime target of the radical feminists of the 1960s and 1970s was the institution of marriage, which involved the self-effacement and loss of identity of women (symbolically through the loss of their maiden names). Associated with this was the broader question of the relations between the sexes. What could be expected of men, and how should they be regarded by women?

Liberal feminists had sought as far as possible to eliminate the differences between men and women, and enlist male aid in the emancipation of women. It was aimed to open up the existing all-male bastions to women to allow free and equal competition, regardless of gender differences. Mill and others argued that the equality of women would ultimately be to the benefit of men and society generally (Mill, 1869, ed. Fawcett, 1971). Many radical feminists assumed by contrast that the advantages men enjoyed by virtue of their power over women would not be readily surrendered. Thus the women's movement would have to depend on women. Indeed, it might entail the positive exclusion of men.

A subject of debate among feminists was the extent to which male nature and behaviour might be modified. There was some talk of the emergence of a 'new man' who might be a fitting equal partner to a liberated woman. Others suggested that the new man was a myth. For a few radical feminists the rejection of the whole male sex was a logical corollary – a factor in the emergence of the hostile caricature of the typical feminist as a lesbian man-hater. While these do exist, they would appear to be a small minority. Some feminists are lesbian in sexual orientation, but this does not prevent them from having warm friendships and co-operative associations with men. The majority probably are heterosexuals who seek more equal and satisfying relationships with men at both the personal and political level. Although lesbianism has understandably been an issue of concern for feminists, and in practice sometimes a source of division between them, it would seem that the rights of individuals, both male and female, to pursue their own sexual preferences as long as these do not involve harm to others, is essentially a different issue from women's rights.

Another closely associated target for radical feminists was the conventional family, perceived as the centre of the inequitable burden of domestic work and child-care imposed on women. In contrast to the arguments of liberals like Betty Friedan, or of the Marxist feminists who sought wages for housework, many radicals denied that women would be able to achieve fulfilment outside the home while they were fettered by domesticity. A meaningful career could not realistically be combined with traditional institutions of motherhood and family. Thus the emancipation of women appeared to some to entail the abolition of the family.

A problem here was that greater involvement of women in child-rearing was clearly in some sense biologically determined. Shulamith Firestone attempted to tackle this problem head-on, arguing that women would not be free until they were liberated from the tyranny of their biology. Pregnancy, she declared, was barbaric, and she looked forward to its ultimate replacement by artificial reproduction. These views have provoked some ridicule, but they do pose in stark form a dilemma for women. Modern forms of contraception have already revolutionised sexual behaviour. Developments in baby-care have facilitated earlier weaning and this and other changes have allowed mothers to leave the babies earlier with child-carers. Test tube babies are already a reality. All such developments enable or oblige choice. It is not impossible that further scientific developments might render human reproduction outside the womb feasible, and enable women to escape from 'the tyranny of reproduction'. As Firestone suggests, 'development of the option should make possible an honest re-examination of the ancient value of motherhood'. While it is possible that the majority of women would indignantly reject the kind of future suggested by Firestone, there can be no certainty unless and until such options were available.

Faced with the diversity within radical feminism, it is difficult to sum up its achievements. Certainly the style of the radicals has provoked a reaction. Arguably, the anger and shock tactics of some radical feminists has had a signal effect on the climate of opinion towards women, and the treatment of women. Those, for example, who attached stickers to posters which declared 'this advertisement degrades women' did arouse some consciousness of the implicit and often quite explicit sexist assumptions behind much of the advertising and media images of women. This has led to some attempt to avoid old stereotypes and provide new, more appropriate, female role models.

Similarly, the campaigns focusing on rape and the general issue of violence against women have contributed to a significant shift in public attitudes and some changes in practice. A major issue for women which was previously ignored or swept under the carpet has been forced onto the political agenda. Violence against women is recognised as a serious problem, and is treated more sensitively by the police than hitherto, encouraging more women to report rape and physical abuse. More support is provided for the victims of violence, both in terms of counselling, and in the provision of refuges.

Nor should the distinctive contributions of feminists to the peace movement, the environmental movement, the animal rights movement, or the left generally be underestimated. All these have been transformed by the active involvement of women, and their involvement has changed the style and content of politics.

The main strength of radical feminism has perhaps always been in action rather than theory, although it could be claimed that it is only radical feminism that can lay claim to a really distinctive political ideology, liberal and Marxist feminism both being essentially derivative. However, radical feminism has perhaps been more impressive in exposing the shortcomings of alternative theoretical foundations than in developing new theory. While there have been attempts to explore the implications of the concept of 'patriarchy', more commonly it has been employed as a catch-all definition and explanation of male dominance. The involvement of some radicals with environmentalism on the one hand, or post-modernism on the other (see below) clearly involves other theoretical connections, but these have contributed to some fragmentation of feminist theory, rather than offering a body of ideas which might be generally acceptable to radical feminism.

Feminists from Wollstonecraft onwards have stimulated a hostile reaction from many men and often also women, so the anti-feminist backlash provoked by the radicals is perhaps scarcely surprising. Yet the crude caricature of the 'Women's Libber' presented by such anti-feminists as Arianna Stassinopoulos (1973) perhaps contains a grain of truth. Moreover, criticism is not confined to anti-feminists. Thus the liberal feminist Betty Friedan (1982) would argue that the shock tactics of the radicals has also alienated support, not least from many women. In particular, Friedan suggests that 'sexual politics has been a red herring', a diversion from the real issues of political and economic exploitation.

Some of this is a criticism of style rather than substance, but there are more fundamental points which go to the heart of the universalist claims of the radical feminists. Thus the preoccupations of some western upper-middle-class feminists, particularly their outright rejection of the institutions of marriage and the family, and even maternity, do sometimes appear remote from the lives and experience of the majority of women, particularly working-class women and women in other cultures. The rejection of patriarchy need not necessarily entail the rejection of motherhood, but a substantial body of feminist writing has involved scorn and derision for the condition and associated maternal values (Freely, 1995), which is unhelpful to the vast majority of women who are mothers or expect to become mothers, whether through their own choice and desire, or through circumstances. Scorn for motherhood is often accompanied by an overidealised perception of the liberating value of a career, which does not recognise that for most women (as for many men) work involves endured tedium, undertaken from financial need, with little prospect of releasing creative energies.

Radical feminists from a relatively privileged background have sometimes been accused of universalising their own highly specific and untypical circumstances as if these were the problems of women everywhere. Yet women may experience very different forms of oppression and have very different needs in different social classes, communities and cultures. The preoccupations of white middle-class feminists do not necessarily coincide with those of black women, and women from the third world, for whom sexual oppression, and the right to personal autonomy are not the first concern (Ramazanoglu,

1989, p. 125). In some cultures women are more exercised over the right to bear children, free from pressures towards family limitation, unsafe contraception, abortion or sterilisation, than they are over the right to abortion.

Some would further argue, with Janet Radcliffe Richards (1982), that exaggeration of the feminist case and neglect of the traditional liberal ideals of reason, justice and fairness, have spoiled the legitimate demands of women for fair and equal treatment. Thus Richards denies that feminism is 'the primary struggle', as some radicals would assert, and rejects the claim of the Redstockings Manifesto that 'All other forms of exploitation and oppression (racism, capitalism, imperialism, etc.) are extensions of male supremacy'. This would seem akin to the vulgar Marxist assertion that all forms of exploitation, including the exploitation of women, derive from conflict between economic classes. Richards similarly castigates demands for the furtherance of women's interests regardless of concerns for justice and morality. Perhaps most significantly, she provides a spirited defence of traditional liberal reason in the face of the deliberate rejection of 'male' logic in favour of feeling and intuition by some radical feminists.

Eco-feminism

Some feminists (who are often also labelled 'radical') have moved in quite a different direction from those radicals who rejected traditional roles associated with motherhood and the family. Traditional feminine attributes are celebrated rather than spurned. Thus child-rearing, far from being stigmatised as demeaning, is once more perceived as a means to fulfilment. Indeed, child-rearing may be seen as the most obvious manifestation of the caring co-operative nature of women, compared with the aggressive, competitive behaviour of men. Far from competing with men, or seeking to be like men, as the liberal feminists appeared to suggest, women should be themselves, and maintain their own distinctive characteristics, values and priorities. This did not necessarily entail a retreat from the political sphere back to the privacy of domesticity, but the promotion of a distinctive alternative female politics of love, peace and care for the environment. The women peace campaigners who symbolically hung baby's bootees and similar objects from the barbed wire surrounding nuclear

	Liberal feminism	Marxist/socialist feminism	Radical feminism
Who?	(first wave) M. Wollstonecraft J.S. Mill H. Taylor suffragettes (second wave) B. Friedan J.R. Richards	(first wave) W. Thompson Engels A. Kollontai (second wave) J. Mitchell M. Barrett	G. Greer K. Millett S. Firestone S. Brownmiller A. Dworkin Eco-feminists
Ideas?	Extension of liberal principles to women: emancipation, equality, civil and political rights	Application of Marxist/ socialist principles to women: economic exploitation, industrial reserve army, domestic labour, reproduction of labour force	Patriarchy and male dominance 'The personal is political' Sexual politics Celebration of women's difference?
Practical concerns	Votes for women Legal rights Outlawing of discrimination Equal opportunities Education for women Equal pay	Unionisation and politicisation of women Child-care for working women Wages for housework? Positive discrimination?	Alternatives to traditional nuclear family Abortion Violence against women: rape, date rape, rape within marriage, pornography Lesbian rights Green issues
Problems	Limitations of legal remedies Failure to explain or remedy continuing sexual inequality Focus on concerns of middle-class and professional career women Neglect of problems of working-class women?	Assumption that end of capitalism and class domination would entail end of exploitation of women Problematic link between gender and class Continued discrimination against women in socialist societies	Insistence on primacy of gender differences over other forms of injustice Remoteness from concerns of 'ordinary' women? Neglect of concerns of black and third world women?

Figure 9.1 Varieties of feminism

missile bases were asserting a different female-oriented value system.

One possible outcome of this kind of radical feminist thinking is what is sometimes referred to as eco-feminism (Plant, 1989; Mies and Shiva, 1993). There is perhaps no logical reason why feminism should entail a concern for the environment. Indeed, some forms of environmentalism have involved a markedly conservative view of the relations between the sexes. The fundamentalist cry 'back to nature' might seem to entail a return to a 'natural' division of labour between the sexes. The image of the earth mother, sometimes associated with eco-feminists, is not one which all feminists find helpful or appealing. Indeed, fascists combined a mystical reverence for the land with some very old-fashioned ideas about the position of women.

Even so, it is clear that women are prominently involved in the Green movement, and for many there is a clear link between their feminist values and their Green commitment. There is a strong female presence likewise in the associated animal rights and vegetarian movements. It may be that experience of pregnancy, giving birth and child nurture do give women a closer sense of kinship with the natural and animal world. Concern for the health of their children entails perhaps a greater awareness of the possible dangers in the environment and in the food chain. Women's nurturing role also gives them a greater felt stake in the future. Moreover, women, it might be suggested, both contribute less to the pollution of the environment and benefit less from those aspects of modern living which are a major cause of pollution, notably the motor car.

Yet arguably the involvement of some feminists in environmentalism has revealed some fissures within the women's movement. There is not a great deal in common between the radical feminism of Shulamith Firestone and that of some of the eco-feminists. The issue of abortion serves to illustrates some of the divisions which have emerged. For many radical feminists of the 1960s and 1970s the demand for abortion was central to female emancipation. Women could not be free unless they had control over their own bodies. Yet for some eco-feminists respect for the life in the unborn foetus was part of their respect for the life of all created things. Those who argue that 'meat is murder' are inclined to think similarly of abortion, which aligns them on this issue with the pro-life 'moral majority' associated with the neo-conservative New Right.

The impact of the New Right – conservative feminism?

This raises the more general question of the impact of New Right ideas on feminism, which has usually been associated predominantly with the left of the political spectrum. As we have seen, feminists were generally radicals in other respects. Mary Wollstonecraft associated with French revolutionaries and married the anarchist William Godwin. Many nineteenth-century American feminist women were closely involved with the anti-slavery movement. Similarly, the second wave of feminism was bound up with civil rights and anti-war protest movements. Thus feminism was associated with other progressive or socialist political causes.

By contrast, the right tended to ignore, scorn, or completely reject the demands of feminists for justice and equality. This was most manifest on the extreme right. The Nazis persecuted feminists, outlawed birth control, condemned women's involvement in politics and recommended a return to the tradition female concerns of *kirche*, *kuche*, *kinder*. Conservatives were less overtly hostile, but generally showed little sympathy for demands for the vote, equal pay and equal opportunities until after they were formally achieved. The British Conservative Party has certainly welcomed women into its ranks, but with a few marked exceptions, of which Mrs Thatcher is the most obvious, has generally assigned them a subordinate role as party workers and fund-raisers, and wives and unpaid political helpmeets of male MPs. Moreover, many Conservative women seem to have accepted their subordinate status uncomplainingly, implicitly and often explicitly rejecting the ideology of feminism.

Thus feminism would seem to have little in common with the right of the spectrum. Yet it would be strange if the ideas of the New Right, which have had such a marked effect on British and western culture generally in recent years, had not had some impact on the women's movement. The initial mainstream feminist reaction was dismissive or hostile to both the neo-conservative and neo-liberal strands of the New Right. Thus Tessa ten Tuscher (in Evans *et al.*, 1986) argued that the agenda of the Moral Majority in the United States and the moral right in Britain was anti-feminist. Georgina Waylen (also in Evans *et al.*, 1986) viewed neo-liberalism as a gender-blind theory which neglected women's concerns but had damaging practical implications for women, who were pushed back into the labour market 'through dire necessity' as a by-product of economic restructuring. These analyses of the twin strands of New Right thinking are penetrating. Yet many women, and even some feminists, have been less antagonistic to some elements of New Right thought.

Neo-liberal free market individualism has some obvious implications for the position of women in the labour market. Discrimination against women simply on the grounds of their gender appears not so much unjust as downright inefficient, involving interference with the operation of the free market and leading to the employment of less able and less productive workers. The increased employment of women, and large-scale unemployment among men is in part a consequence of the greater flexibility of the female workforce, and a greater readiness to accept the competitive market rate for the job (i.e. lower pay), characteristics applauded by neo-liberal economists, although likewise deplored by many feminists as exploitation. However, there are arguably positive aspects for women in this restructuring of the labour market. The world of employment is no longer pre-eminently a man's world. Women are as a consequence not only breadwinners in their own right, but often the main breadwinners in the household. A small proportion of women, moreover, have spectacularly benefited from the new meritocratic competition for career advancement. The economic position of women generally has been transformed. Their purchasing power in the economy is increasingly evident not only in the advertising of traditional female products, but in the promotion of cars, banks and insurance policies.

The neo-conservative aspects of the New Right perhaps have more ostensibly damaging implications for most women, however. The reaction against 'permissiveness', the proclaimed concern for the silent or moral majority, and the 'back to basics' campaign have involved a reaffirmation of traditional and particularly family values. Thus the breakdown of marriage and the traditional family have been widely deplored. As gender relationships within marriage and the nuclear family have been a major target for radical feminists, it might be imagined that the attitudes of feminists and neo-conservatives are diametrically opposed. Indeed, this is still largely the case. However, radical feminists have sometimes found themselves in the same camp as neo-conservatives, notably over pornography, which many feminists have vigorously denounced, for the image it portrays of women, for the encouragement it might offer to the sexual abuse of women, and for the exploitation of women employed as models. Thus some feminists find themselves aligned with neo-conservative opponents of sexual permissiveness, which was once commonly associated with women's liberation.

Additionally, some feminists have had second thoughts over the attacks on the family and the values of traditional motherhood associated with the 1960s and early 1970s. Then the family was seen by radical feminists as a prison. Women's emancipation therefore entailed the destruction of the conventional family. Yet some have argued that men have been the main beneficiaries of sexual liberation. The freedom from conventional ties have not been liberating for all women, particularly those forced into the dual role of sole bread-winner and carer in lone-parent households. Moreover, while escalating divorce statistics and the growing phenomenon of the one-parent family suggested that the traditional family was dead or dying, experimentation with alternative lifestyles by some feminists were not altogether successful. Other feminists rediscovered the satisfactions of motherhood.

Thus Betty Friedan, who encouraged a generation of American women to ambitions and careers outside the narrow confines of conventional domesticity has in a later book (1982) reaffirmed the values of the family and marriage. For Friedan, who was always a liberal feminist with a reformist rather than a revolutionary agenda, this was only a change of emphasis. Rather more surprising perhaps, Germaine Greer, who remains a scathing critic of the western nuclear family, has become an enthusiast for the extended family as a source of comfort, support and fulfilment for women. Other feminists, while seeking a broader, more inclusive, and more tolerant definition of the family, have cautiously endorsed family values. Thus they have sometimes appeared as ideological bedfellows of New Right neo-conservatives. Indeed, there are some female Conservative politicians for whom the term 'conservative feminist' may not be inappropriate, in that they combine traditional family values with a concern for women's issues, which has sometimes led them into cross-party alliances with other women politicians (Walter, *Guardian*, 9/11/95).

Yet for most feminists any ideological fellow-travelling with the New Right is strictly limited. While some policy prescriptions may coincide, underlying assumptions tend to remain very different. To many neo-conservatives the institution of the family is valued for its presumed capacity to restore the authority and social order which they see as lacking in society. It is a means of disciplining the young, and the restoration of paternal discipline is key facet of this neo-conservative agenda. Hence it is urged that 'families need fathers'. At another level support for the traditional two-parent family may be seen as means to limiting the escalating social welfare budget. Family breakup and single parenting is perceived as a significant burden on the state and the taxpayer. By contrast, feminists seek increased support for lone parents. While they too advocate more help for families, that presupposes a broader conception of the family.

The tensions can be seen in attitudes to the Child Support Agency. This was supported in principle by many feminists, who have long campaigned for more realistic maintenance payments for child support, and better enforcement of court orders. Yet the targets given to the Agency by the government, and the way in which those targets were in practice implemented, suggested that the main aim was not to benefit lone parents (most of whom are women) but to save the Exchequer money. Women bringing up children on their own discovered that any increased contributions from 'absent fathers' were offset by reductions in welfare benefits, so commonly they were no better off financially, while relations with former partners were soured. Meanwhile, second wives and the children of second marriages suffered from a marked reduction in family income. Thus an ostensibly pro-family measure actually made many families, and many women, worse off.

In other respects also the practical consequences of New Right policies have had damaging consequences for many women. While the ideas behind 'care in the community' were compatible with many feminist concerns, the reality has often involved a greater burden on principally female relatives of those requiring care, with only inadequate support services from the state. At the same time the effective privatisation of much geriatric institutional care has provided a bonanza for the owners of homes, yet these financial benefits have not generally percolated through to the army of largely part-time low-paid female staff, some of whom previously enjoyed better pay and conditions in the public sector. Thus for many old campaigners in the women's movement, the notion of conservative feminism still appears a contradiction in terms.

Feminism and post-modernism

It has been observed that feminism has always appeared a particularly
action-oriented ideology, with immediate practical concerns generally
taking priority over the elaboration of feminist theory, which indeed
has sometimes been criticised as relatively thin or essentially derivative. Some feminists have found new theoretical insights in the ideas
associated with post-modernism.

Post-modernism is difficult to pin down and define. The term has
been employed in a wide variety of contexts: in architecture, in
literary criticism and the study of popular culture, and in philosophy
and politics. While there is a clear family resemblance between the
various usages, there are also differences of emphasis. Thus post-
modernism means different things to different people, which is
perhaps hardly surprising as its major thrust is to question the whole
search for meaning and purpose in art and life.

Post-modernism essentially involves a reaction against the post-
Enlightenment faith in rationalism and progress. Post-Enlightenment
rationalism was sceptical in the sense that it rejected traditional
authority, particularly the 'revealed truths' of religion. Yet it was not
sceptical over the search for truth itself, through the exercise of
human reason and science. Post-modernism, by contrast, rejects all
'metanarratives', or universal explanations, including those derived
from post-Enlightenment science and rational enquiry. It undermines
the assumptions of truth and authority in male-oriented western
culture, and even the assumptions of both Christians and humanists of
a universe centred on the human species. Thus just as sceptical post-
Enlightenment rationalism was a critical weapon in the struggle
against the received wisdom of the age, so post-modernism is a useful
intellectual tool for anyone, including feminists, Greens, and post-
colonial opponents of cultural imperialism who wishes to challenge
prevailing orthodoxies in the modern world.

Thus it is perhaps unsurprising that some feminists have been
attracted to post-modernism. Women have not always conspicuously
benefited from the progress entailed in industrialisation and modernisation. As we have seen, some feminists have seen rationalism as
'male logic', antipathetic to feminine feeling and intuition. Moreover,
well before post-modernism became fashionable, feminists spelled
out in some detail the unfavourable image of women presented both
in 'serious' literature and popular culture, while others pointed to a

persistent male bias in conventional estimates of literary worth. Post-modernist literary criticism has provided feminists with a powerful conceptual framework to reveal the gender bias in the use of language, to uncover new messages in and behind texts, and to attack traditional male-oriented canons of literary excellence.

Some feminists have undoubtedly found the debunking thrust of post-modernism stimulating and liberating (McRobbie in Perryman, 1994). Women, they argue, can only benefit from the rejection of received intellectual authority, from the undermining of old assumptions, and the breaking down of old barriers between disciplines. Moreover, the rejection of 'metanarratives' is useful for those feminists seeking to escape the universalist assumptions of Marxism and older forms of radical feminism, with their neglect of women's needs and feelings in other cultures. In this intellectual atmosphere new diverse ways of thinking can flourish.

Yet others have been more cautious or downright hostile. The relativism implicit in post-modernism is ultimately, they argue, not only destructive of 'male-stream' assumptions but of any alternative, including feminism itself. If the message is 'Anything goes!' then demands for women's rights can be dismissed as just one other subjective perspective, with no other claims on allegiance. Thus feminists 'must be wary of throwing out reason and justice in their entirety' (Bryson, 1992). Post-modernism could prove an intellectual cul-de-sac, and a distraction from the immediate practical issues and broader struggle previously associated with the women's movement.

Feminism and the future

The outlook for feminism now seems more problematic than in the 1960s and 1970s. Some apparent victories achieved by the women's movement then have proved cosmetic, illusory or double-edged. Moreover, feminists have provoked a strong anti-feminist backlash, from men, particularly in the United States, and even from some women. Radical feminists might see this backlash as evidence of their own success in challenging the assumptions behind a patriarchal society, but the altered moral and political climate has led to some setbacks on traditional feminist issues. Thus it is those who still champion the freedom of women to control their own bodies who have been pushed onto the defensive by the increasingly militant pro-life campaigners against abortion.

The women's movement also seems more uncertain and divided than it was. There have long been differences in underlying theoretical assumptions between those rather arbitrarily classified as liberal, Marxist and radical feminists. Eco-feminists, post-modernists and others have added further distinctive and sometimes provocative contributions to feminist theory. Such theoretical debates may be dismissed as relatively unimportant and secondary to practical issues in what has always been an action-oriented ideology. Yet significantly there are now more differences than there were on policy: on, for example, wages for housework, pornography and censorship, abortion, child support and the family. There are also divergences over tactics.

Perhaps this only serves to illustrate that feminism is an ideology like any other, with its own different strands and conflicting tendencies. Moreover, the diversity in feminist thought can be viewed more positively as an indication of its essential strength and vitality. Nor, at another level, should the actual progress secured by women in some areas be underestimated. Changes in language and the portrayal of women both reflect and assist changes in attitudes. Significant barriers to the appointment and promotion of women in many occupations and professions have been broken. There is rather more sensitivity towards the feelings of women on sexual violence and pornography. There is a greater awareness of the disproportionate burden placed on women in domestic labour, the upbringing of children, and the care of the old and disabled, and this has led to some changes in practice. The continuing discrimination and oppression suffered by women should not obscure some real if modest gains, secured in large part by the agitation of feminists.

There has also been some real progress for women in the conventional political arena scorned by some radicals. Thus there have been significant recent increases in the numbers of women elected to Parliaments and other representative institutions over much of the world. Until recently this was less evident in the UK (Randall, 1987). However, both the 1987 and 1992 elections involved a modest but significant rise in the number of women MPs. The adoption by the Labour Party of deliberate positive discrimination involving all-women shortlists for many winnable seats seems likely to raise the parliamentary representation of women to somewhere close to Scandinavian levels. As so much of the early struggle for women's rights centred on the franchise, and as its achievement resulted in some disappointment with the results in terms of parliamentary politics, this advance in the involvement of women in the conventional political sphere represents a belated victory for the old suffragettes.

Ongoing changes in society, such as changes in the pattern and structure of employment, increased diversity in household units, and an ageing population, have particular implications for women and feminist theory. Some of these developments could involve yet higher burdens on women in their traditional parenting and caring role, unless men are persuaded to take a greater share of responsibility. Others have already led to the scapegoating of some women, such as those heading one-parent families who are dependent on state welfare. Newly fashionable communitarian ideas may involve a retreat from the competitive individualism associated with the New Right, but they may equally point to the replacement of state welfare by care in the family and the community. As many women have learned to their cost, care in the community too often involves in practice care by unpaid female relatives, with little or no outside assistance.

Guide to further reading

Good introductions to feminist politics are provided by Vicky Randall (1987), April Carter (1988) and Joni Lovenduski and Vicky Randall (1993). For a broad and lucid introduction to feminist political theory Valerie Bryson (1992) is invaluable. Diana Coole (1988) focuses enlighteningly on women in the history of traditional political theory, from Plato onwards.

For those who wish to sample the range of feminist thinking, there are a number of readers which can be recommended, including *British Feminist Thought* edited by Lovell (1990), *Feminisms* edited by Maggie Humm (1992) and *Women's Studies* edited by Stevi Jackson *et al.* (1993).

Liberal feminism may be explored through the classic texts of Wollstonecraft and Mill, and the more recent work of Betty Friedan (1977, 1982) and Janet Radcliffe Richards (1982). Aspects of Marxist feminism are examined by Juliet Mitchell (1974), who combines psychological analysis with a Marxist framework, and Michelle

Barrett (1980). L. Sargent (1981) has edited a collection of essays on *The Unhappy Marriage of Marxism and Feminism*.

The modern radical feminist classics by Kate Millett, Germaine Greer, Shulamith Firestone and Eva Figes are all still readily available. Other important texts are Susan Brownmiller (1977) on rape and sexual violence and Andrea Dworkin (1981) on pornography. Arianna Stassinopoulos (1973) provided an early populist assault on modern feminism. Books which are more thoughtfully critical of some aspects of radical feminism include Richards (1982, above), Caroline Ramazanoglu (1989), who points to the diversity of women's experiences and particularly to the different preoccupations of women from ethnic minorities and the third world, and Maureen Freely (1995) who champions motherhood.

Books on eco-feminism include *Healing the Wounds*, a collection of essays and readings edited by Judith Plant (1989) and *Ecofeminism* by Maria Mies and Vandana Shiva (1993). The implications of post-modernism for feminism are explored critically by Bryson (1992, above) and Judith Grant (1993) and more enthusiastically by Angela McRobbie (in M. Perryman, 1994).

Finally, a number of fairly recent books examine aspects of feminist theory in ways which cut across conventional classifications. Judith Evans *et al.* (1986), includes among other essays two feminist perspectives on the New Right. Carol Lee Bacchi (1990) critically examines the debate over sexual equality and difference. Michelle Barrett and Anne Phillips (1992) edit a wide range of essays from different feminist perspectives.

10

GREEN IDEOLOGY

Introduction

Any survey of modern ideologies would be incomplete without an examination of Green thinking, which in some forms at least now clearly constitutes an important and distinctive political philosophy, and presents a profound challenge to virtually all longer-established political creeds. While its roots can be traced back a long way, to pantheism, romanticism and the rediscovery of nature, Malthusianism, elements of anarchism, and even aspects of fascism, it is essentially a new ideology. It has brought together a number of more specific concerns – over, for example, conservation, pollution, energy, population growth and animal rights – and woven these together into a coherent and distinctive political philosophy, which, in a comparatively brief period, has achieved a remarkable impact over much of the world.

Inevitably, as with other ideologies, there are problems of definition and terminology. The label 'Green' is a broad one, and is not easily adapted into an 'ism'. Thus some commentators have preferred the term 'environmentalism' or 'ecologism' to describe the political ideology which is here simply described as 'Green'. Yet these alternatives are not only awkward and less familiar, but also carry their own baggage of associations. The term 'Green' by contrast is freely adopted by pressure groups and political parties, and both the name and the colour has become powerfully associated in the public mind both with specific environmental concerns and a more general political outlook. All familiar labels involve some problems and ambiguities, but there seems no compelling reason artificially to substitute another term for one which is so universally recognised. Here the term 'Green' will be freely and perhaps indiscriminately applied not just to specific causes, groups or parties commonly described as 'Green' but to the underlying political philosophy which relates the concerns of humanity to the world of which it forms a part.

Of course there is a need for some further distinction and sub-classification of Green thinking. Political ideologies are expressed at various levels and involve sharp internal tensions and conflicts. The Greens are no exception. There are considerable differences among them in terms of analysis, policy prescription and strategy. There is no generally accepted terminology. Distinctions have been drawn between dark Greens and light Greens (e.g. Porritt and Winner, 1988) deep and shallow Greens, ecologists and environmentalists (Dobson, 1995), radicals and reformists (e.g. Garner, 1995), ecocentrics and technocentrics (O'Riordan, 1976), fundamentalists and realists (among German Greens). The pairs of terms overlap, but each has particular connotations, and they are not necessarily interchangeable. Most are relative terms, implying a spectrum of attitudes, not sharp distinctions. At one end there are those whose concern over one or more specific environmental issues gives their general political outlook a greenish tinge. At the other end there are those who hold a coherent and distinctive Green philosophy which colours their whole personal and political perspective on life.

This Green philosophy is clearly marked off from other political ideologies. All other political creeds focus on the presumed interests, needs or rights of the human species, or more narrowly, of sections of human society: such as a particular race, nation, class, or gender. The Greens effectively marginalise virtually all these interests and virtually all the fundamental issues of traditional political theory by focusing instead on the universe or the planet. Mainstream political ideologies are dismissed as anthropocentric – they assume that humankind is the centre of the universe, rather than one species among countless others. To Greens the overriding political issue is the relationship of the human species with its environment.

The Green message is a stark one. It is that a continuation of unthinking and unlimited human exploitation of the natural environment spells disaster for the planet and for its human inhabitants.

Impending disaster can only be averted by a sharp change of direction, preserving rather than destroying the environment, using renewable rather than non-renewable resources, and adopting sustainable rather than non-sustainable lifestyles. There are massive implications for all areas of public policy, but particularly industrial and agricultural policy, energy policy and transport policy.

Green and other ideologies

One way of classifying older or more established mainstream political ideologies is by locating them on the familiar left–right political spectrum, although, as has been seen, there are some difficulties in placing nationalism and feminism. The Greens are similarly awkward to place. Indeed, many Greens would argue that they represent a radically different departure from the old politics, and they are 'neither left nor right but forward'. Yet although some Greens would prefer to dismiss as irrelevant other ways of thinking about politics, it is inevitable that Green ideas should be related to other ideologies.

In the first place, to state the obvious, no ideology can be wholly new. Ideas derive from somewhere, and in exploring the roots of Green thinking, inevitably connections are made with thinkers, values and interests which are more familiarly associated with other ideologies or traditions of thought. Secondly, virtually all political creeds now proclaim a concern for the environment, which in turn requires some analysis of the green credentials of mainstream ideologies. Thirdly, those who reject older ideologies and identify themselves as 'Green' generally also have views on political issues which are not essentially or exclusively Green, and which tend to place them on the 'left' or the 'right'. Finally, in terms of practical politics it is very difficult for Greens to avoid making tactical alliances with other interests and parties. Almost inevitably they are forced to choose, and further consequences flow from choice. Thus Greens are likely to be associated with the political company they keep.

Aspects of Green thinking can be derived from a very diverse range of sources. A pantheistic concern for the universe can be found among Greek stoics. The revolt against rationalism, industrialism and modernism can be discerned in such thinkers as Rousseau, Carlyle, Ruskin or Disraeli. The notion of limits to growth was famously

articulated by Malthus. A preference for the small scale and community values can be derived from Kropotkin or William Morris. To
name such thinkers is to touch off further associations. Thus aspects
of Green thinking can be derived from those who regarded themselves or have been commonly regarded as conservatives, liberals,
socialists and anarchists. There are also links with some forms of
nationalism and even fascism. More recently, as has been noted, there
is a marked compatibility with a significant strand of feminism.

Greens and the right

At the Conservative Party Conference of 1988 Mrs Thatcher startled
commentators by proclaiming her party's Green credentials (Mc-
Cormick, 1991, ch. 3). This was surprising in the sense that the free
market strand of conservatism with which Mrs Thatcher has been
particularly associated has generally seemed the political ideology
least obviously compatible with Green ideas (Hay, 1988). The freedom of market forces and associated notions of legitimate profit
maximisation does not apparently sit easily with controls over pollution and environmental exploitation. Yet some neo-liberal economists
argue that through the market solutions will be found for problems of
resource depletion and pollution. Thus market pressures will oblige
entrepreneurs to find innovative alternatives to scarce resources,
while experience has demonstrated the profit potential of environmentally friendly goods. Moreover, ways can be found of making
polluters pay (Ashford, 1989). More fundamentally, it is suggested
that private interest and ownership is more conducive to environmental preservation than common ownership (Hardin, 1968). There is
something in such arguments, although they do not provide easy
answers to either long-term resource depletion and pollution issues on
the one hand, or sudden environmental disasters on the other. On
balance, Green solutions would appear to require rather more interference with free market forces than neo-liberals are generally prepared to countenance (Martell, 1994, pp. 63–72).

Yet arguably mainstream conservatism shows more affinities with
Green thinking. Traditional conservatism involved a reaction against
post-Enlightenment rationalism, science, industrialism, modernism
and faith in progress, and much of this would be shared by modern
Greens. Almost by definition, conservation is a key value, and

traditional conservatives have had a strong interest in the land, and the preservation of the environment. In some cases this has taken the form of support for groups such as the Council for the Protection of Rural England, or the National Trust. Further to the right on the political spectrum, some nationalists or fascists would proclaim an almost mystical association between race and environment, of 'blood and soil'.

There are indeed some Greens whose views are compatible with the traditional or even the fascist right. However, many Greens would argue that the conservative interest in the land is essentially self-interested and exploitative. The concern is for the rights of land-owners, including their rights to exploit the land for their own profit and pleasure, conserving game for example, so they can subsequently hunt or shoot, and restricting access to the countryside. Many Greens would reject the assumptions of natural hierarchy and inequality associated with the right. In terms of practical politics, although Greens might sometimes enter tactical alliances with local right-wing preservation groups opposed to new roads, housing or retail develop-ments, the grounds of Green concern are fundamentally different from those of self-interested NIMBYs. Thus although Greens share some conservative values, they are not essentially defenders of the status quo, but radicals, seeking a very different future.

Greens and the left

In practice, Green activists are more commonly associated with other radicals and the left rather than the right, with anarchists, socialists, social democrats and radical liberals. 'Red-greens' are a more famil-iar phenomenon than 'blue-greens', at almost every level of political activity. There are socialists with a strong green commitment, active in groups such as SERA. Some Greens were previously members of left-wing parties or groups, and retain an affinity with their former political allegiance. Other Greens have worked closely with socialists of all kinds in the peace movement or the women's movement. In terms of analysis, Green concerns with certain aspects of indus-trialism overlap with the fundamental socialist critique of capitalism. Some Marxists have argued that not only are Marx's ideas compatible with environmentalism, but that his analysis is highly relevant to modern Green thinking (Pepper, 1993). In terms of prescription both socialists and Greens seek radical change.

Yet some strands of socialism are clearly more compatible with Green ideas than others. Greens tend to be individualist rather than collectivist, with a mistrust of large bureaucratic organisations, whether these are major industrial unions or government departments. Anarchism, and the bottom-up decentralised approach of Owen, William Morris or the Guild Socialists would seem to have more in common with Green thinking than the centralised state socialism or labourism which have been dominant strands in the British socialist tradition. Moreover, for all their critique of capitalism, most socialists (including Marx) belong firmly to the modernist, rationalist and essentially optimistic post-Enlightenment tradition. Their objections to the private ownership of capital does not extend to the industrialisation associated with capitalism. On the contrary, they tend to be fervent believers in modernisation, progress and growth. Indeed, the leading socialist revisionist, Crosland (1956), hoped to promote greater equality in large part through redistributing the product of economic growth. At a practical level the interest of the labour movement in jobs and living standards has not always been compatible with Green concerns.

Thus Greens would argue that although other political creeds might proclaim some environmental concerns, some of this is relatively shallow and cosmetic 'greenspeak'. For both conservatives and socialists, green issues are at best always likely to have a lower priority than core ideological concerns, for private property and the free market on the one hand, or social reform and equality on the other. Only for the Greens are environmental issues central and fundamental rather than essentially peripheral. Only the Greens (or perhaps some Greens) articulate a coherent alternative ecological ideology.

Key elements of Green thinking

It is now necessary to identify the core ingredients of this Green ideology. The key elements of Green thinking have been variously identified. Lists of core principles generally include the assumption that there are limits to growth, and the corollary of 'sustainability', an ecocentric rather than anthropocentric view of the relationship between humans and their environment, and a 'holistic' rather than piecemeal approach to the analysis of environmental issues and problems. Some would add a preference for small-scale and local organisation and activity. Other principles sometimes mentioned might be regarded as essentially derivative – thus limits to population might be seen as an application of sustainability (see e.g. Dobson, 1995; Kenny in Eccleshall *et al.*, 1994; and Garner, 1995).

While all the above have been regarded as core Green principles, it should be noted that they are principles of different kinds. The holistic approach is a fundamental methodological assumption which suggests that problems cannot be tackled in isolation, but are only explicable as parts of a whole. The notion of 'limits to growth' can be interpreted by contrast as a scientific hypothesis, in principle suscept-ible to empirical investigation. The ecocentric view, crudely ex-pressed in the slogan 'Earth first', asserts a moral principle, although it may also be interpreted as a means to the anthropocentric end of human survival. The emphasis on the small scale and the local might be interpreted as a fundamental political principle or alternatively as a point of strategy – a means to an end.

Green thinking is sometimes associated with post-modernism, naturally enough, as the targets of post-modernists are largely targets of Greens also: post-Enlightenment assumptions over science, reason and progress (Pepper, 1993, pp. 55–8). Yet ultimately post-modern-ism is a rather dubious ally, as it implies a moral relativism which is at odds with the Greens' essentially ethical message, and as it rejects all metanarratives or universal explanations, and environmentalism is above all a metanarrative. While Greens reject current orthodoxies, they have their own truths to proclaim. It is now necessary to explore these truths in rather more detail.

Limits to growth – sustainability

The Greens' challenge to the near universal assumption of the benefits to be derived from growth is a crucial element of their distinctive ideological approach. The notion that cumulative growth is both possible and desirable is relatively recent and the product of industrialisation and modernisation. In predominantly agrarian com-munities output and income waxed and waned largely according to climatic conditions. Malthus (1970, ed. Flew) supplied a plausible theoretical account of the practical limits to growth through the notion of diminishing returns, which was particularly applicable to agriculture, where land was a relatively fixed factor of production. However, the experience of the industrialising western world in the nineteenth century seemed to suggest the possibility of virtually limitless improvements in growth and living standards. Since then, high growth has become a tacit and often explicit objective of governments across the ideological spectrum, and a crucial component of a revisionist social democratic creed which sought to promote greater equality and provide social benefits without making anyone worse off through the distribution of the products of planned growth.

Modern Greens have rediscovered the essentially Malthusian assumption that there are limits to the increases in productivity to be derived from the exploitation of finite natural resources. They have also identified significant costs associated with the pursuit of growth, in terms of damage to the environment, and risks to health. The limits to and costs of growth have been vividly dramatised in some celebrated attempts to predict the consequences of present trends, such as the Club of Rome report 'The Limits to Growth' (Meadows *et al.*, 1972). While the more pessimistic doomwatch scenarios have been partially discredited as predictions of the imminent exhaustion of natural resources have been proved wrong (Maddox, 1972), Greens would argue that the fundamental point remains unchallenged and unchallengeable – that non-renewable resources such as fossil fuels are finite and will ultimately be exhausted.

The Greens' alternative to the pursuit of growth is the principle of sustainability. Humanity should only adopt those policies which can in the long run be sustained without irreversible damage to the resources on which the human species and other species depend. The practical implications are more contestable. There is a school of thought, known as 'ecological modernisation', which suggests that environmental protection and sustainability is compatible with real growth and improvements in living standards (Weale, 1992, ch. 3). Another line of argument suggests that the pursuit of material prosperity is ultimately not fulfilling for human beings, who increasingly prize a quality of life which involves environmental protection. Indeed, the involvement in Green parties and causes of a growing section of the middle classes in advanced industrial societies provides some supporting evidence for this assumption (Martell, 1994). One issue at stake here is what 'growth' actually involves, and how it should be measured.

Yet if economic growth is measured in conventional economic terms, most Greens would probably concede that sustainability can only be achieved with (for developed nations at least), zero or negative growth, with lower material living standards, and a reduction in population levels. This is, needless to say, a difficult message to sell. Politicians have generally sought power by promising to make people better off in material terms. Greens are effectively promising to make people worse off (although, as already noted, there is some scope for argument as to whether a reduction in material consumption would involve a higher or lower quality of life). It is widely assumed, particularly by neo-liberals, that human beings are naturally self-seeking and acquisitive, and on these assumptions it is difficult to see how they can be persuaded to forego current consumption in the interests of generations yet unborn, still less other species, or the long-run survival of the planet. Thus even if the economic case for long-run limits to growth are accepted, there seems little prospect of a fundamental change in human behaviour without some assumptions about guiding moral principles, which takes the argument from the economic into the ethical sphere.

Ecocentrism

Some would argue that an ecocentric rather than an anthropocentric approach is the defining characteristic of a distinctive Green philosophy (Eckersley, 1992). An anthropocentric view puts humankind firmly at the centre of the universe. Green policies of pollution control and resource conservation are justified in terms of human interests – both present and future generations. An ecocentric view does not accord any priority to humanity, but emphasises the intrinsic value of the natural world, and the need of men and women to live in harmony with the universe. The distinction seems clear, but in practice, like other attempts to categorise Greens, involves a subtle gradation of positions. Further sub-divisions can be discerned within both anthropocentrism and ecocentrism (e.g. Eckersley, 1992, ch. 2). Moreover, there are some Greens who would reject anthropocentrism without endorsing a pure ecocentric position. Supporters of animal rights occupy an important intermediate position (Martell, 1994). As they argue animals should be valued for their own sake, they are clearly not anthropocentric, but in confining their concerns to sentient beings which can experience pain and pleasure, they fall far short of the ecocentric perspective which values the whole universe, including non-sentient nature (e.g. trees) and inanimate objects (e.g. rocks).

It can be argued that ecocentrism is ultimately a moral principle, requiring human beings to place the interests of the planet above their own self-interest. It is a moral principle which runs counter to key assumptions of post-Renaissance humanism, Baconian science and post-Enlightenment modernism, and indeed to most religions and philosophical systems which have held sway in the world, although some attempt has been made by Green writers to relate their ethical principles to those of 'primal' peoples, such as pre-Christian Celts or American Indians.

Mainstream religion and mainstream political thought is anthropocentric: it focuses on humanity and human needs. It is implicitly and often explicitly assumed that the rest of the natural world exists to serve the needs of humankind. It follows that men and women are free to exploit natural resources in whichever way they please to suit their own interests. Scientific advances have enabled humanity to overcome specific problems and exploit the resources of the natural world more effectively. Industrialisation and modernisation has involved the apparent taming of nature in the service of man.

In place of this anthropocentric approach, the ecocentric view places the human species in the context of its environment. 'Earth first' is a shorthand slogan which requires humans to consider first and foremost the future of the planet rather than their own immediate requirements. They have no claim to primacy over other species. Indeed, some Greens argue, it is the human species which has provided the main threat to the long-run survival of the planet. If the Earth is to survive, human beings must learn to live in harmony with their natural environment, rather than seeking to exploit it.

One version of the ecocentric approach is the Gaian hypothesis, which suggests that the Earth – personified as the Goddess Gaia – is a complex super-organism which requires other organisms to operate so as to keep the planet fit for life (Lovelock, 1979). Greens who oppose spiritual values to the materialist values they see embedded in modern society have sometimes tended to deify nature, which apparently provides a quasi-religious foundation for their ethical assumptions. Yet defining exactly what is 'nature' or 'natural', and identifying right with nature involves familiar philosophical difficulties. Another militant interpretation of the injunction 'Earth First!' is provided by extremists within the American group of that name who have used sometimes violent and dangerous direct action techniques to protect the environment from man.

The notion of animal rights might be considered as either an important subsidiary application of the ecocentric principle, or a distinctive political perspective. While perhaps all Greens would share a concern for animal welfare, at least rejecting unnecessary cruelty, and would support the aims of established pressure groups such as the RSPCA and the League Against Cruel Sports, not all would go further to endorse animal rights. Greens in practice adopt a variety of positions with regard to the treatment of animals (Singer, 1990; Regan, 1988; Garner, 1995; Martell, 1994). Thus many, but by no means all, Greens are vegetarians or vegans. For some this is a matter of simple preference or health or efficient resource utilisation. For others it is a critical ethical issue: 'meat is murder'. They view the rearing and killing of animals for human consumption as morally on the same level as the deliberate murder of fellow humans. Similarly, the use of animals in experiments to test new beauty treatments or medicines is regarded by some animal rights activists as akin to Nazi medical experiments on the Jews. A few who take this view have been prepared to indulge in acts of violence, including even murder, against those who are perceived to abuse animals.

Ultimately 'Earth first' or 'Animal Rights' are fundamental moral principles not susceptible to scientific verification or falsification, to be held irrespective of their consequences. Clearly they are moral principles which some people hold and at least try to act upon, even where they may conflict with their own tastes and instincts. Yet such principles are not widely held, and it is difficult to see how the majority of humanity might be persuaded to adopt them, particularly in the absence of religious sanctions. In practice, despite their explicit rejection of the anthropocentric approach, in order to persuade others, and perhaps also to persuade themselves, many Greens tend to fall back on human-centred justifications for their injunctions. Thus human beings should refrain from exploiting and polluting in their own long-term interests, or those of their children and grand-children.

The holistic approach

The holistic approach requires that problems should not be analysed in isolation but related to the whole of which they are a part. The whole in question here is the universe or the ecosystem. Thus holism might be derived from the ecocentric perspective. Yet although it has moral overtones, it is essentially a matter of methodology.

The need to analyse environmental problems in context is sometimes seen as the defining characteristic which marks off genuine ecologists, deep or dark Greens from those who have particular and limited environmental concerns. Thus light or shallow Greens are commonly associated with particular single issues, such as live calf exports, or new roads, or nuclear power, while deep or dark Greens have a holistic concern for the environment, of which such specific issues are at best only a part, and at worst a dangerous diversion from more fundamental objectives.

This can be illustrated by reference to the campaign for lead-free petrol. In this campaign the harmful consequences of lead additives to petrol for children's health in particular were demonstrated and publicised, resulting in public pressure on government to encourage lead-free petrol through a tax incentive. At one level it was a textbook example of a successful single issue campaign (Wilson, 1984). From a light Green or environmentalist perspective the problem was virtually solved. Yet dark Greens would perceive the problem against the general context of resource conservation, waste and pollution. One possibility is that lead might be effectively replaced by other equally environmentally harmful additives. Yet, more to the point, the removal of lead from petrol may be perceived as at best a palliative which does not tackle the fundamental problem of resource depletion, waste and pollution associated with human dependence on the motor car. At worst it might be regarded as ecologically counter-productive, encouraging false assumptions about green fuels and green motoring.

In one sense the need to see problems in context and relate issues to the wider whole is simply common sense, and may help to avoid counter-productive strategies. Yet taken to extremes it might inhibit any action, because it would be impossible to calculate all the possible environmental implications and side-effects of any policy initiative compared with all the alternatives. Moreover, any personal or local initiative might be regarded as 'a drop in the ocean' and irrelevant to the real issue.

In practice, even those Greens most insistent on a holistic approach tend to become involved in single-issue campaigns, which can often be justified not only in terms of incrementalist reform, but also for raising environmental consciousness. Thus pure or dark Greens may frequently become involved in tactical alliances with others whose commitment to a wider green agenda may be vestigial. Indeed, any specific environmental issue, such as opposition to a new road, tends to attract a coalition of interests, including NIMBYs with little or no general concern for the environment, people seeking to preserve particular areas of countryside or wildlife habitats, specialist pressure groups such as Transport 2000, as well as committed Green activists for whom the proposed new road is only an illustration of much wider issues of pollution and resource depletion. For Greens, such tactical alliances present awkward questions of political strategy which might be perceived as particularly problematic for the green movement generally.

Small is beautiful?

Sometimes regarded as a core principle, sometimes seen as an issue of strategy is the widespread green preference for the small scale, decentralised and local. An influential text was Schumacher's (1973) *Small is Beautiful* which challenged the then fashionable presumption in favour of large-scale enterprise. Since then the mass production associated with Fordism has increasingly given way to the small-scale and flexible high tech and service enterprises considered character-istic of a post-Fordist economy. To that extent the previously heret-ical assertion 'small is beautiful' has become the new orthodoxy.

Schumacher was an economist, and much of the argument can be couched in terms of economic theory. Conventional economic theory suggested that there were economies of scale to be gained from larger-scale production, although it was always recognised that be-yond a certain point there might be diseconomies of scale. Theory seemed to be abundantly confirmed by the expansion of manufacturing industry through the mass production of standardised products, such as the family Ford car, which in western capitalist societies brought what were previous luxury items into the reach of those on average income. Standardisation and large-scale operations also seemed to yield benefits in such areas as retailing and catering, and even in government, where it was suggested that larger departments, larger local authorities, and larger units for administering specific services such as education, health or police would likewise yield economies of scale.

There were always those who held a more sceptical or hostile perspective on this trend towards larger-scale production and organisation in the modern world. Burke spoke eloquently of the love of the little platoon. Toulmin Smith fulminated against the centralising tendencies of the Victorian era. William Morris reaffirmed the value of individual craftsmanship in an age of mass production. Anarchists rejected the growing power of the modern centralised nation-state.

These often appeared to be minority voices vainly protesting against the onward march of progress and modernisation. Yet modern Green preferences for the small scale and local seem rather more consistent with prevailing trends. Thus the Fordist assumptions behind mass production, standardisation, specialisation and the division of labour have given place to a post-Fordist emphasis on innovation, flexibility and autonomy in the workplace. To an extent, small has become fashionable. Mainstream analysis accords a leading role to small to medium enterprises in fostering economic development. Modern management theory suggests the need for flatter hierarchies which accord more autonomy to front-line staff. Current political wisdom reaffirms the need for government close to the people through decentralisation.

All this would seem abundantly to justify the common Green preference for community-based action at the local level, and bottom-up rather than top-down political strategies. Indeed, Green political activity seems largely to fit neatly into a post-industrial, post-Fordist, post-modern world. Their own organisational structures tend to be decentralised, with few concessions to the conventional requirements for discipline, unity and leadership. Thus the British Green Party has shown a marked reluctance to recognise leaders, and a distaste for actual or potential political stars. Green activists generally follow the injunction to 'think global, act local'.

A possible corollary of decentralisation is greater self-sufficiency or autarky. Indeed, unless there is to be considerable co-operation among self-governing small-scale communities, an increased level of self-sufficiency is essential. Yet some Greens would point also to substantial positive benefits from greater self-sufficiency in terms of resource conservation. Less fuel and other resources would be needed to transport goods and people. One version of this approach is described as 'bioregionalism' (Eckersley, 1992, pp. 167–70; Martell, 1994, pp. 51–3), which seeks the integration of human communities within their distinctive regional environment. Thus the inhabitants of a particular region would utilise the specific resources of the region at a sustainable level, rather than relying on international trade to fulfil their needs. Bioregionalism rejects the general assumptions of the benefits to be derived from specialisation and comparative advantage in conventional economic trade theory. It also incidentally involves a critique of mass travel and tourism.

Although many Greens seem to favour greater decentralisation and self-sufficiency, there are some who would deny that it is or should be an integral element of a Green ideology (Eckersley, 1992; Goodin, 1992; Martell, 1994). The preference for the small scale, decentralised and local is reminiscent of anarchism, and indeed there are close links in theory and practice between Greens and anarchists (Bookchin, 1982). Yet for anarchists the decentralisation of power is clearly their fundamental principle: it is what anarchism is essentially about. For Greens the ultimate objective is saving the planet, and 'small is beautiful' would seem an essentially subordinate principle to this overriding end.

Decentralisation, particularly if combined with increased self-sufficiency, has for some Greens uncomfortable implications for the distribution of resources between different regions and communities. Thus 'insisting too emphatically on decentralization, local political autonomy, and direct democracy can ... compromise the ecocentric goal of social justice' (Eckersley, 1992, p. 175). It is difficult to see how considerable inequalities between regions could be avoided. Those from poorer underdeveloped regions of the world would be effectively prevented from benefiting from the only assets they could offer richer areas: cheap raw materials and cheap labour.

Moreover, it may be questioned whether decentralisation is a political strategy which is likely to further other, more fundamental Green objectives. It is at least arguable that if drastic and urgent action is needed to save the planet this may be more effectively achieved by centralised and even dictatorial methods. Most modern Greens seem temperamentally averse to such an approach. To a degree it was attempted by the Nazi and fascist regimes of between the wars, and this has provided further reasons for modern Greens to distance themselves from centralised and authoritarian methods. The issue does, however, raise in acute form the problem which has already been alluded to in the above analysis: what is an appropriate strategy for the Greens?

Green strategy

It has been suggested that all political ideologies contain (implicitly or explicitly) three main elements: a critique of existing society, a vision of the future and a strategy for moving from the present to the desired future, what is often termed the problem of agency. The first two are very clearly evident in Green thinking, but Green strategy often appears relatively weak and undertheorised.

Strategy is particularly problematic for those ideologies which assume a need for radical change. For example, many socialists have envisaged a future society very different from the world in which they lived, which inevitably raises acute questions over the means of achieving objectives, the agency for change. Indeed, socialists have often been more bitterly divided over strategy rather than ultimate ends. Greens similarly seek a very different future. They seek massive economic and social change. Their political philosophy has far-reaching implications for industrial policy, agricultural policy, energy policy, transport policy and taxation policy. Virtually all Greens, apart from the most optimistic reformists, believe that radical changes in government policy and human lifestyles are urgently required. Indeed, many Greens would argue that the Green revolution they seek is more fundamental and far-reaching than a socialist revolution. Nor, if their analysis is correct, do Greens have time on their side. Those who subscribe to the Green ideology readily proclaim that change is urgent now if catastrophe is to be avoided in the future. This is scarcely compatible with the kind of gradualism acceptable to a Fabian socialist.

Yet it is not just the radical and urgent nature of the change envisaged which makes strategy particularly problematic for Greens.

The early socialists portrayed a potential future which was very different, but in many ways attractive to the mass audience at which it was directed, if threatening to established wealth- and power-holders. They were promising a better life. Greens by contrast seek a future which is widely perceived as involving a worse rather than a better life for the majority of humanity. While it may be objected that the perception is not necessarily accurate, it is still an intrinsically difficult message to put across.

A variety of strategies, not necessarily mutually exclusive, are adopted in practice, including personal commitments to a green lifestyle, education and rational persuasion, grassroots community action, single issue and broader pressure group campaigns, and involvement in party politics. Most of them neglect or skate round the problem of power. All of them raise awkward questions.

Green convictions clearly may involve some implications for personal behaviour. Just as high living seems inconsistent with socialist views, so Greens indulging in conspicuous consumption and environmental degradation invite charges of hypocrisy. Many Greens in practice agonise over the concessions and compromises which they make to modern consumerism. Others prefer to express their convictions almost entirely through their lifestyles, giving up their cars and reducing their consumption of non-renewable resources, becoming vegetarian and growing organic food. Some join communes of like-minded people. Like medieval monks or nuns, they have opted out of conventional values and materialistic lifestyles (Eckersley, 1992, pp. 163–7). However, their individual commitment, while affording some personal satisfaction, is unlikely by itself to promote any wider change, beyond the limited influence of their example.

Broadly compatible with the politics of personal commitment is involvement in local initiatives within the immediate community. This sometimes involves a conscious rejection of conventional national politics for a bottom-up grassroots political strategy, much as some of the early socialists sought to fulfil their ideals through self-help friendly societies, cooperatives and educational projects. The question here is the extent to which the cumulative impact of such local initiatives can possibly achieve the extent and pace of change required by Green analysis. 'Think global, act local' is an appealing slogan, but if the scale of the problem is global rather than local, it seems unlikely that local initiatives can produce global solutions.

Another strategy, similar to that adopted by some early socialists, is to rely essentially on education and rational persuasion. While Green thinking often appears antipathetic to the post-Enlightenment rationalism, some Greens in practice place a heavy dependence on the power of reason, assuming that people will be convinced of the need for massive changes in their current materialist lifestyles if they can only be persuaded to grasp the facts. Yet of course the 'facts', however persuasive to Greens, involve assumptions and projections which are disputable. Most people may prefer to believe what they want to believe. There are optimistic as well as pessimistic perspectives on the future, and most human beings may understandably be inclined to accept interpretations which have less uncomfortable implications for their own sense of well-being. Thus Greens may be doomed to play the role of Cassandras, perhaps accurately forecasting the future, but ignored. Alternatively, in order to dramatise their case more effectively they may be tempted to exaggerate risks and dangers, risking loss of credibility if their claims are disputed or disproved (Maddox, 1972).

At the other extreme to the employment of rational persuasion is the use of direct and sometimes violent action by a minority of Green extremists, presumably perceived as a shock tactic to raise public consciousness of environmental degradation or the exploitation of animals, and as a deterrent to those directly engaged in pollution or exploitation. Yet such tactics would seem generally counter-productive, and indeed have been roundly condemned by the great majority of Greens.

The most high profile manifestation of Green politics has perhaps been through pressure groups such as Greenpeace and Friends of the Earth operating at a genuinely international level. Their activities have certainly raised public consciousness of green issues, and have often had an apparent influence on both business practice and government policy. Pressure group politics involve some familiar dilemmas: whether, for example, to seek increased influence on government through securing insider status, involving some compromise of ideals and possible incorporation, or to maintain ideological purity at the expense of effective exclusion from the decision-making process. While Greenpeace has maintained its provocative radical outsider stance, Friends of the Earth has become more involved in the consultative process. Only time will tell which is the more effective strategy in terms of changing policy.

Pressure group politics is almost by definition the politics of influence rather than the politics of power. Indeed, it could be argued that none of the approaches discussed above really address the problem of political power. Greens need some effective leverage on centres of power if they are to have any hope of forwarding their extensive and urgent agenda for change. In countries like the United Kingdom which are at least nominally democratic, this would appear to require some involvement in conventional electoral and parliamentary politics, either through existing political parties, or through the relatively new Green Party.

The extent of the compatibility of Green ideas with older established political ideologies is, as has been noticed above, a contentious issue, and the potential for working through existing parties will depend in part on the view taken. The early Fabians initially sought to spread their socialist ideas through their 'permeation' of other parties and institutions, and some who hold Green views may seek a similar permeation of the older parties. Indeed, there are Green (or Greenish) groups operating in all major British parties, although the extent of their influence is contentious (Robinson, 1992).

There are others of course who would argue that Green convictions are fundamentally inconsistent with the established political parties and their underpinning ideological assumptions. The logical corollary for those who accept nevertheless the need for involvement in electoral and parliamentary politics is a separate Green Party. Green parties have enjoyed some electoral success in other countries, most notably in Germany, where they have secured representation in local, state, and (intermittently) federal elections. Such relative success in conventional politics inevitably forces some hard choices and compromises which are not always palatable to Green purists, and indeed the political record of the German Greens has not always won the approval of Greens inside and outside Germany.

In Britain familiar problems of competing with established parties are compounded by an electoral system which effectively penalises national parties without a strong regional base. The Greens achieved a remarkable 15 per cent of the poll for the 1989 European elections, which would have secured respectable representation in Strasbourg in any other country in the European Union, but resulted in no MEPs, and proved something of a false dawn, as the party has achieved nothing remotely comparable since.

Lack of success should not perhaps be blamed solely on the electoral system. The Green electoral cause has scarcely been helped by their disregard for the conventional imperatives of party politics, for which some Greens have a marked distaste. While the party's avoidance of hierarchical organisation, discipline and leadership is true to their decentralist philosophy, it scarcely assists their electoral appeal in an environment where politics is personalised and is increasingly about image and presentation. Indeed, the whole approach to politics of many Greens is schizophrenic. They reject not only conventional political parties and their associated philosophies but the whole existing political process as outdated and morally bankrupt, yet their own ideas have massive political implications which require active involvement in that political process.

The real problem for any Green Party is that the message they seek to present is at odds with prevailing materialist values, with the immediate apparent interests of the bulk of the electorate, and with dominant assumptions about political motivation. For most people, it seems, the good life is about increased income and wealth, and the enjoyment of more and better consumer goods and services. Parties, it is assumed, win votes by appealing to the self-interest of individuals, groups and classes, promising to protect or raise living standards, reduce taxation, improve benefits and services. Even when politicians demand sacrifices in immediate consumption, this is usually on the expectation of some tangible benefit in the not too distant future, such as stable prices, increased employment, steady growth. The Greens, by contrast, are effectively promising to make people worse off in material terms. The sacrifices they call for are not for an immediate better future, but to avert a potential environmental catastrophe which might not affect current voters. It is not an easy political message to put across.

Other political ideologies are linked to a particular social class or an identifiable sectional interest within society. Indeed, as has been noted, an influential interpretation is that political ideologies are essentially rationalisations of interest. Now there are some who would link environmentalist concerns with class interests. Some Greens indeed have seen the middle classes in advanced capitalist countries as credible agents of change, providing the political muscle for a transition to a green (or greener) society. By contrast, critics of Greens from both the left and the right have sometimes sought to portray preservationists as selfish well-heeled people concerned to

Strategy	Examples	Problems
Personal	Green lifestyle No car, etc. Vegetarianism Join commune	Monastic withdrawal? Lack of impact on environmental problems

Local or community	'Think global, act local'
	'Small is beautiful'
	Local initiatives, self-help
	Anarchism
		Difficulty in co-ordinating
		  local initiatives
		Negligible impact on global
		  environmental problems

Pressure group activity –
  orthodox
	Rational persuasion
	Education
	Lobbying Parliament,
	  Whitehall, parties, public,
	  etc.
	Seek insider status for
	  purposes of consultation
		Unpalatable messages not
		  believed or rejected
		Short-term horizons of
		  public, politicians, etc.
		  (but over-dramatising or
		  exaggerating may be
		  counter-productive)
		Danger of incorporation

Pressure group activity –
  direct action
	Demonstrations
	Obstruction, sabotage
	Damage to property
	Violence to people (e.g.
	  those involved in
	  experiments on animals)
		May be counter productive,
		  alienate sympathy, etc.
		Gives cause a bad name
		Remedy worse than
		  problem?

Regional strategy	Regional government?
	'Bio-regionalism', autarky
	Limits on travel and trade
	Encourage close relationship
	  between people and
	  region
	Regional diversity
		Cuts across conventional
		  wisdom on free trade
		Challenges existing
		  economic and political
		  interests
		Would lead to
		  unacceptable inequalities
		  between regions

National strategy	Involvement in conventional
	  electoral politics
	Either seek to convert major
	  parties to green ideas, or
	  support Green Party
		Strength of vested interests
		  in traditional parties –
		  green policies only
		  cosmetic?
		Electoral system and other
		  factors hinders Green
		  Party

International strategy	'Think global': influence and
	  involvement on
	  international organisations
	  and multinational
	  corporations, international
	  pressure groups
		Lack of political clout
		Problems of co-ordination
		Differences between rich
		  and poor nations:
		  western paternalism

Figure 10.1 Varieties of Green strategies

protect their own property values and lifestyles against the poor or aspiring. On a global scale it is sometimes alleged that western concerns with destruction of the Amazonian rain forests or pollution in the third world reflect neo-colonial attitudes, designed to keep other countries poor and underdeveloped. There is something in the allegation. Green politics would seem to appeal more to the haves than the have-nots, both within and between countries.

Yet, ostensibly, in so far as the Green ideology serves an interest at all, it would appear to be an interest which transcends present society or even humanity itself. It is concerned with generations yet unborn, with other species, and with the future of the planet. This poses a problem for conventional politics. There is no mechanism for taking into account the interests of future generations, still less threatened fauna and flora, in either the economic or political market-place. The radical Greens require a collective sacrifice of current consumption and immediate aspirations on the part of humanity in the interests of an unknown and unknowable future. Such heroic unself-ishness does not fit easily with the assumptions about humankind which are implicit or explicit in mainstream western political ideo-logy. Yet unless these assumptions prove mistaken, it is difficult to see a realistic political strategy for the Greens.

Guide to further reading

There are useful introductory short chapters on what is described as ecologism or environmentalism in Heywood (1992), Vincent (1995), and Eccleshall *et al.* (1994, chapter by Michael Kenny). There are a number of recent accessible books on green politics, including Porritt and Winner's *The Coming of the Greens* (1988), John McCormick's *British Politics and the Environment* (1991) and Robert Garner's *Environmental Politics* (1995). Garner has a particularly useful chap-ter on 'Green thinking', a topic which is explored in more detail in Andrew Dobson's *Green Political Thought* (1995), R. Goodin's *Green Political Theory* (1992) and Robyn Eckersley's *Environmen-talism and Political Theory* (1992). Andrew Dobson has also edited *The Green Reader* (1991) which includes extracts from several key modern green classics.

Among books which have almost acquired the status of modern Green classics are Rachel Carson's *The Silent Spring* (1962), the Club of Rome's *The Limits to Growth* report (Meadows *et al.*, 1972), Edward Goldsmith's *A Blueprint for Survival* (1972), E. F. Schumacher's *Small is Beautiful* (1973), T. O'Riordan's *Environmentalism* (1976), and J. E. Lovelock's *Gaia: A New Look at Life on Earth* (1979).

More specialist recent books include Albert Weale's *The New Politics of Pollution* (1992), David Pepper's *Eco-socialism* (1993), M. Robinson's *The Greening of British Party Politics* (1992) and Luke Martell's *Ecology and Society* (1994). Although apparently less strictly relevant to a book on British political ideologies some of the literature on the German Greens raise important issues particularly surrounding political strategy which British Greens may be forced to confront in the future.

BIBLIOGRAPHY AND REFERENCES

Abrams, M., Rose, R. and Hinden, R. (1960), *Must Labour Lose?*, Penguin.

Adams, I. (1993), *Political Ideology Today*, Manchester University Press.

Adelman, P. (1970), *Gladstone, Disraeli and Later Victorian Politics*, Longman.

Adelman, P. (1986), *The Rise of the Labour Party*, 2nd edn, Longman.

Adonis, A. and Hames, T. (1994), *A Conservative Revolution? The Thatcher–Reagan Decade in Perspective*, Manchester University Press.

Almond, G. and Verba, S. (1963), *The Civic Culture*, Princeton University Press.

Alter, P. (1989) *Nationalism*, Arnold.

Anderson, B. (1983), *Imagined Communities*, NLB/Verso.

Arblaster, A. (1984), *The Rise and Decline of Western Liberalism*, Blackwell.

Arendt, H. (1967), *The Origins of Totalitarianism*, Allen and Unwin.

Ashford, N. (1989), 'Market liberalism and the environment: a response to Hay', *Politics*, vol. 9, no. 1.

Ayer, A. J. (1988), *Thomas Paine*, Faber and Faber.

Bacchi, C. L. (1990), *Same Difference: Feminism and sexual difference*, Allen and Unwin.

Barker, R. (1978), *Political Ideas in Modern Britain*, Methuen.

Barrett, M. (1980), *Women's Oppression Today: Problems in Marxist feminist analysis*, Verso.

Barrett, M. and Phillips, A. (eds) (1992) *Destabilizing Theory: Contemporary feminist debates*, Polity Press.

Barry, N. P. (1986), *On Classical Liberalism and Libertarianism*, Macmillan.

Beer, S. H. (1982), *Modern British Politics*, Faber and Faber.

285

Behrens, R. (1989), 'Social democracy and liberalism' in Tivey, L. and Wright, A. (eds), *Party Ideology in Britain*, Routledge.

Bell, D. (1960), *The End of Ideology*, Free Press.

Benewick, R. (1972), *The Fascist Movement in Britain*, 2nd edn, Allen Lane.

Bentley, M. (1984), *Politics without Democracy*, Fontana.

Bentley, M. (1987), *The Climax of Liberal Politics: British liberalism in theory and practice, 1869–1918*, Edward Arnold.

Berlin, I. (1967), 'Two concepts of liberty', in Quinton, A. (ed.), *Political Philosophy*, Oxford University Press.

Bernstein, G. L. (1986), *Liberalism and Liberal Politics in Edwardian England*, Allen and Unwin.

Birch, A. H. (1977), *Political Integration and Disintegration in the British Isles*, Allen and Unwin.

Blake, R. (1966), *Disraeli*, Eyre and Spottiswoode.

Blake, R. (1985), *The Conservative Party from Peel to Thatcher*, Fontana.

Bookchin, M. (1982), *The Ecology of Freedom*, Cheshire Books.

Bosanquet, N. (1983), *After the New Right*, Heinemann.

Bottomore, T. (1991), *A Dictionary of Marxist Thought*, Blackwell.

Bradley, I. (1981), *Breaking the Mould: The birth and prospects of the Social Democratic Party*, Martin Robertson.

Bradley, I. (1985), *The Strange Rebirth of Liberal Britain*, Chatto and Windus.

Branson, N. (1979), *Poplarism 1919–1925*, Lawrence and Wishart.

Breuilly, J. (1993), *Nationalism and the State*, 2nd edn, Manchester University Press.

Brockway, F. (1977), *Towards Tomorrow*, Hart-Davis MacGibbon.

Brownmiller, S. (1977), *Against Our Will*, Penguin.

Bryson, V. (1992), *Feminist Political Theory: An introduction*, Macmillan.

Buck, P. W. (1975), *How Conservatives Think*, Penguin.

Bullock, A. and Stallybrass, O. (eds) (1977), *The Fontana Dictionary of Modern Thought*, Fontana/Collins.

Bulpitt, J. (1987), 'Thatcherism as statecraft', in Burch, M. and Moran, M. (eds), *British Politics: A reader*, Manchester University Press.

Burke, E. (1790), *Reflections on the Revolution in France*, edited by Hill, B. W. (1975), Fontana/Harvester Wheatsheaf.

Butler, D. and Butler, G. (1994), *British Political Facts 1900–1994*, seventh edition, Macmillan.

Callaghan, J. (1987), *The Far Left in British Politics*, Basil Blackwell.

Callaghan, J. (1990), *Socialism in Britain*, Basil Blackwell.

Carson, R. (1962), *The Silent Spring*, Riverside Press.

Carsten, F. L. (1967), *The Rise of Fascism*, Batsford.

Carter, A. (1988), *The Politics of Women's Rights*, Longman.

Challinor, R. (1977), *The Origins of British Bolshevism*, Croom Helm.

Charvet, J. (1982), *Feminism*, Dent.

Clarke, J., Cochrane, A. and Smart, C. (1987), *Ideologies of Welfare*, Hutchinson.

Clarke, P. F. (1971), *Lancashire and the New Liberalism*, Cambridge University Press.
Coates, D. (1980), *Labour in Power?*, Longman.
Coole, D. H. (1988), *Women in Political Theory*, Harvester Wheatsheaf.
Cowling, M. (ed.) (1978), *Conservative Essays*, Cassell.
Cranston, M. (1967), *Freedom*, 3rd edn, Longman.
Crick, B. (1987), *Socialism*, Open University Press.
Crick, B. (ed.) (1991), *National Identities*, Blackwell.
Crick, B. (1993), *In Defence of Politics*, 4th edn, Penguin.
Crosland, C. A. R. (1956), *The Future of Socialism*, Jonathan Cape.
Crossman, R. H. S. (1981), *The Backbench Diaries of Richard Crossman*, edited by Morgan, J., Hamish Hamilton and Jonathan Cape.
Cust, R. and Hughes, A. (1989), *Conflict in Early Stuart England*, Longman.
Dahrendorf, R. (1990), *Reflections on the Revolution in Europe*, Chatto and Windus.
Dangerfield, G. (1966), *The Strange Death of Liberal England*, MacGibbon and Kee.
Dearlove, J. and Saunders, P. (1984), *Introduction to British Politics*, Polity Press.
Deutscher, I. (1954), *The Prophet Armed: Trotsky 1879–1921*, Oxford University Press.
Deutscher, I. (1959), *The Prophet Unarmed: Trotsky 1921–1929*, Oxford University Press.
Deutscher, I. (1963), *The Prophet Outcast: Trotsky 1929–1940*, Oxford University Press.
Dickens, A. G. (1959), *Thomas Cromwell and the English Reformation*, English Universities Press.
Dinwiddy, J. (1989), *Bentham*, Oxford University Press.
Disraeli, B. (1844), *Coningsby*, 1983 edn, Penguin.
Disraeli, B. (1845), *Sybil*, 1980 edn, Penguin.
Dobson, A. (ed.) (1991), *The Green Reader*, Andre Deutsch.
Dobson, A. (1995), *Green Political Thought*, 2nd edn, Routledge.
Donald, J. and Hall, S. (eds) (1986), *Politics and Ideology*, Open University Press.
Downs, A. (1957), *An Economic Theory of Democracy*, Harper and Row.
Drucker, H., Dunleavy, P., Gamble, A. and Peele, G. (1983), *Developments in British Politics*, Macmillan.
Drucker, H., Dunleavy, P., Gamble, A. and Peele, G. (1986), *Developments in British Politics 2*, Macmillan.
Dunn, J. (1969), *The Political Thought of John Locke*, Cambridge University Press.
Dworkin, A. (1981), *Pornography*, Women's Press.
Eatwell, R. (1995), *Fascism: A history*, Chatto and Windus.
Eccleshall, R. (1977), 'English conservatism as ideology', *Political Studies*, vol. xxv, no. 1.
Eccleshall, R. (1986), *British Liberalism: Liberal thought from the 1640s to the 1980s*, Longman.

Eccleshall, R. (1990), *English Conservatism since the Reformation: An introduction and anthology*, Unwin Hyman.

Eccleshall, R., Geoghegan, V., Jay R., Kenny, M., MacKenzie, I. and Wilford R. (1994), *Political Ideologies, an Introduction*, 2nd edn, Routledge.

Eckersley, R. (1992), *Environmentalism and Political Theory: Towards an ecocentric approach*, UCL Press.

Edgar, D. (1984), 'Bitter harvest' in Curran J. (ed.), *The Future of the Left*, Polity Press/New Socialist.

Elton, G. R. (1953), *The Tudor Revolution in Government*, Cambridge University Press.

Ensor, R. C. K. (1936), *England 1870–1914*, Oxford University Press.

Etzioni, A. (1995), *The Spirit of Community*, Fontana Press.

Evans, B. (1984), 'Political ideology and its role in recent British politics', in Robins, L. (ed.), *Updating British Politics*, The Politics Association.

Evans, J., Hills, J., Hunt, K., Meehan, E., Tuscher, T. ten, Vogel, U. and Waylen, G. (1986), *Feminism and Political Theory*, Sage Publications.

Figes, E. (1970), *Patriarchal Attitudes*, Faber & Faber.

Finer, S. E. (1952, 1970), *The Life and Times of Edwin Chadwick*, Barnes and Noble.

Finer, S. E. (ed.) (1975), *Adversary Politics and Electoral Reform*, Wigram.

Firestone, S. (1979), *The Dialectic of Sex*, The Women's Press.

Flew, A. (ed.) (1979), *A Dictionary of Philosophy*, Pan/Macmillan.

Foot, M. and Kramnick, I. (eds) (1987), *The Thomas Paine Reader*, Penguin.

Foote, G. (1986), *The Labour Party's Political Thought*, Croom Helm.

Franklin, B. (1994), *Packaging Politics*, Edward Arnold.

Fraser, D. (1984), *The Evolution of the British Welfare State*, Macmillan.

Freeden, M. (1978), *The New Liberalism: An ideology of social reform*, Oxford University Press.

Freeden, M. (1986), *Liberalism Divided: A study in British political thought 1914–1939*, Oxford University Press.

Freely, M. (1995), *What About Us? An Open Letter to the Mothers Feminism Forgot*, Bloomsbury.

Friedan, B. (1965), *The Feminine Mystique*, Penguin.

Friedan, B. (1977), *It Changed my Life*, Victor Gollancz.

Friedan, B. (1982), *The Second Stage*, Michael Joseph.

Fukuyama, F. (1989), 'The End of History?', *The National Interest*, no. 16, Summer.

Fukuyama, F. (1992), *The End of History and the Last Man*, Hamish Hamilton.

Gamble, A. (1974), *The Conservative Nation*, Routledge and Kegan Paul.

Gamble, A. (1988), *The Free Economy and the Strong State*, Macmillan.

Garner, R. (1995), *Environmental Politics*, Harvester Wheatsheaf.

Gellner, E. (1983), *Nations and Nationalism*, Basil Blackwell.

George, V. and Wilding, P. (1985), *Ideology and Social Welfare*, Routledge and Kegan Paul.

Gilmour, I. (1978), *Inside Right*, Quartet Books.

Gilmour, I. (1992), *Dancing with Dogma: Britain under Thatcherism*, Simon and Schuster.

Glasgow University Media Group (1976), *Bad News*, Routledge.

Glasgow University Media Group (1982), *Really Bad News*, Writers' and Readers' Publishing Co-operative Society.

Goldsmith, E. (ed.) (1972), *A Blueprint for Survival*, Penguin.

Goldsmith, E. (1992), *The Way: An ecological world view*, Rider.

Goodin, R, (1992), *Green Political Theory*, Polity Press.

Goodwin, B. (1992), *Using Political Ideas*, 3rd edn, John Wiley and Sons.

Grant, J. (1993), *Fundamental Feminism*, Routledge.

Gray, J. (1986), *Liberalism*, Open University Press.

Gray, R. (1981), *The Aristocracy of Labour in Nineteenth-Century Britain c. 1850–1914*, Macmillan.

Green, D. G. (1987), *The New Right*, Harvester Wheatsheaf.

Green, T. H. (1881), *Lectures on the Principles of Political Obligation*, edited by Harris, P. and Morrow, J. (1986), Cambridge University Press.

Greenleaf, W. H. (1973), 'The character of modern British conservatism', in Benewick, R., Berkhi, R. N. and Parekh, B. (eds), *Knowledge and Belief in Politics*, Allen and Unwin.

Greenleaf, W. H. (1983), *The British Political Tradition, Vol. 1, The Rise of Collectivism, Vol. 2, The Ideological Heritage*, Methuen.

Greer, G. (1970), *The Female Eunuch*, MacGibbon and Kee.

Hall, S. and Jacques, M. (eds) (1983), *The Politics of Thatcherism*, Lawrence and Wishart.

Hamilton, M. B. (1987), 'The elements of the concept of ideology', *Political Studies*, vol. xxxv, no. 1, March.

Hampsher-Monk, I. (1992), *A History of Modern Political Thought: Major political thinkers from Hobbes to Marx*, Blackwell.

Hardin, G. (1968), 'The tragedy of the commons', *Science*, vol. 162.

Harrison, W. (1965), *Conflict and Compromise: History of British political thought*, The Free Press/Collier-Macmillan.

Hattersley, R. (1987), *Choose Freedom: The future of democratic socialism*, Michael Joseph.

Hattersley, R. (1995), *Who goes home?*, Little, Brown.

Hay, J. R. (1983), *The Origins of the Liberal Welfare Reforms, 1906–1914*, Macmillan.

Hay, P. R. (1988), 'Ecological values and the western political traditions from anarchism to fascism', *Politics*, vol. 8, no. 1.

Hayek, F. (1975), 'The principles of a liberal social order', in Crespigny, A. and Cronin, J. (eds), *Ideologies of Politics*, Oxford University Press.

Hayek, F. A. (1976), *The Road to Serfdom*, Routledge and Kegan Paul.

Healey, D. (1989), *The Time of My Life*, Michael Joseph.

Heywood, A. (1992), *Political Ideologies: An introduction*, Macmillan.

Hill, C. (1980), *The Century of Revolution*, Van Nostrand Reinhold (International).

Hindess, B. (1971), *The Decline of Working Class Politics*, MacGibbon and Kee.

Hobhouse, L. T. (1911), *Liberalism*, with a new introduction by A. P. Grimes (1964), Oxford University Press.
Hobhouse, L. T. (1918), *The Metaphysical Theory of the State*, Macmillan.
Hobsbawm, E. J. (1969), *Industry and Empire*, Penguin.
Hobsbawm, E. J. (1988), *The Age of Capital 1848–1875*, Cardinal.
Hobsbawm, E. J. (1989), *Politics for a Rational Left*, Verso.
Hobsbawm, E. J. (1990), *Nations and Nationalism since 1780*, Cambridge University Press.
Hobsbawm, E. J. (1992), *The Age of Revolution 1789–1848*, Abacus.
Hobsbawm, E. J. (1994a), *The Age of Empire 1875–1914*, Abacus.
Hobsbawm, E. J. (1994b), *Age of Extremes: The short twentieth century 1914–1991*, Michael Joseph.
Hogg, Q. (1947), *The Case for Conservatism*, Penguin.
Holland, S. K. (1975), *The Socialist Challenge*, Quartet Books.
Honderich, T. (1990), *Conservatism*, Hamish Hamilton.
Hume, L. J. (1981), *Bentham and Bureaucracy*, Cambridge University Press.
Humm, M. (ed.) (1992), *Feminisms: A reader*, Harvester Wheatsheaf.
Hutchinson, J. (1994), *Modern Nationalism*, Fontana Press.
Hutchinson, J. and Smith, A. D. (eds) (1994), *Nationalism*, Oxford University Press.
Hutton, W. (1986), *The Revolution that Never Was*, Longman.
Hutton, W. (1995), *The State We're In*, Jonathan Cape.
Jackson, S. *et al.* (eds) (1993), *Women's Studies: A reader*, Harvester Wheatsheaf.
Jenkins, R. (1991), *A Life at the Centre*, Macmillan.
Jennings, Sir I. (1966), *The Law and the Constitution*, 6th edn, University of London Press.
Joll, J. (1979), *The Anarchists*, 2nd edn, Methuen.
Jones, B., Gray, A., Kavanagh, D., Moran, M., Norton, P. and Seldon, A. (1994), *Politics UK*, 2nd edn, Harvester Wheatsheaf.
Joseph, K. (1976), *Stranded on the Middle Ground*, Centre for Policy Studies.
Kavanagh, D. (ed.) (1982), *The Politics of the Labour Party*, Allen and Unwin.
Kavanagh, D. (1990), *Thatcherism and British Politics*, 2nd edn, Oxford University Press.
Kavanagh, D. and Morris, P. (1994), *Consensus Politics*, 2nd edn, Blackwell.
Kavanagh, D. and Seldon, A. (1994), *The Major Effect*, Macmillan.
Kedourie, E, (1991), *Nationalism*, 4th edn, Blackwell.
Keegan, W. (1984), *Mrs Thatcher's Economic Experiment*, Allen Lane.
Kellas, J. G. (1991), *The Politics of Nationalism and Ethnicity*, Macmillan.
King, D. S. (1987), *The New Right*, Macmillan.
Kirk, R. (1982), *The Portable Conservative Reader*, Viking Penguin.
Kitchen, M. (1976), *Fascism*, Macmillan.
Kogan, D. and Kogan, M. (1982), *The Battle for the Labour Party*, Kogan Page.

Laqueur, W. (ed.) (1979), *Fascism: A reader's guide*, Penguin.
Laybourn, K. (1988), *The Rise of Labour*, Edward Arnold.
Layton-Henry, Z. and Rich, P.B. (eds) (1986), *Race, Government and Politics in Britain*, Macmillan.
Leach, R. (1995), *Turncoats: Changing party allegiance by British politicians*, Dartmouth.
Levitas, R. (ed.) (1986), *The Ideology of the New Right*, Polity Press.
Lichtheim, G. (1970), *A Short History of Socialism*, Weidenfeld and Nicolson.
Locke, J. (1689), *A Letter Concerning Toleration*, edited by Gough J. W. (1966, with *Second Treatise of Civil Government*), Basil Blackwell.
Lovell, T. (ed.) (1990), *British Feminist Thought: A Reader*, Basil Blackwell.
Lovelock, J. E. (1979), *Gaia: A new look at life on earth*, Oxford University Press.
Lovenduski, J. and Randall, V. (1993), *Contemporary Feminist Politics*, Oxford University Press.
McCormick, J. (1991), *British Politics and the Environment*, Earthscan Publications Ltd.
McCrone, D. (1992), *Understanding Scotland*, Routledge.
MacDonald, J. R. (1911), *The Socialist Movement*, Home University Library.
Mackenzie, J. M. (ed.) (1986), *Imperialism and Popular Culture*, Manchester University Press.
McKenzie, R. T. (1963), *British Political Parties*, 2nd edn, Heinemann.
McKenzie, R. T. and Silver, A. (1968), *Angels in Marble*, Heinemann.
MacKinnon, C. (1989), *Towards a Feminist Theory of the State*, Harvard University Press.
McLellan, D. (1976), *Karl Marx*, Paladin, Granada Publishing.
McLellan, D. (1979), *Marxism after Marx*, Macmillan.
McLellan, D. (1986), *Ideology*, Open University Press.
Macpherson, C. B. (1962), *The Political Theory of Possessive Individualism*, Oxford University Press.
Maddox, J. (1972), *The Doomsday Syndrome*, Macmillan.
Malthus, T. (1970), *An Essay on the Principle of Population*, edited by Flew, A., Penguin.
Manning, D. J. (1976), *Liberalism*, Dent.
Mannheim, K. (1960), *Ideology and Utopia*, Routledge and Kegan Paul.
Marquand, D. (1977), *Ramsay MacDonald*, Jonathan Cape.
Marquand, D. (1988), *The Unprincipled Society*, Fontana.
Marr, A. (1992), *The Battle for Scotland*, Penguin.
Martell, L. (1994), *Ecology and Society: An introduction*, Polity Press.
Marx, K. *Selected Writings*, edited by McLellan, D. (1977), Oxford University Press.
Marx, K. and Engels, F. (1962), *Selected Works*, 2 vols, Lawrence and Wishart.
Meadows, D. H., Meadows, D. L., Randers, D. L. and Behrens III, W. (1972), *The Limits to Growth*, Earth Island.

Michels, R. (1915, 1962), *Political Parties*, Free Press.

Middlemas, K. (1979), *Politics in Industrial Society: The experience of the British system since 1911*, Deutsch.

Mies, M. and Shiva, V. (1993), *Ecofeminism*, Fernwood Publications, Zed Books.

Miliband, D. (ed.) (1994), *Re-inventing the Left*, Polity Press.

Miliband, R. (1972), *Parliamentary Socialism*, 2nd edn, Merlin Press.

Miliband, R. (1994), *Socialism for a Sceptical Age*, Polity Press.

Mill, J. S. (1859), *On Liberty*, with introduction by M. Warnock (1962), Collins.

Mill, J. S. (1861), *Utilitarianism*, edited by Warnock, M. (1962), Collins.

Mill, J. S. (ed. Fawcett) (1971), *On Liberty, Representative Government, The Subjection of Women*, three essays, Oxford University Press.

Millett, K. (1977), *Sexual Politics*, Virago.

Minkin, L. (1978), *The Labour Party Conference*, Allen Lane.

Minkin, L. (1991), *The Contentious Alliance: Trade unions and the Labour Party*, Edinburgh University Press.

Minogue, K. R. (1967), *Nationalism*, Batsford.

Minogue, K. (1985), *Alien Powers: The pure theory of ideology*, Weidenfeld and Nicolson.

Mitchell, J. (1974), *Psychoanalysis and Feminism*, Penguin.

Mitchell, J. and Oakley, A. (eds.) (1976), *The Rights and Wrongs of Women*, Penguin.

Mitchell, J. and Oakley, A. (1986), *What is Feminism?*, Blackwell.

Morgan, K. O. (1992), *The People's Peace: British history, 1945–1990*, Oxford University Press.

Morris, W. (1962), *Selected Writings and Designs*, edited by Briggs, A., Penguin.

Mosley, O. (1970), *My Life*, Nelson.

Nairn, T. (1981), *The Break-up of Britain*, NLB and Verso.

Newton, K. (1969), *The Sociology of British Communism*, Allen Lane.

Nisbet, R. (1986), *Conservatism*, Open University Press.

Nozick, R. (1974), *Anarchy, State and Utopia*, Blackwell.

Oakeshott, M. (1962), *Rationalism in Politics and other Essays*, Methuen.

O'Riordan, T. (1976), *Environmentalism*, Pion Ltd.

O'Sullivan, N. (1976), *Conservatism*, Dent.

Owen, D. (1981), *Face the Future*, Oxford University Press.

Owen, R. (1991), *A New View of Society and Other Writings*, edited by Claeys, G., Penguin.

Paine, T. (1791–2), *The Rights of Man*, edited by Collins, H. (1969), Penguin.

Pares, R. (1953), *George III and the Politicians*, Oxford University Press.

Parkin, F. (1972), *Class, Inequality and Political Order*, Paladin, Granada Publishing.

Pearson, R. and Williams, G. (1984), *Political Thought and Public Policy in the Nineteenth Century*, Longman.

Pelling, H. (1965), *The Origins of the Labour Party*, Oxford University Press.

Pepper, D. (1993), *Eco-Socialism: From deep ecology to social justice*, Routledge.

Perryman, M. (ed.) (1994), *Altered States: Postmodernism, politics, culture*, Lawrence and Wishart.

Pierson, S. (1973), *Marxism and the Origins of British Socialism*, Cornell University Press.

Pimlott, B. (1977), *Labour and the Left in the 1930s*, Cambridge University Press.

Pimlott, B. (1992), *Harold Wilson*, Harper Collins.

Plamenatz, J. P. (1963), *Man and Society: A critical examination of some important social and political theories from Machiavelli to Marx*, two volumes, Longmans.

Plant, J. (ed.) (1989), *Healing the Wounds: The promise of ecofeminism*, Green Print, The Merlin Press.

Plumb, J. H. (1966), *The Growth of Political Stability in England*, Macmillan.

Pois, R. A. (1986), *National Socialism and the Religion of Nature*, Croom Helm.

Popper, K. R. (1962), *The Open Society and its Enemies*, 4th edn, 2 vols., Routledge and Kegan Paul.

Porrit, J. and Winner, D. (1988), *The Coming of the Greens*, Fontana/Collins.

Punnett, R. M. (1987), *British Government and Politics*, 5th edn, Gower.

Quinton, A. (1978), *The Politics of Imperfection*, Faber and Faber.

Ramazanoglu, C. (1989), *Feminism and the Contradictions of Oppression*, Routledge.

Randall, V. (1987), *Women and Politics*, Macmillan.

Rawls, J. (1971), *A Theory of Justice*, Harvard University Press.

Regan, T. (1988), *The Case for Animal Rights*, Routledge and Kegan Paul.

Richards, J. R. (1982), *The Sceptical Feminist*, Penguin.

Riddell, P. (1983), *The Thatcher Government*, Martin Robertson.

Robinson, M. (1992), *The Greening of British Party Politics*, Manchester University Press.

Rowbotham, S. (1973), *Hidden from History: 300 years of women's oppression and the fight against it*, Pluto Press.

Royle, E. (1986), *Chartism*, Longman.

St John-Stevas, N. (1982), 'Tory philosophy – a personal view', *Three Banks Review*, June, no. 134.

Sandbach, F. (1980), *Environment, Ideology and Policy*, Basil Blackwell.

Sargent, L. (ed.) (1981), *The Unhappy Marriage of Marxism and Feminism: A debate on class and patriarchy*, Pluto Press.

Saville, J. (1988), *The Labour Movement in Britain*, Faber and Faber.

Schultz, H. J. (1972), *English Liberalism and the State: Individualism or collectivism?*, Heath.

Schumacher, E. F. (1973), *Small is Beautiful*, Sphere Books.

Schumpeter, J. A. (1943), *Capitalism, Socialism and Democracy*, Allen and Unwin.

Schwarzmantel, J. (1991), *Socialism and the Idea of the Nation*, Harvester Wheatsheaf.

Scruton, R. (1980), *The Meaning of Conservatism*, Macmillan.

Scruton, R. (1983), *A Dictionary of Political Thought*, Macmillan/Pan.

Seldon, A. and Ball, S. (1994), *Conservative Century: The Conservative Party since 1900*, Oxford University Press.

Seliger, M. (1976), *Ideology and Politics*, Allen and Unwin.

Seyd, P. (1987), *The Rise and Fall of the Labour Left*, Macmillan.

Seymour-Ure, C. (1974), *The Political Impact of the Mass Media*, Constable.

Shaw, E. (1994), *The Labour Party since 1979*, Routledge.

Singer, P. (1990), *Animal Liberation*, Cape.

Skidelsky, R. (1967), *Politicians and the Slump*, Penguin.

Skidelsky, R. (1990), *Oswald Mosley*, 3rd edn, Macmillan.

Skidelsky, R. (ed.) (1988), *Thatcherism*, Chatto and Windus.

Skinner, Q. (1978), *The Foundations of Modern Political Thought*, 2 vols, Cambridge University Press.

Smith, A. (1776), *The Wealth of Nations*, edited with an introduction by E. Cannan (1976), University of Chicago Press.

Smith, A. D. (1991), *National Identity*, Penguin.

Smith, P. (1967), *Disraelian Conservatism and Social Reform*, Routledge.

Stassinopoulos, A. (1973), *The Female Woman*, Davis-Poynter.

Stephenson, H. (1982), *Claret and Chips: The rise of the SDP*, Joseph.

Talmon, J. L. (1960), *The Origins of Totalitarian Democracy*, Praeger.

Tawney, R. H. (1921), *The Acquisitive Society*, Fontana.

Tawney, R. H. (1938), *Religion and the Rise of Capitalism*, Penguin.

Tawney, R. H. (1964), *Equality*, Unwin.

Taylor, S. (1982), *The National Front in English Politics*, Macmillan.

Thatcher, M. (1977), *Let Our Children Grow Tall*, Centre for Policy Studies.

Thompson, E. P. (1980), *The Making of the English Working Class*, Penguin.

Thompson, K. (1986), *Beliefs and Ideology*, Ellis Horwood and Tavistock Publications.

Thomson, D. (1966), *Political Ideas*, Penguin.

Thurlow, R. C. (1987), *Fascism in Britain: A history 1918–1985*, Basil Blackwell.

Tivey, L. (ed.) (1981), *The Nation State*, Martin Robertson.

Tivey, L. and Wright, A. (1989), *Party Ideology in Britain*, Routledge.

Tomalin, C. (1974), *The Life and Death of Mary Wollstonecraft*, Weidenfeld & Nicholson.

Vincent, A. (1995), *Modern Political Ideologies*, 2nd edn, Blackwell.

Vincent, J. (1966), *The Formation of the Liberal Party, 1857–1868*, Constable.

Waldegrave, W. (1978), *The Binding of Leviathan*, Hamish Hamilton.

Walker, M. (1977), *The National Front*, Fontana.

Watson, J. S. (1960), *The Reign of George III*, Oxford University Press.

Weale, A. (1992), *The New Politics of Pollution*, Manchester University Press.

Weatherall, D. (1976), *David Ricardo*, Martinus Nijhoff.

Williams, R. (1976), *Keywords: A vocabulary of culture and society*, Fontana/Croom Helm.

Williams, S. (1981), *Politics is for People*, Penguin.

Wilson, D. (1984), *Pressure: The A to Z of campaigning in Britain*, Heinemann.

Wollstonecraft, M. (1792), *A Vindication of the Rights of Women*, edited by Brody, M. (1975), Penguin.

Woodcock, G. (1963), *Anarchism*, Penguin.

Wright, A. (1983), *British Socialism*, Longman.

Wright, A. (1987), *Socialisms: Theories and practices*, Oxford University Press.

Wright, D. G. (1970), *Democracy and Reform, 1815–1885*, Longman.

Young, H. (1989), *One of Us*, Macmillan.

INDEX

right *see* conservatism; far right; new right
Ritchie, D.G. 87, 88, 192
Robinson, M. 279
Rodgers, B. 167
romanticism 261
Romilly, Sir S. 75
Rosebery, A.P.P. 92–3
Rousseau, J.-J. 24, 176, 263
Royal Mint 85
Ruskin, J. 158, 263
Russell, J. 87
Russia *see* former Soviet Union

Saatchi & Saatchi 19
St John-Stevas, N. 112
Saint-Simon, C. 144
Salisbury 27, 114, 120, 122–3
Samuel, H. 88
Sargent, L. 242
Saunders, P. 30, 53
Saville, J. 135, 161
Scandinavia 215, 226, 258–9
Scargill, A. 187
Schlesinger, P. 227
Schultz, H.J. 88, 90, 92
Schumacher, E.F. 273
Schumpeter, J.A. 115
Schwarz, B. 62, 124
Scotland
  empire, legacy of 64
  Enlightenment 80
  ideological difference and consensus 6
  nationalism 199, 206, 213, 215, 216, 217–23
  religion 43
Scott, Sir W. 219
Scruton, R. 117, 126
Seliger, M. 16

Senior, Nassau William 27, 80, 81
sexual violence *see* rape
Seyd, P. 168
Seymour-Ure, C. 30
Shaftesbury 78
Shaw, E. 168
Shaw, G.B. 146, 153
Shiva, V. 251
Silver, A. 114, 124
Singer, P. 271
Single European Act 131
Skidelsky, R. 159, 192
Slovakia 229
Slovo, J. 213
Smiles, S. 27, 41, 82
Smith, A. 17, 28, 56, 125, 126
  liberalism 67, 79, 80, 81–2, 85
Smith, A.D. 202, 227
Smith, J. 11, 152, 170
Smith, P. 120
Smith, T. 274
Snowden, P. 156
social democracy *see* socialism, revisionist
social reform 119, 120, 121
social welfare reforms 91, 93
socialism 176
  and anarchism 185
  centralised state 229
  Christian 152, 170, 171
  Civil War and Glorious Revolution 49
  and conservatism 100, 109, 111–12, 116, 121, 123–5, 130
  constitution and political tradition 52–3
  demise 196